The Dynamics of Standards

The Dynamics of Standards

Edited by

Tineke M. Egyedi

Senior Researcher, Standardization, Delft University of Technology, The Netherlands, President of the European Academy for Standardization and Vice-chair of the International Cooperation for Education about Standardization

Knut Blind

Chair of Innovation Economics, Berlin University of Technology, Head of the Competence Center 'Regulation and Innovation', Fraunhofer Institute for Systems and Innovation Research, Berlin, Germany and Endowed Chair of Standardization, Rotterdam School of Management, Erasmus University, The Netherlands

Edward Elgar

Cheltenham, UK • Northampton, MA, USA

Published by
Edward Elgar Publishing Limited
The Lypiatts
15 Lansdown Road
Cheltenham
Glos GL50 2JA
UK

Edward Elgar Publishing, Inc.
William Pratt House
9 Dewey Court
Northampton
Massachusetts 01060
USA

A catalogue record for this book
is available from the British Library

Library of Congress Control Number: 2008932872

ISBN 978 1 84720 486 8

Printed and bound in Great Britain by MPG Books Ltd, Bodmin, Cornwall

Contents

List of Figures vii
List of Tables viii
List of Boxes x
List of Contributors xi
Foreword xiii
Acknowledgements xv
List of Abbreviations xvii

1. General Introduction 1
Tineke M. Egyedi and Knut Blind

PART ONE THE PROBLEM OF CHANGING STANDARDS

2. The Sustainability of Digital Data: Tension Between the Dynamics and Longevity of Standards 15
Kees van der Meer
3. An Implementation Perspective on Sources of Incompatibility and Standards' Dynamics 28
Tineke M. Egyedi

PART TWO CAUSES OF CHANGE

4. + vs –: Dynamics and Effects of Competing Standards of Recordable DVD-Media 47
Stephan Gauch
5. Internet Addressing Standards: A Case Study in Standards Dynamics Driven by Bottom-Up Adoption 68
Jos Vrancken, Marnix Kaart and Michel Soares
6. Incompatible Successors: The Failure to Graft XML onto SGML 82
Tineke M. Egyedi and Arjan Loeffen

PART THREE CHANGE IN AN IMPLEMENTATION CONTEXT

7. The IEEE 802.11 WLAN Installation at RWTH Aachen University: A Case of Voluntary Vendor Lock-In 99
Kai Jakobs
8. A Case Study of the Adoption and Implementation of STEP 117
Josephine W. Thomas, Steve Probets, Ray Dawson and Tim King

PART FOUR SCALE OF CHANGE

9. How stable are IT standards? 137
Tineke M. Egyedi and Petra Heijnen
10. Factors Influencing the Lifetime of Telecommunication and Information Technology Standards 155
Knut Blind

PART FIVE CONCLUSION

11. Conclusion 181
Tineke M. Egyedi

Bibliography 190
Index 205

Figures

1.1	Three categories of standards change: implementation change, maintenance and succession in the extended life cycle of a standard	5
3.1	Schematic representation of the phases leading up to the standard implementation	30
4.1	Relationship of standards, consortia and actors in the context of DVD recordable standardization	56
5.1	Network structure	71
5.2	Connecting a LAN via a NAT gateway	74
6.1	The relative importance of domains of use in SGML and XML	93
7.1	Timeline of the project and of availability of 802.11-based product	107
7.2	The dimensions of dynamics	109
9.1	Number of standards documents published per year	143
9.2	Number of changes over time: withdrawals, supplements and editions	145
9.3	Aggregate number of changes per year and the number of unchanged main documents	147
9.4	Mean age of withdrawn documents	151
9.5	Comparison of computed age based on withdrawn standards and standards that are 'still active'	151
10.1	Survival times of telecommunication and information technology standards in years by country	164
10.2	Survival times of international telecommunication standards by area of standardization	165
10.3	Survival times of international information technology standards by area of standardization	167

Tables

1.1	Main functions of compatibility standards	4
2.1	The 15 simple DC elements	21
3.1	Typification of three standardization approaches in the mid-1990s	32
3.2	Causes of incompatibility and their origins	38
3.3	Recommendations	40
4.1	Overview of DVD recordable standards and supporting consortia	50
4.2	DVD Forum core members	52
4.3	Members of the DVD+RW Alliance	53
4.4	Members of the DVD 6C patent pool	54
4.5	Structure of the ECMA TC 31 – optical discs and disc cartridges	55
4.6	Overview of DVD recordable standardization history	60
5.1	Pros and cons of top-down and bottom-up	78
6.1	Characterization of relationships between standards based on the dimensions of functionality and compatibility, and examples of associated phenomena	84
6.2	Taxonomy of successor standards	85
6.3	Aims of the SGML and XML standardizers	87
6.4	Overview of some of the main aspects of SGML and XML	88
6.5	Overview of the state of compatibility between the most relevant combinations of documents and software that conform to SGML to XML 1.0	92
6.6	Causes for discontinuity: differences between the problems, context of use, and standardization setting of SGML and XML	94
7.1	Purpose of the 802.11a/b standards projects	104
7.2	Characteristics of 802.11 and 802.11a/b/g	104
9.1	Overview of the changes at stake	143
9.2	Example of a forward document revision	145
9.3	Example of a backward document revision	145
9.4	Designated time for standards development	147
9.5	Main documents	149

9.6 Comparisons between types of standards and number of changes 149
9.7 Mean number of supplements, withdrawals and new editions 149
9.8 Mean age of withdrawn standards 150
9.9 Recoded ICS levels: number of changes 151
9.10 Significant differences between means in technical areas 152
10.1 Average publication and withdrawal dates in telecommunications differentiated by area of standardization 159
10.2 Average publication and withdrawal dates in telecommunications for various countries 160
10.3 Average publication and withdrawal dates in information technology differentiated by area of standardization 161
10.4 Average publication and withdrawal dates in information technology differentiated by country 162
10.5 Meanings and names of exogenous variables 171
10.6 Results of Cox regression analysis for telecommunication standards 172
10.7 Results of Cox regression analysis for information technology standards 173
11.1 Areas of dynamics which the chapters primarily address 183

Boxes

3.1 Dilemmas regarding the implementability of standards 40
9.1 Eurocentrism and the co-operation agreements between formal European and international standards bodies 144

Contributors

Knut Blind, Chair of Innovation Economics, Faculty of Economics and Management, Berlin University of Technology, Fraunhofer Institute for Systems and Innovation Research, Berlin, Germany and Endowed Chair of Standardization at the Rotterdam School of Management, Erasmus University, The Netherlands

Ray Dawson, Loughborough University, Department of Computer Science, UK

Tineke M. Egyedi, Faculty of Technology, Policy and Management, Section of Information and Communication Technology, Delft University of Technology, The Netherlands, President of the European Academy for Standardization and Vice-chair of the International Cooperation for Education about Standardization

Stephan Gauch, Fraunhofer Institute for Systems and Innovation Research, Karlsruhe, Germany

Petra Heijnen, Delft University of Technology, Faculty of Technology, Policy, and Management, Section of Energy and Industry, The Netherlands

Kai Jakobs, RWTH Aachen, Computer Science Department, Informatik 4, Germany

Marnix Kaart, Delft University of Technology, Faculty of Technology, Policy, and Management, Section of Information and Communication Technology, The Netherlands

Tim King, LSC Group Limited, Lichfield, Staffordshire, UK

Arjan Loeffen, Valid/Vision, Amsterdam, The Netherlands

Kees van der Meer, Delft University of Technology, Department Computer Science, Netherlands, DECIS, The Netherlands and Antwerp University, Institute OIOW, Section IBW, Belgium

Steve Probets, Loughborough University, Department of Information Science, UK

Michel Soares, Delft University of Technology, Faculty of Technology, Policy, and Management, Section of Information and Communication Technology, The Netherlands

Josephine W. Thomas, Rolls-Royce plc, Derby, UK

Jos Vrancken, Delft University of Technology, Faculty of Technology, Policy, and Management, Section of Information and Communication Technology, The Netherlands

Foreword

Scholars in science and technology studies have been interested in standards and standardization processes for a relatively short time. Much of the seminal literature stems only from the 1980s and early 1990s, spurred to a large extent by the tremendous growth and diversification that occurred in the information and communication technology industries. These developments crystallized interest in the roles of regulation and technological co-ordination in the innovation process in an especially forceful way. In this tumultuous and exciting new industrial environment, issues like voluntary industry standards, which heretofore had attracted little analytical interest except perhaps on the part of engineers, began to be seen as critical factors in the formation of technology markets and in the business strategies of high-technology companies. The public interest implications of standards became highlighted also. Over more than three decades, a rich and sophisticated theoretical and empirical literature has emerged from a broad cross-section of science and technology perspectives and disciplines. But a great many intriguing questions still persist.

This is an important new book that directly addresses probably the most significant and longstanding lacuna in our understanding of standards. Most previous studies have focused upon the problems of how standards are acquired in the first place; mainly upon problems of technology selection, actor co-ordination and institutional dynamics. The key observations that most of the impact of a standard occurs after it has been established, and that most standards do not retain their original form throughout their lifetimes, was always staring us in the face. That until now few scholars have addressed this issue specifically is itself perhaps a 'standards' problem. With the maturation of any field of scientific enquiry, certain 'standard' problems and approaches become entrenched, many scholars becoming more intent upon refining methods and 'improving' knowledge than upon posing radical new questions.

The contributors to this volume must be commended for taking this much needed next step boldly and with the confidence that can be born only of extensive knowledge and experience acquired over many years. In many respects, the contributors set out a new paradigm for the investigation of standards. They open the door to new kinds of questions about the function and role of standards in rapidly changing technological and business environments and new approaches to the investigation of standardization phenomena. The scientific implications will be far reaching. But so also will the practical implications as the major strategic and public interest issues in the ICT industries shift from traditional problems of coordinating hardware, software and infrastructure to concerns about the role of standards in the management of digital content, especially concerning ownership rights and digital permanence. We can all look forward to the many elaborations of this new paradigm that I am sure will begin to emerge within a very short time.

Richard Hawkins,
Professor and Canada Research Chair in Science, Technology and Innovation Policy, University of Calgary, Canada

Acknowledgements

This volume builds on two projects. First, it draws heavily on a European Union project funded under the Information Society Technologies priority of the 6th Framework Programme. The project, called 'Networking Organizations – Research into Standards and Standardization' (NO-REST, project co-ordinator: Knut Blind, 2004–06) was a co-operation between the Fraunhofer Institute (Knut Blind and Stefan Gauch), Aachen University (Kai Jakobs), TNO Institute for Strategy, Technology and Policy (Richard Hawkins), Delft University of Technology (Tineke Egyedi and Jos Vrancken), STEP SINTEF (Eric Iversen and Richard Tee), the University of Edinburgh (Ian Graham, Raluca Bunduchi and Martina Gerst), and ETSI (Yves Chauvel). It focused on the supply and demand side of information and communication technology (ICT) standards for networked organizations and on their interaction, which is an important source of standards' dynamics. 'Standards' dynamics' is a term that refers to what happens to standards once they have been developed. It has received very little scholarly attention despite the difficulties surrounding it. Standards' dynamics was the theme of the NO-REST work package led by Tineke Egyedi. Most of the contributions to this work package have since evolved into chapters in this volume. In the context of the NO-REST project our gratitude goes to the European Commission for funding the project, and to our NO-REST colleagues for their support, feedback and discussions.

Second, the volume capitalizes on research performed by the Delft University of Technology (Tineke Egyedi) and sponsored by Sun Microsystems (interoperability project, 2003–04 and 2006–07). We are particularly grateful to John Hill, Carl Cargill and Emil Sarpa for their relentless interest in and support for this strand of research.

Two external contributors, Kees van der Meer and Josephine Thomas, who were not involved in either of the above projects, have been invited to contribute because of the high interest of their work for our theme. We are proud to include their chapters in this volume.

Finally, we sincerely thank our reviewers and colleagues Jan van den Berg (Delft University of Technology), Raluca Bunduchi (University of Aberdeen Business School), Martina Gerst (University of Edinburgh), Ole Hanseth (University of Oslo), Arjan Loeffen (Valid/Vision), Jaroslav Spirco (Delft University of Technology), Mostafa Hashem Sherif (AT&T), Nelson Enano (student at Delft University of Technology) for their useful reviews of earlier chapter versions; Donna Mehos for her valuable feedback about language use in two of the chapters; and, not least, Brigitte Essoun and Sabine Wurst for helping us with cumbersome aspects of the editorial work.

Tineke M. Egyedi and Knut Blind
Delft/Berlin, 2008

Abbreviations

AAP	American Association of Publishers
AFNOR	Association Française de Normalisation
AIM	Application Interpreted Model
ALG	Application Level Gateway
AMS	Acquisition Management Systems
ANSI	American National Standards Institute
AP	Access Point
ARM	Application Reference Model
ASN.1	Abstract Syntax Notation 1
ATA	Air Transport Association
Amd	Technical Amendment
BSI	British Standards Institute
CALS	Continuous Acquisition and Life cycle Support
CCC	RWTH's Computing and Communication Centre
CCITT	Comité Consultatif International Téléphonique et Télégraphique (now ITU-T)
CDMA	MoD Central Data Management Authority
CDMA2000	Code Division Multiple Access 2000
CE	Conformité Européenne
CEN	Comité Européen de Normalisation
CEN/ISSS	CEN/Information Society Standardization System
CENELEC	Comité Européen de Normalisation Electrotechnique
CIDR	Classless Interdomain Routing
CSS	Cascading Style Sheets
Cor	Technical corrigendum
DC	Dublin Core
DCMI	Dublin Core Metadata Initiative
DCQ	Dublin Core Qualifiers
DECT	Digital Enhanced Cordless Telecommunications
DIN	Deutsches Institut für Normung
DIS	Draft International Standard
DNS	Domain Name System
DOI	Diffusion of Innovation
DSSSL	Document Style Semantics and Specification Language
DTD	Document Type Definition

DVD	Digital Versatile Disc
DVD+RDL	DVD Recordable Dual Layer
DoD	US Department of Defense
ECMA	European Computer Manufacturers Association (now ECMA International)
ECMA TC31	ECMA Technical Committee 31
EMC	Electromagnetic Compatibility
ERB	Editorial Review Board
ESPRIT	European Strategic Program of Research and Development in Information Technology
ETSI	European Telecommunications Standards Institute
Ed.	Edition
FCD	Final Committee Document
FDIS	Final Draft International Standard
GCA	Graphic Communications Association
GML	Generalized Markup Language
GSM	Global System for Mobile communications
HIPERLAN	HIgh PErformance Radio Local Area Network standard
HTML	HyperText Markup Language
HyTime	Hypermedia Time based structuring language
ICANN	Internet Corporation for Assigned Names and Numbers
ICS	International Classification for Standards
ICT	Information and Communication Technology
IEC	International Electrotechnical Commission
IEEE	Institute of Electrical and Electronics Engineers
IETF	Internet Engineering Task Force
IMAP	Internet Message Access Protocol
IP	Internet Protocol
IPR	Intellectual Property Right
IPT	Integrated Project Team
IPv4	Internet Protocol version 4
IPv6	Internet Protocol version 6
IR	Infrared
IS	International Standard
ISDN	Integrated Services Digital Network
ISO	International Standardization Organization
ISP	International Standardized Profile (Chapter 9)
ISP	Internet Service Provider (Chapter 5)
IT	Information Technology
ITU	International Telecommunication Union
ITU-T	International Telecommunication Union – Telecom standardization sector

IrDA	Infrared Data Association
JTC 1	Joint Technical Committee 1 of ISO/IEC
LAN	Local Area Network
LLC	Logical Link Control
MAC	Medium Access Control
MAN	Metropolitan Area Networks
MES	Metadata Element Set
MMCD	MultiMedia Compact Disc
MODS	Metadata Object Description Schema
MoD	Ministry of Defence (UK)
MoPS	Mobile Professors and Students
NAT	Network Address Translation
NATO	North Atlantic Treaty Organization
NIST	National Institute of Standards and Technology (US)
OCLC	Online Computer Library Center
ODA	Open Document Architecture
ODF	Open Document Format
ODIF	Open Document Interchange Format
OMG	Object Management Group
OOXML	Office Open XML
OSI	Open Systems Interconnection
PC	Personal Computer
PDA	Personal Digital Assistant
prEN	Draft European standards
RAMP	Rapid Acquisition of Manufactured Parts
RFC	Request For Comments ('Internet standards' are also RFCs)
RIPE	Réseaux IP Européens
RUP	Rational Unified Process
SC	SubCommittee
SD	Super Density
SDIF	SGML Document Interchange Format
SDL	Specification and Description Language
SDO	Standards Development Organization
SGML	Standard Generalized Markup Language
SIP	Session Initiation Protocol
SMTP	Simple Mail Transfer Protocol
SOAP	Simple Object Access Protocol
SOHO	Small Office or Home Office
SRU	Search/Retrieve via URL
SRV	SeRVice (part of data record in DNS)
SRW	Search/Retrieve Web service

SSE	Support Solutions Envelope of MoD
STEP	STandard for the Exchange of Product model data
TCP	Transport Control Protocol
TEI	Text Encoding Initiative
TOE	Technology, Organization, Environment
TPAD	Terminal Packet Assembly/Disassembler
TR	Technical Report
TWG	Technical Working Group
UML	Unified Modelling Language
UNICODE	Unique, universal, and uniform character encoding
URMEL	Ubiquitous RWTH for Mobile E-Learning
USPI-NL	Dutch Process and Power Industry Association
VPN	Virtual Private Network
W-CDMA	Wideband Code Division Multiple Access
W3C	World Wide Web Consortium
WAN	Wide Area Networks
WEP	Wired Equivalent Privacy
WG 8	Working Group 8
WLAN	Wireless Local Area Network
WORM	Write Once Read Many times
XML	EXtensible Markup Language
XML WG	XML Working Group
ZING	Z39.50 International Next Generation

1. General Introduction

Tineke M. Egyedi and Knut Blind

Our society is imbued with standards. Where successful, they go unnoticed. We do not need to think twice about which one is the cold water tap or what to do when we get a green traffic light signal (United Nations 1949). In this respect: 'standards are like keys always hung at the same nail – they free up our mind for more useful thoughts'.[1]

Standards allow us to deal with our environment in an almost unconscious way. Regrettably, though, they forcibly make their way to our senses when they do not perform as expected or are not being complied with. Their existence may show up in small, seemingly inconspicuous daily events – such as when we unsuccessfully try to push open an exit door when leaving a public building.[2] We assume exit doors will swing outward. This is standard procedure and so engrained in our minds that in such a situation most of us will first try to push open the door a second time before pulling it open. The significance of this standard and the full drama of non-compliance only reveals itself when an emergency situation arises in a public building. With other examples, such as driving on the wrong side of the road, the consequences of non-compliance are more immediately evident.

Not only do we notice standards when they do not perform as expected and are not complied with, we also become aware of them when they change. Standards' change is the main subject of this book. To an onlooker, changing standards may seem to contradict the intuitive perception that standards are stable entities. In practice, nevertheless, standards are not static. They are updated, revised and replaced by new standards. They are dynamic and *do* change.

Standards' change can be a source of irritation and a highly unsettling experience. The impact of change can be illustrated by the switch which some countries have made from the imperial to metric measurement units. Two news events come to mind. First, in 1999 NASA lost a spacecraft for orbiting Mars because certain data on rocket thrust were mistakenly taken to be expressed in metric units. Second, in 2001 a plane crashed into a house after it ran out of fuel because the pilot 'had miscalculated the conversion from US gallons to litres when requesting fuel before taking off'.[3] The two accidents are somewhat out of the ordinary but they are symptomatic of the daily difficulties which people have adjusting to standards' change. The phenomenon would therefore seem to deserve more systematic scrutiny.

Although there is a growing body of knowledge about standards and their development, standards' change is a new area of research. A number of fundamental questions still need to be answered. In this volume we focus on the causes of standards' change and explore why standards are not stable. This question, in turn, raises a string of other questions such as: Under what circumstances is change (un)desirable and (un)avoidable? What determines the impact of standards' change? Together, we hope to offer a set of key concepts, insights and thought-provoking illustrations that help us understand and cope with the phenomenon of standards' dynamics.

In this introductory chapter, we aim to develop the common ground necessary for analysing the problem of standards' change, and for situating the following chapters. We explain what we mean by a standard and specify the kind of standards on which this volume focuses; we address the value of standards and how it relates to their stability; and we discuss issues of standards' change, possible types of change, and the problems and possible impact of change. We also argue why the field of information and communication technology (ICT) is specifically suited to study standards' change, and conclude by presenting an overview of the subjects covered in the individual contributions.

WHAT IS A STANDARD?

The metaphor of 'keys always hung at the same nail' might refer not only to standards but also to the benefits of acquiring a habit. What, then, characterizes a standard and distinguishes it from, say, a habit, a regulation or a treaty? Many standardization scholars have struggled with this question. There are several definitions, all of which have their value and constraints (e.g. de Vries 1999, p. 15). In this volume, we use the term 'standard' in two main senses, namely in the sense of committee standards[4] and in the sense of *de facto* standards.

A committee standard is a very specific type of agreement. It is a specification developed by a committee for repeated use. It can be: 'a document established by consensus and approved by a recognized body, that provides, for common and repeated use, rules, guidelines or characteristics for activities or their results, aimed at the achievement of the optimum degree of order in a given context' (ISO/International Electrotechnical Commission [IEC] 2004, p. 8). However, the element of 'approval by a recognized body' in this definition only covers standards developed by the formal standards bodies such as the International Organization of Standardization (ISO). That is, in this volume we also address committee standards from, for instance, standards consortia (e.g. World Wide Web Consortium [W3C]) and professional organizations (e.g. Institute of Electrical and Electronics Engineers [IEEE]). We therefore prefer a slightly adapted ISO/IEC definition of 'committee standard': a document established by consensus that provides, for common and repeated use, rules, guidelines or characteristics for activities or their results, aimed at the achievement of the optimum degree of order in a given context. Committee standards are usually meant for voluntary use. We will not be addressing standards that are developed by government committees and which are therefore more likely to become mandatory through regulation.

Laypersons often use the term 'standard' in the second sense of *de facto* standard. *De facto* standards are widely adopted (specifications or company standards that underlie) products, services and practices. Examples are the cold water tap placed on the right-hand side and the portable document format (PDF) specification of Adobe – which by the way has recently been formalized by ISO.[5] In economic terms, *de facto* standards have a significant market share. Because the relevant products, services or practices are widely applied, their specifications are referred to and built to by other parties. *De facto* standards, too, undergo changes (e.g. software updates). Moreover, as several chapters will show, sometimes specifications derived from *de facto* standards are fed into standards committees and become committee standards.

Apart from the distinction between committee and *de facto* standards, standards may cover a whole range of areas and specifications. The most elaborate taxonomy classifies and sub-classifies standards according to the subject matter they address, the way standard development takes place (e.g. open or restricted participation), and how standards are used (de Vries 2006). To illustrate the latter, standards serve different purposes. Without aiming for completeness, there are: behavioural standards such as 'hazard analysis critical control points (HACCP)' that specify how to handle food in hospitals; interface and compatibility[6] standards such as 'global system for mobile communications (GSM)' for mobile telephony and the ISO standard for freight container dimensions; 'threshold limit values', and 'maximum allowable concentration values' that specify reference values, for example, for a smog alert; and classification standards such as colour codes for paint (e.g. RAL) and the 'international statistical classification of diseases and related health problems' (Bowker and Star 1999). In this volume, we focus on compatibility standards in the field of ICT, including consumer electronics.

THE VALUE OF STANDARDS

Standards make life easier because we can refer to them implicitly and explicitly, and thus reduce what economists term the informational transaction costs (Kindleberger 1983).[7] Moreover, they create compatibility (i.e. interoperability). They allow products to work together and equipment parts to be replaced. In anonymous markets, complementary products can be used together based on standard interfaces. As points of reference, standards co-ordinate technology development (Schmidt and Werle 1998). They structure and co-ordinate the way markets develop. Standards-based clusters of economic activity emerge, such as the product cluster for paper processing equipment such as printers, copiers and fax machines that is based on the common A-series of paper formats (ISO 216).

There are many economic benefits to standards. As Table 1.1 indicates, standards facilitate trade and allow economies of scale. They increase economic efficiency and contribute significantly to economic growth (see Blind 2004 for a more comprehensive treatment and Department of Trade and Industry [DTI] 2005).

Table 1.1 Main functions of compatibility standards

Function of standards	Effect on the market
Information	Reduce transaction costs, correct adverse selection,[8] facilitate trade
Compatibility	Create network externalities,[9] avoid lock-ins
Variety reduction	Allow economies of scale, build critical mass

Source: Blind (2004), adapted.

INTRODUCING STANDARDS' CHANGE

To be of value, however, standards need to be stable – at least for a certain period of time. The problem is that often they are not. Standards are revised, extended, replaced, succeeded, withdrawn, reinstated, etc. In short, they are dynamic. We reserve the term 'standards' dynamics' for the changes to and interaction between standards, that is, to what happens to standards once they have been set. It includes the changes which standards undergo, competition between standards, and the interaction and friction between complementary standards. It takes standards development into account as a source of dynamics in existing standards.

Categories of Change

Although certain chapters also address other elements of standards' dynamics,[10] the emphasis in this book is on standards' change. We distinguish three categories of change each of which can be plotted onto the standard's

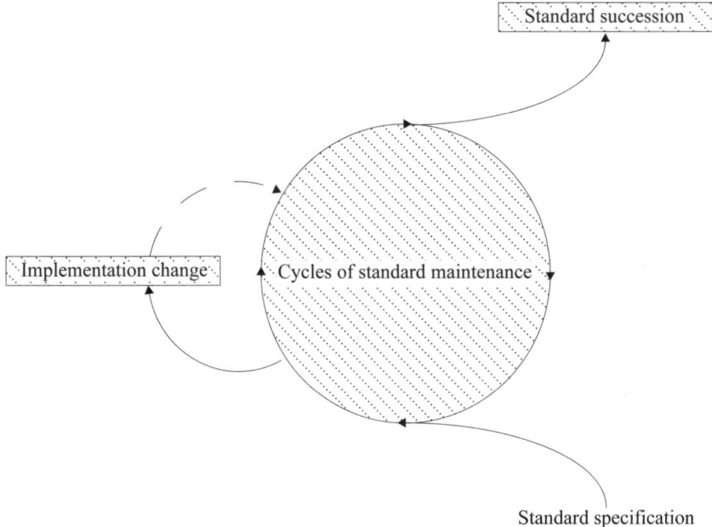

Figure 1.1 *Three categories of standards change: implementation change, maintenance and succession in the extended life cycle of a standard*

life cycle (Figure 1.1), that is, implementation change, standard maintenance and standard succession.

The life cycle starts with the development of a specification and its publication. Standards' change, which is our main interest, refers to what follows. When a standard is used, that is, implemented in a product, a service or a practice, it may undergo changes. The specification may only partly be implemented in order to suit the local situation (e.g. Timmermans and Berg 1997); or it may be extended and implemented in a way that ties customers to a producing company ('extend and embrace' strategy). In such situations, where the implementation deviates from the standard, we speak of 'implementation change'.

The second category of change falls within the scope of 'standard maintenance'. It includes: developing a new standard edition, a corrigendum, an amendment or a revision; merging and splitting standards: getting a standard accepted by another standards body; and withdrawing and reinstating a standard.

The third category of change is closely related and is that of 'standard succession'. The term refers to the replacement and substitution of one standard by another in an area of standardization, and includes what may be recognized in retrospect as the next generation of the standard. Where developed by the same committee, standard succession can be viewed as an extension to, and special case of, standard maintenance. However, different committees and even competing standards bodies may be involved in developing successors.

Figure 1.1 visualizes the relation between the three categories of standards dynamics. From the moment the standard specification has been defined, the cycles of standard maintenance start. Feedback from implementers may be the reason to revise a standard (dotted arrow); while too many maintenance cycles may indicate that a more radical change, i.e. a new standard is required. From the perspective of standards change, succession is viewed as an extension of the standard's life cycle.

PROBLEMS OF STANDARDS' CHANGE

Standards' change is a double-edged sword. On the one hand, there is a definite positive side to certain changes. Standards change accompanies innovation in science and technology. A self-evident example in the field of medicine is that new research might well result in a changed reference value for medical treatment. It may mean a lower dose of medication and fewer side-effects for patients. In the field of ICT, the updates to the standard for character encodings (Unicode 2006) illustrate that change is an ongoing activity in this field. In such cases, standards' change is a regular occurrence and standards maintenance is part of what Kuhn (1970) calls 'normal problem solving'. Some regulatory and policy areas greatly depend on standards, and therefore need to find ways to cope with standards change. In this vein, the European Union has decided not to include standards in regulation precisely because standards change so often. Redrafting regulation would require too much time and effort. Therefore a referential approach has been developed, which allows standards to evolve without affecting the regulatory framework. This referential approach, confirmed in 1985 and called the New Approach, is still in place.

On the other hand, there has been little systematic scrutiny of the problematic side of standards' change – let alone of strategic policy on how to deal with its negative impact. For, while stable standards create transparency and reduce informational transaction costs, changing standards have the opposite effect; they decrease transparency (e.g. due to lack of insight in the functional differences between versions) and increase transaction costs. Standards' change involves new costs (e.g. costs of updating the standard) and devaluates earlier investments (i.e. sunk costs). It diminishes self-evident interoperability. That is, uncertainty may arise about the interoperability of products complying with different standard versions. There is more at stake than the difficulty of getting used to changes – however bothersome and time-consuming that can be. The consequence of standards change in ICT, for example, may well be that we cannot access our documents anymore (van der Meer, Chapter 2).

Below, we highlight two problematic aspects to give a first sense of the range of issues that may arise: the economic costs of switching to the revised standard, and the question who actually benefits from and who carries the burden of change.

Switching Costs

Although no studies exist that specifically focus on standards' change, the work of economists on switching between competing *de facto* standards (e.g. Farrell and Saloner 1985) provides a useful theoretical underpinning for understanding the difficulty of switching to a new standard version. The costs involved in switching from one standard to another are called 'switching costs' (e.g. von Weizsacker 1982). Literature informs us that whether or not a party switches standards depends, in particular, on the size of the installed base, the improvements offered by the competing standard, and the speed with which network externalities are expected to be realized. In addition to a likely loss of past investments in terms of time, effort and money, new investments in equipment and training have to be made. When the sum of these switching costs become too high, 'lock-in' occurs (Farrell 1990).

Arguably, doubts and deliberations that make it difficult for parties to switch between competing standards, like the need to depreciate earlier investments, also apply to switching from an old to a new standard's version. Similar switching costs are involved.

Who is Most Affected by Change?

Standards' change influences some groups more than others and thus raises questions of who benefits from, and who bears the costs of, change. Usually, some parties have more to gain from standards change than others. The stakes are distributed asymmetrically not only between those who develop and change standards (the developers), but also between developers, standard implementers (i.e. those who adopt standards in products, services, regulation, etc.), and those who buy the standard-compliant products and services, or are affected by them (end-users such as consumers).

Those who initiate the change are seldom the ones who bear its costs. In particular where lack of quality of an initial standard is the reason for a revision, the people responsible may not be the ones to pay (Sherif, Jakobs and Egyedi 2007). As Jakobs puts it: '[U]sers [...] are the ultimate sponsors of standardization (the costs of which are included in product prices). [...]

Moreover, users will suffer most from inadequate standards that will leave them struggling with incompatibilities' (Jakobs 2005b, p. 5).

We experience the mismatch between those who initiate change and those who pay for it in our daily lives. Microsoft products have become a *de facto* standard in both the home and the work environment. Users are required to download updates in response to software bugs and virus attacks. In addition, new software releases have kept many large organizations in an almost constant flux of information technology (IT) projects that usually not only involve the roll-out of software and adapted configurations but also include renewal of the stock of personal computers (Egyedi 2002). Not the producer but the consumer bears the costs of change. In the case of proprietary products, change of the *de facto* standard is likely to be part of the company's business model. The company therefore will not recognize change as a problem nor want to solve it.

WHY FOCUS ON ICT STANDARDS?

This book focuses on ICT standards because ICT plays a crucial role in today's societies not only as an industry but also as a mover of other economic sectors and of the societal infrastructure. Standards are essential for ICT because they ensure interoperability between the numerous technical components, products, services, architectures and infrastructures in increasingly complex and networked environments. The degree of heterogeneity and complexity of ICT environments severely challenges ICT standardization.

Moreover, a set of interrelated developments further increases the pressure on the stability and longevity of standards as well as on standards organizations. First, the speed of technology development has increased dramatically leading to a further shortening of technology and product life cycles. This phenomenon is especially notable in the ICT sector. In certain areas of ICT, the shorter life cycles have challenged standards bodies to speed up the sometimes time-consuming, inclusive consensus process and better cater to the interests of ICT industry. Some of them have adopted new, more informal and flexible standards development procedures. In addition, since the 1990s, many so-called 'standards consortia' have emerged, most of which focus on a specific area in IT. This has led to differentiation in the landscape of ICT standardization organizations.

The worldwide diffusion of ICT systems has been the basis for the second development: the globalization of production. This has also created challenges for the standardization system. The worldwide, distributed production of goods and services, including the outsourcing of research and development (R&D), is creating additional demand for ICT standards. A further differentiation of the value chain requires new interfaces between the organizational units involved. Next to the growth in number of standards, the qualitative requirement of acquiring consensus among a higher number of stakeholders and the increased heterogeneity of their preferences is even more challenging. And even if consensus is reached, the diverse framework conditions of those implementing the ICT standards increase the likelihood of different implementation.

Related to the above two developments is a third one: the deregulation of many industries, in particular, the telecommunication sector. Publicly-owned companies have been privatized and legal frameworks have been substituted by self-regulatory schemes that include standardization. Therefore, the need to develop standards has increased while the stability of the surrounding conditions has decreased.

Because the rate of standards change is particularly high in the field of ICT, this area is well-suited for doing research on standards' dynamics.

RESEARCH QUESTION

With the increasing speed of technological change and globalization, both of which require more standards while leading to more competing standards, standards' dynamics – a new field of research – comes centre stage. This volume aims to lay a basis for understanding phenomena of standards' dynamics. In particular, it focuses on standards' change in the context of standard setting and use. Illuminating processes of change will help parties deal with change (i.e. develop company and policy strategies), where possible prevent unnecessary change – however difficult to define – and steer change in ways more acceptable to industry and society at large.

STRUCTURE OF THE BOOK

The field of standardization studies is interdisciplinary. The chapters contributed to this book have been written by economists, social scientists, computer scientists and engineers. They take different approaches and cover a wide range of committee and *de facto* standards. The chapters are organized into five parts.

The first part takes the problem-centred approach. It examines two prototypical problems that illustrate the impact of standards change in the field of ICT. The first, increasingly urgent, problem is that of sustainable digital data. In Chapter 2 van der Meer analyses how to maintain access to archival digital data over time (i.e. 'longevity'). He studies standards that facilitate the interchange and identification of documents and data, and their uniform retrieval (i.e. open document architecture/open document interchange format [ODA/ODIF], standard generalized markup language [SGML], the Dublin Core metadata element set, and the Z39.50 protocol), and analyses the revisions that these standards have undergone. In most cases, the changes to these standards make it very difficult to retain access.

A second problem area is that of standard-compliant, but incompatible, IT products and services (Chapter 3). In this chapter, Egyedi focuses on sources of incompatibilities that arise from implementation change. She derives her arguments from a panel discussion among experts, institutional analysis, and case studies of SGML and extensible markup language (XML), the open systems interconnection (OSI) model and the unified modelling language (UML). The study shows that heterogeneous implementation increases the need for *post hoc* changes, while improving the drafting process and ensuring the interoperability and implementability of standards would decrease the need to change standards.

Part 2 contains case studies that highlight different causes and kinds of change. In Chapter 4, Gauch illustrates the dynamics of competing standards for recordable digital versatile disc (DVD) technology. He analyses the underlying characteristics of the market structure in this area (including patent clusters), distinguishes between horizontal and vertical dynamics, and explains standards dynamics as part of a technology race. His longitudinal approach shows at what moments standards' dynamics is likely to occur and how the way standards are implemented may prolong the technology and standards race.

In Chapter 5, Vrancken, Kaart and Soares analyse two competing successors for the Internet protocol version 4 (IPv4) addressing scheme. These are IPv6, the 'official' successor to IPv4, and network address translation (NAT), a technical solution to address space shortage within IPv4. The authors arrive at a set of criteria that clarify why users are more likely to choose one standard solution over another. They explain the slow uptake of IPv6, and shed light on mechanisms that underlie the bottom-up adoption of new standards.

In Chapter 6, Egyedi and Loeffen analyse two successive standards on structured information exchange (i.e. SGML and XML), and demonstrate why, despite all efforts to the contrary, continuity and compatibility between them was not maintained. The authors use the distinction between different types of succession (i.e. graft, shift and revolution) to explain causes of discontinuous change and the impact of incompatible standards' succession on the market.

Part 3 focuses on the context in which standards are implemented and the implementation change which this may involve. The contribution by

Jakobs (Chapter 7) addresses the dynamics of the standards' implementation and installation in the case of the IEEE 802.11 wireless local area network (WLAN) standard. The study illustrates both the problem of implementing an evolving standard in a large setting, and the non-obvious solution to this problem: a standards-based single vendor strategy to avoid incompatible standard implementations.

In Chapter 8, Thomas, Probets, Dawson and King analyse the adoption and implementation of the standard for the exchange of product data (STEP) in the defence environment to identify factors unique to its adoption. They distinguish between and examine the issues that arise during primary adoption (the decision to adopt a standard) and secondary adoption (implementation of the project in an organization). Among other things, the study illustrates the complexities of coping with compatibility between different standard versions over time.

The fourth part of the book focuses on the scale of change. The case studies mentioned above would seem to indicate that many standards undergo changes, and that some standards even change often. However, quantitative research is needed to generalize from specific cases. This part presents the results of two quantitative studies of formal standards – since databases of informal and consortia standards are not available – each of which focuses on a different aspect of standards' dynamics. Egyedi and Heijnen analyse the scale of change of formal international IT standards with a focus on the type and number of changes that occur, while Blind analyses the lifetime of ICT standards and uses survival analysis to examine the causes of standards dynamics.

The conclusion presents a synthesis and characterization of the causes of standards change in the context of standard setting and use. It also explores areas for future research.

NOTES

1. Anonymous, quoted in Hurd and Isaak (2005, p. 68).
2. E.g. the Dutch 'Arbeidsomstandighedenbesluit, Artikel 3.7'.
3. 'Pilot cleared of crash charges', http://news.bbc.co.uk/1/hi/england/southern_counties/3081612.stm
4. We will avoid using the term 'open standards', because it raises more questions than it provides answers, and the term committee standard suffices for our purposes. For the interested reader we point to Krechmer (2006), who distinguishes different aspects of openness and angles (openness from the perspective of standard creators, implementers, and users).
5. In 2008 the Adobe PFD 1.7 Reference was published as ISO 32000.
6. Compatibility refers to: 'the suitability of products, processes or services for use together under specific conditions to fulfil relevant requirements without causing unacceptable interactions' (ISO/IEC 1991, 2.2).

7. Transaction costs are costs such as the time and resources required to establish a common understanding. Standards reduce transaction costs of negotiation because: 'both parties to a deal mutually recognize what is being dealt in' (Kindleberger 1983, p. 395). Standards reduce transaction costs between producers and costumers by improving recognition of technical characteristics and avoidance of buyer dissatisfaction (Reddy 1990). They reduce e.g. search costs since there is less need for customers to spend time and money evaluating products (Jones and Hudson 1996).
8. Adverse selection takes place if a supplier of inferior products gains market share through price competition because the supplier of high quality products has no means to signal the superior quality of its products to consumers. Quality standards support the latter in signalling activities, foster the co-existence of low and high quality market segments, and therefore minimize the likelihood that consumer selection is based on wrong assumptions.
9. The term network externalities refers to the situation that every new user in the network increases the value of being connected to the network (Farrell and Saloner 1985).
10. Standards' competition and change are both addressed in Gauch and in Vrancken et al. in this volume.

PART ONE

The Problem of Changing Standards

2. The Sustainability of Digital Data: Tension Between the Dynamics and Longevity of Standards

Kees van der Meer

INTRODUCTION: TAKING A BYTE OUT OF HISTORY

As a result of the innovation urge that characterizes ICT, the lifetime of information objects that are digital, like digital documents or computer programmes, is short. It may be some five years. By contrast, information objects that are archived – whether they be digital or not – may be expected to have a shelf life in excess of a century. Of course not all information objects need to be archived and preserved. Once an information object is no longer useful, it should be discarded. However, technical obsolescence is surely no reason to do so. The problems that arise from the difference between the lifetimes of digital and archival objects can be studied well in the area where digital and archival practices overlap: digital archival objects. 'Taking a byte out of history' is the catchy title of an article from 1990 that addresses the problem of valuable but unreadable and unprocessable old bit streams (US Government 1990):

1. Governments, publishers, ship-building companies, garages, and all kinds of other organizations have experienced difficulties reading digital texts in obsolete formats.
2. The original UK Domesday book of 1086 was readable for centuries and it still is. When the original celebrated its 900 year anniversary, in 1986, a kind of update in electronic form was produced. Ironically, the digital version of the Domesday Book became nearly unusable within a decade. Around 1998, a major effort had to be made to produce a new version that will hopefully last a bit longer.
3. Digital image collections have been made from original historical photos. The process of making digital surrogates is expensive, the reproduction of colours is demanding, and the handling requires care, because the original photos are vulnerable. Despite the efforts required to produce surrogates

from historical photos, several collections are under threat of becoming inaccessible because of the obsolescence of the image format, storage medium and access to the images (van Horik 2005).

4. The accessibility problem even shows up for digital-born data (i.e. digital materials like word processor documents, digital materials that have not been created by conversion of an analogue source). There is at present a growing worldwide interest in climatic change. New climatic models will be developed in the coming decades. These models are longitudinal in nature, and they must run on climatic data for many years to come (i.e. from the future past); and as these data cannot be reproduced once they are lost, they must be harvested and stored now. This means that right now, data concerning precipitation, terrain drain and river flow are harvested and archived for a distant future. The data must be archived in such a way that they can be read and processed for many years.

It is possible to prolong the lifetime of digital information objects and their building blocks. There are various strategies that are used to do so: refreshment, i.e. the bit stream is transferred to a new copy of the original medium; migration and conversion, i.e. the bit stream is transferred to a new medium, new format or new platform; and emulation, i.e. a computer system behaves like an earlier computer system. Strong general-purpose operational emulators exist (Hoeven et al. 2005; Kol et al. 2006).

Standards are building blocks for digital information objects, that is, for digital texts, the digital Domesday Book, digital copies of historical photos, climatic data and all kinds of other digital objects. Because contributions to digital information objects can come from colleagues everywhere and the objects may be used all over the world, there should be no obstruction in time or place. Standards are meant to improve interoperability independent of time and place. However, standards do not last forever. They may be subject to change and replacement in a time that is considered short in terms of the lifetime of digital archival objects. Therefore, the longevity of standards for digital archival objects must be considered.

Technical aspects of digital longevity are discussed by Meeuws et al. (2003). Digital longevity refers to the continuity of the building blocks of digital information objects: content, structure, layout, context and behaviour. Only if all these building blocks are preserved, will it be possible to inform correctly, timely, precisely, completely, and in a controllable way in the future. Digital longevity includes the notion of a records continuum (Upward 1996 and 1997), the control of 'records' in time and space for as long as they are valuable, with an emphasis on metadata management.

The question that arises is: how have standards for digital information objects taken in longevity requirements in the past, and what options are there for improvement? The statistics with regard to standards that have become obsolete (replaced, corrected, amended, etc.) indicate that the average lifetime of standards is five years (Egyedi and Heijnen, this volume). This means that the problem regarding the continuity and availability of information that in itself is not obsolete, is becoming urgent.

The question has been studied before by Egyedi and Loeffen (2002), who take a look at the efforts made to graft extensible markup language (XML) onto standard generalized markup language (SGML). 'Grafting' means developing a successor standard based on a predecessor standard with the aim of improving its functionality and/or usefulness while preserving compatibility (Egyedi and Loeffen, this volume).

We investigate this problem further. Four standards are considered: ODA/ODIF, SGML, the Dublin Core metadata element set, and the Z39.50 protocol. We describe how the demands for upgrading or modernization of these standards have been met in practice. The focus is on archival requirements. After a description and discussion of the current practices, we will reflect on the consequences of and present recommendations regarding how to deal with the tension between the dynamics and the longevity of standards for the sustainability of digital data.

DYNAMICS OF FOUR STANDARDS FOR DIGITAL ARCHIVAL OBJECTS

The four standards mentioned here focus on interrelated aspects of information management: the composition, labelling, retrieval and dissemination of documents. ODA/ODIF defines the architecture of documents and how their information and layout can be interchanged. SGML focuses on document structure and interchange, and so partly overlaps with ODA/ODIF. The Dublin Core standard introduces categories for labelling information components such as documents, in order to facilitate retrieval of those components from large collections. And finally Z39.50 defines a 'language' (protocol) for passing retrieval requests to information retrieval systems.

ODA/ODIF

ODA/ODIF, the open document architecture/open document interchange format, ISO standard 8613, first issued in 1989, was developed in a common effort by various standards organizations, including Comité Consultatif International Téléphoniquen et Télégraphique (CCITT) and European Computer Manufacturers Association (ECMA). ODA/ODIF describes a general information architecture to be used as an encoding framework for document interchange between open information processing systems. The standard includes a framework for document data models, layout structures and the interchange format, i.e. the construction of a data stream that enables the recipient to reconstruct the entities that have been sent. The standard describes a large number of functions and possibilities in a detailed way. After interchange has taken place a document including graphics and raster elements can even be presented as the sender intended the layout to be (formatted), it can allow processing like editing and reformatting (processable) to take place, or even both (formatted-processable) (Hunter et al. 1989).

ODA/ODIF was a well-known standard. INSPEC®, the bibliographic database of worldwide literature on physics, electronics and computing, lists no fewer than 84 references to scientific articles that have ODA in the title and that are about the office document architecture over the years 1986–96 (INSPEC 2007). In 1988, Carr stated that collaborative projects demonstrated the usefulness of the standard and that manufacturers were developing editors and translators (Carr 1988). Many ODA and ODIF tools were developed in the then well-known European strategic programme of research and development in information technology (ESPRIT) projects; ODA/ODIF even made it possible to interchange multimedia compound documents, to convert them to and from other formats, and to process them (ESPRIT 1990–93).

Few articles referred to actual use of ODA/ODIF in companies. Nevertheless, the developments on ODA/ODIF continued. The 1993–94 revision of the ODA/ODIF standard improved some of the minor defects in the 1989 standard and extended the facilities for colours, security, styles, probably hypermedia documents and others (Appelt 1993). In 1996, the number of articles on ODA/ODIF declines sharply. ODA/ODIF as such vanishes from the scientific literature.

Why did ODA/ODIF not become the commercial success it was supposed to be? The ODA/ODIF standard must have been too big: some ten thick volumes. Also, it must have been too complex: using ODA/ODIF required a software system that was expensive to build for a supplier, that was expensive to maintain for an ICT department, and that would have involved a lot of change and education requirements for the end-users.

The work on ODA/ODIF contributed to the insight into the area of digital object structures. Moreover, operational tools have been developed. However, no agreement was reached concerning a strategy to archive and update ODA/ODIF tools. At the moment it has already become difficult to process ODA/ODIF encoded documents. In a few decades, most ODA/ODIF developers will have retired, which means that an entire data storage and processing solution has come and gone in a few decades. If anyone wanted to access ODA/ODIF encoded documents (historical research on the genesis of digital object structures), they would most likely require a major reconstruction programme. From the point of view of digital longevity of ODA/ODIF encoded documents, the short lifetime of the ODA/ODIF standard is disastrous.

SGML

SGML is the standard generalized markup language, ISO standard 8879:1986. SGML was initiated as early as 1969 by Goldfarb, Mosher and Lorie. It offers a framework for data models of encoded (text) objects, like title, author, introduction, and paragraph. The framework allows for a description by names in markup tags.

Unlike ODA/ODIF, SGML is not intended to describe the layout structure or the interchange format. Other building blocks exist for the layout structure. For example, hypertext markup language (HTML, ISO 15445:2000) is an application of SGML for the representation of web pages and the placing of references in documents that can point to other documents; DSSSL, the document style specification and semantics language (ISO 10179:1996) is a standard for formatting (resulting in the layout) of SGML documents; and SDIF, the SGML document interchange format standard (ISO standard 9069:1988) aims at the reconstruction of the bit stream. In the early days of digital documents, a framework to structure document information was very welcome. Because, compared to ODA, SGML is a lightweight architecture, it was more successful than ODA. Elsevier, HMSO ('Her Majesty's Stationery Office', the UK government office for public sector information), the American Association of Publishers (AAP), ISO itself and many other publishers used SGML. In addition, many organizations dealing with the maintenance of complex and sizeable technical products, for instance ships, airplanes, medical cameras for body scans, and complex software, used SGML for the maintenance supporting technical documents.

In response to difficulties in using SGML in other application areas and in the World Wide Web environment (Egyedi and Loeffen, this volume), two things were done. Firstly, the SGML standard was revised in 1996 and 1999 (ISO/IEC 2007), and secondly, and probably more importantly, XML, a W3C Recommendation, was developed (XML is no ISO standard, SGML was and is!).

We highlight some prominent differences between SGML and XML:[1]

1. Firstly, in SGML, many encoding constructs, as well as the character set, had to be declared prior to processing. For example, the fact that a tag was identified by pointed brackets was explicitly declared. SGML systems that catered for many such variant declarations were hard to build. It soon

turned out that companies used the same SGML declaration. The pressure to introduce this level of abstraction (as the standard required) kept the software market from delivering SGML tools. In contrast, XML uses a fixed lexical form, i.e. a fixed set of delimiters and the 'unique, universal, and uniform character encoding' (UNICODE) character set.

2. As a second example, in SGML a tag that had not been introduced in the grammar prior to the document could not be used. This meant that in the SGML definition all the possible cases had to be modeled as a 'document grammar'. This resulted in extremely high demands for requirements engineering and/or in lots of updates of operational SGML software. In contrast, XML does not require a grammar to be present; it therefore allows the introduction of undeclared tags. That is, the document will no longer be valid but may still be 'well-formed' (a well-known concept in computer science), in which case the application does not stop the execution of the application as it did with SGML.
3. As a final example, in SGML sections did not have to be marked explicitly by start- and end-tags (this can still be seen in HTML, which conforms to the old SGML). The SGML system was under some specific circumstances able to determine the start or end of a text element automatically. Of course, this was attractive from the manual editing perspective. However, XML documents are not expected to be manually coded. The XML standard dropped the nasty task of determining element start and end positions without explicit codes. All codes are entered explicitly.

As a result of such changes, an XML parser will normally not be able to parse an original SGML document, due to the absence of closing tags (and possibly for other reasons as well); and an original SGML parser cannot parse a common XML document that contains empty elements because the empty element syntax is unknown to (old) SGML.

The differences make it necessary to convert SGML software and information objects to XML. For several years, organizations have kept SGML applications running for their dynamic archive, to process SGML files and to use the functions in the SGML tools. The difficulties eventually could be overcome in a structured way; converters have been built. Nevertheless, it took a lot of work and trouble to 'translate' SGML to XML: both transition of Gigabytes of SGML files to XML in their local environment, and changes in software and work processes are costly; moreover, there are related changes, e.g. the standards related to SGML, such as DSSSL, 'hypermedia time based structuring language' (HyTime) and the character set to the standards related to XML. For the owners of SGML software and files, the transition from SGML to XML proved a costly affair. A second disadvantage is that not all SGML information objects that should have been kept have been or will be converted. Common practice tends to treat objects that have an obsolete format as garbage. By contrast, based on experience, best practices for records management adhere to the maxim of 'better safe than sorry' when it comes to keeping documents. A third problem is that the reprocessing of old files to make them readable may affect the legal status of the digital object. This problem may still come up, e.g. if life insurance documents or technical drawings of buildings or any other old information objects are SGML-encoded and the authentic information object is wanted in a legal conflict.

The transition from SGML to XML did not end in disaster. Although the backward compatibility of XML to the original SGML is limited, at least it is possible to convert most files. Having said that, the major drawbacks originating from the partial lack of backward compatibility should not be neglected.

The Dublin Core Metadata Element Set

Metadata are structured data that describe the characteristics of an information object. Metadata are important: archiving makes no sense and digital longevity requirements can be discarded if one cannot find the digital archival object in the future. This is one of the reasons why the records continuum emphasizes metadata management. The Dublin Core metadata element set, 'Dublin Core MES' or even 'DC', issued as the ISO standard 15836:2003, describes web publications. The metadata are not only meant to describe text, but also images, video, sound and web pages. The original 'core', also known as 'simple' DC, consists of 15 elements (Dublin Core Metadata Initiative [DCMI] 2007), see Table 2.1. The list has been stable since shortly after it was set up in 1995, after the Online Computer Library Center (OCLC) conference in Dublin (Ohio).

Table 2.1 The 15 simple DC elements

1. Title	6. Contributor	11. Source
2. Creator	7. Date	12. Language
3. Subject	8. Type	13. Relation
4. Description	9. Format	14. Coverage
5. Publisher	10. Identifier	15. Rights

Few early users found that these 15 elements satisfied all their needs. There were many ideas with regard to expanding the list to make it better suited to more types of digital objects, including software components and cultural heritage materials. However attractive these ideas might seem, the resulting expansion would have robbed the 'simple' DC of its charm of simplicity and orderliness. Therefore a strategy was adapted that introduced optional expansions, while keeping the original setup intact. The 'qualified DC' (DC Qualifiers [DCQ] 2007) introduces the idea of 'element refinement, encoding scheme, and expansion'.

1. An example of the DCQ 'element refinement' – the descriptor 'DC: date' – can be used more specifically. In DCQ, 'DC: date' may have the narrower terms 'created, valid, available, issued, and modified', as well as 'date-Accepted, dateCopyrighted and dateSubmitted' (DCQ 2007).
2. An example of the DCQ 'encoding scheme': in DCQ the 'DC: date' or its narrower terms are required to be represented according to the 'W3C date and time format', which is a specification of ISO standard 8601:1988.
3. An example of the DCQ 'expansion': DCQ has the extra element of 'provenance'. Simple DC cannot describe and is also not designed to describe ownership and custody of or any changes in a resource. For archival information objects, the ownership and custody are important: they could support their legal evidential value. That is why 'provenance' is needed. There are other 'expansion' elements; in January 2007 DCQ had 22 elements.

The approach presented above shows a way of adapting changing demands for, in this case, the Dublin Core MES. The question is whether or not the longevity demand for the metadata has now been solved now. We discuss two objections: the role of alternative metadata element sets and the value of the metadata.

Firstly, metadata must be useful in retrieving information. DC was not readily accepted for web publications. Lawrence and Giles (1999), in their classical article in *Nature*, reported that in February 1999 only 0.3 per cent of the websites contained DC metadata. Although the number of websites with DC metadata is growing, most of them still contain no DC metadata at all. Is it worthwhile to add DC metadata to your website? Zhang and Dimitroff (2004) analysed whether the inclusion of the DC subject field improved the retrieval of websites in search engines. Although in general they found this to be the case, the results are not conclusive. In his article 'Dublin Core: an obituary', Beall (2004) was not enthusiastic about the DC. He argues that: 'the Dublin Core metadata standard has rapidly become obsolete', due to 'the bloated, European-style bureaucracy' of the Dublin Core initiative. It will 'soon be popularly replaced by the Metadata Object Description Schema (MODS)' (see also MODS 2007). Incidentally, a 'crosswalk', a Dublin Core MES mapping to MODS, has been published; and also, just in case, a mapping back from MODS to Dublin Core MES (Mapping 2007). These studies indicate that an alternative to DC/DCQ may be developed in the future. Although a crosswalk between DC and its successor seems possible, the result could be as ambiguous as it was in the case of the SGML-XML transition.

Secondly, the metadata element fields must have a value. The standardization efforts to describe unambiguously the assigned value of the metadata of a digital object are the domain of ISO 11179 metadata registries. This is essential for archival purposes (van Horik 2005). This work is still in progress. ISO 11179 is still partly under construction.

We can conclude that the problem of digital longevity of metadata has not been completely solved yet. Nevertheless, the way in which the original, 'simple' DC has been elaborated into a larger tool, DCQ, in a way that ensures that there is no objection to using the original DC, is an example of how to adapt a standard without negative consequences for the longevity of the digital information objects.

The Z39.50 Protocol

Z39.50 is the protocol for information retrieval from remote databases; Z39.50 describes the rules for exchanging information for connection-oriented, programme-to-programme communication for information retrieval. A protocol is a type of object like http (port 80), ftp (port 21), SMTP (port 25), and Internet message access protocol (IMAP) (port 143). Z39.50 has port number 210 and has been issued as ISO 23950:1998, although usually called Z39.50.

There have been various versions of Z39.50 (Needleman 2000): *Version 1* was created in 1988, before the widespread adoption of the Internet. The library automation communities and online information specialists used national and international networks to query bibliographic data bases like INSPEC, ChemAbs, and Medline. In those days, few people had heard of Z39.50. *Version 2* was a combination of Z39.50 mark 1 and the search and retrieve protocols ISO 10162:1992 and ISO 10163:1993; the latter were later withdrawn by ISO. Some organizations offered their own add-ons to the Z39.50 protocol, and a meeting in 1995 of the Z39.50 Implementators Group (ZIG) led to *Version 3* of the Z39.50 standard (Over et al. 1995). In 1999–2002, there were discussions on *Version 4*. It included removal of unwanted duplicates in a search result from several sources.

Z39.50 is widely used and in various ways in libraries. Library queries conform to Z39.50; personal bibliographic managers such as EndNote, ProCite, and Reference Manager use Z39.50 to access bibliographic data bases; and union catalogues, describing holdings of several libraries, are addressed by Z39.50 queries. Libraries can keep only a fraction of the books and other information objects their clients may want, so they have to use electronic facilities for loans and information exchange. Because the process of cataloguing books has always been labour-intensive, they welcome the chance to reuse cataloguing data from elsewhere.

In spite of all the work on Z39.50 and the many users, its use is going to decline. Z39.50 has been assigned to port 210, whereas port 80, the http port for the World Wide Web, has become immensely popular. Since 2001, in the framework of 'Z39.50 international next generation (ZING)', SRU/SRW ('search/retrieve via URL' and 'search/retrieve web service', via 'simple object access protocol [SOAP]') are being developed. The result should be the reuse of the query facilities of Z39.50 while replacing the outdated port.

Libraries have invested millions of their moderate budgets in complying with the Z39.50 standard. Disinvestment as a result of the conversion of Z39.50 to SRU/SRW is unlikely to make them happy.

A significant but as yet underexposed aspect of digital longevity concerns the behaviour of a system in response to queries (e.g. a Z39.50 query). The behaviour of a dynamic digital information object, namely an information system, has to be preserved. Z39.50 has always been interpreted differently by different vendors. One of the peculiarities of Z39.50 is that a target server receiving queries has some liberty to map a query to the indexes it has available. Different servers may thus yield different results. This means that with Z39.50 it is difficult to prove that a person or an organization had access to certain sources of information (the web services of SRW, Z39.50's successor, could bring about a change in this respect). The privacy of a person may be violated if it can be proved that certain information can be accessed; the responsibility of an organization may be different in a dispute on whether it really has not been aware of certain facts. How long will people remember the peculiarities of Z39.50 after it has been superseded?

Apart from differences between the query results of different Z39.50 implementations, a change in standards (e.g. from Z39.50 to SRW) may also give a different result, which affects digital longevity. Although changes in dynamic objects like information systems as yet have no legal impact, this may change in the future. The legal consequences of the lack of preservation of dynamic aspects, that is, the 'behaviour' of digital information objects, remains to be studied in the future.

TOWARDS LONGEVITY OF STANDARDS

Longevity requirements on information objects have existed for ages. They represent the following values:

1. The informational value, which is lost if the information object can no longer be read.

2. The legal status of information objects, which is tainted if one cannot prove that the information object is authentic (that is, if it cannot be proven that the information object is what it purports to be). This is an important issue as laws (e.g. in the US: Sarbanes-Oxley) and managerial best practices demand that the legal status of information be guaranteed.
3. The cultural historical value, which is often felt to be the most important value, albeit for a much smaller number of information objects.

These values are seriously threatened if the content, structure, layout, context and behaviour change or have not demonstrably been preserved.

Based on the examples ODA/ODIF, SGML, Dublin Core MES, and Z39.50 protocol, we can examine the intersection of the dynamics and the longevity of standards in the light of the sustainability of digital data. The fast developments in ICT in the last few decades have led to a very visible change in the amounts and types of information objects. It has also led to profound changes in the structure and use of digital information objects. The digital information objects and their usage are supported by building blocks that have been developed into standards, like ODA/ODIF, SGML, the Dublin Core MES, and the Z39.50 protocol. These standards apparently are under pressure to being changed, updated, extended and/or expanded every few years.

The four examples yielded the following results:

1. ODA/ODIF-encoded documents are hardly readable anymore and may soon be regarded as lost. This is the worst case scenario.
2. SGML-encoded documents may be transferred to XML but not without costs and problems, due to the differences in details between the SGML standard and the XML standard. This means that with SGML it has been possible to ensure some of the longevity of digital information objects.
3. The DC metadata can be used without drawbacks by any artifact that requires DCQ metadata. The DC standard is preserved in DCQ. This is the best case scenario. DC descriptions will not always comply with DCQ, but DC descriptions remain useable in DCQ.
4. The Z39.50 standard operates on a dynamic digital information object, and the result is likely to be different from that of its successor SRW. Although this constitutes a change, the behaviour of digital archival objects is such a new topic that society does not consider it a problem yet. However, it may be a problem in the future.

In an ideal world, standards are stable. Standards are not too bulky, complex or difficult to use, and never need revision. But new societal demands emerge continuously. From the viewpoint of memory institutions like archives, this world is less than ideal. Here, a standard may have to change. In that case, a new version of the standard should offer backward compatibility with the former version. The upgrade of the Dublin Core standard does this. It is the grafting situation that Egyedi and Loeffen describe in this volume. Backward compatibility ensures the longevity of the digital information objects to be used in a distant future. A worse situation is the case of SGML. Omitting the need to include the closing tag was a sensible decision in 1986; the revision of that decision in 1996, making the closing tag compulsory, was sensible as well, it helped the further development of SGML/XML. But in this and comparable cases, we should be aware that improving a standard to make it more suitable for future use may be detrimental with regard to the future use of today's assets. Many standards have been converted and many will follow. We recommend that the costs involved in adapting to a new situation in terms of the loss of existing valuable digital data be taken into account before a decision is made to convert a standard. The history of ODA/ODIF is the worst case: documents based on the ODA standard will probably be lost.

Many users – archivists and records managers, computer scientists, standardization staff, and end-users – encounter problems when digital information objects can no longer be read or used because the standard in question has become obsolete. Ultimately, all these users have to pay the price for the conversion and/or the loss of data, which means that they all have a vested interest in strategies aimed at keeping standards backwards compatible. This must be a topic for every course on standards and standardization.

CONCLUSION

Our research question was: how have standards for digital information objects taken in longevity requirements in the past, and what options are there for improvement? We studied the changes in ODA/ODIF, SGML, the Dublin Core MES, and the Z39.50 protocol, four standards that are building blocks for digital information objects. We have concluded that there are serious issues at stake with regard to the interoperability of standards for digital information objects over time. The changes in standards, even within a single generation indicate that within a few generations it may no longer be possible to access information that we use today. The content, structure, lay-out, context and/or behaviour of digital information objects are at risk as a result of the changes in standards. That risk puts a burden on the dynamics of standards. Backward compatibility is to be preferred. In cases where that may not be attainable, we still recommend restraint; standards developers, specialists and end-users should be aware that improving a standard may have a serious effect on the accessibility of historical information. If a change in a standard is considered, the consequences of conversion of archived digital information objects and possible losses should explicitly be taken into account. In this way, a trade-off can be brought about in the demands for the dynamism and the longevity of standards for the sustainability of digital data.

NOTE

1. Clark (1997, Chapter 1) contains a complete list of changes.

3. An Implementation Perspective on Sources of Incompatibility and Standards' Dynamics[1]

Tineke M. Egyedi

INTRODUCTION

Standard-compliant products do not always interoperate, as most IT users will have experienced. This is a frustrating problem, and sometimes drastic measures are taken to circumvent it. In a well-documented case study a university decided to adopt a standards-based single-vendor solution for its local area network (IEEE 802.11b; see Jakobs, Chapter 7, on voluntary vendor lock-in). The single-vendor 'solution', whether based on open or *de facto* standards, is a fairly widespread defensive procurement strategy. Although it may resolve incompatibility in the short run, it undermines an important asset of open standards, namely that they allow us to combine the best of different vendors and protect us from vendor lock-in – a different, but equally frustrating problem.

In this chapter we take a closer look at the problem of standard-compliant – but incompatible – IT products and services and analyse the causes of incompatibility in order to better understand how we can deal with them.

Some companies introduce changes to standards to frustrate the development and adoption of competitive products, or to lock users into a proprietary technology. They, for example, elaborate standards by adding extra functionalities (embrace-and-extend strategy), implement only part of the standard (embrace-and-omit strategy), or introduce local adaptations to the standard (embrace-and-adapt). In all three situations the integrity of a standard is at stake.[2] Sometimes interoperability can be recreated, but this requires a great deal of additional effort. A more common result is market fragmentation.

What Sherif et al. (2005) argue with regard to standards quality, namely that there is no corrective market incentive to address lack of standards quality, also applies to the corrupt use of standards.

> The diverse interests that affect standardization, the distributed nature of its management process and the time lag between a standard and its implementation in

> products and services mean that there is no clear accountability in terms of profit and loss responsibilities due to deficiencies in an ICT standard. In some cases, those who pay the cost of the lack of quality are not those who made the decisions. Thus, market mechanisms will rarely provide the driving incentive to carry out the intensive planning and coordination across organizational boundaries that are needed to produce a quality standard. (Sherif et al. 2005, p. 230)

The voluntary consensus standard process and open standards are vulnerable to malevolent attacks. Little can be done when harm is intended. But such attacks, however spectacular, are the exception rather than the rule. In this chapter we focus on the large majority of incompatible implementations that may come about unintentionally or for perfectly viable economic, functional or other reasons. (Let it be noted that although the consequences may be the same as those of malevolent attacks, namely incompatibility and in its wake uncertain exchangeability, loss of self-evident interoperability, increased transaction costs and possible market fragmentation,[3] the non-malevolent nature of these deviations offers more leeway for addressing their causes.)

FRAMEWORK AND METHODOLOGY

If standard implementations are not interoperable, the cause may lie in one or more of the phases leading up to standard implementation. Schematically speaking, the average standards committee starts with an idea, adopts it as a work item and then passes it through the successive stages of standardization. The result is a document known as the standard specification. The standard is then implemented in a product or service. The implementation process results in a standard implementation.[4] Figure 3.1 highlights the three main states of a standard: the conceptual idea, the specification, and the implementation; and the two translation processes between these states: the standard or standard maintenance process, and the implementation process. The examples below illustrate how each phase can be the source of implementation problems:

- The idea that underlies a standard may not be implementable (e.g. too comprehensive).
- The ideal of consensus decision-making may affect the standards process (e.g. lead to too many options) and, indirectly, the implementability of standards.
- Different use of terminology in a standard specification may lead to problems of interpretation, implementation and interoperability.
- Modest user requirements and cost-constraints in the implementation process may lead to partial standard compliance and incompatible implementations.

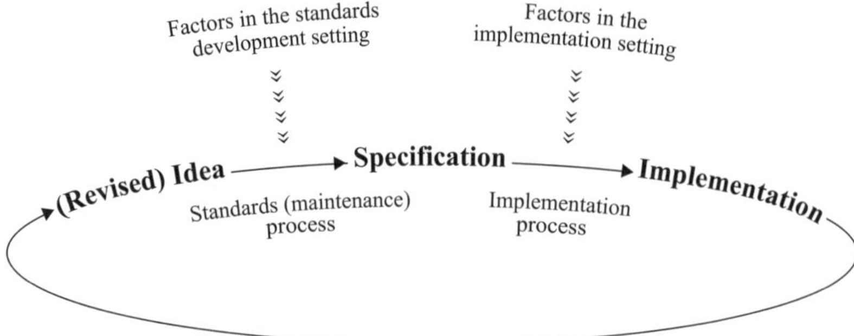

Figure 3.1 Schematic representation of the phases leading up to the standard implementation

As Figure 3.1 indicates, the immediate cause of incompatibility may primarily lie in the standard implementation setting, but the underlying causes may be related to factors that affect standard development.

We have used three complementary methodologies to gather data about possible causes of incompatibility. Firstly, to investigate whether certain institutional characteristics of standardization can lead to problems of interpretation and implementation, we analysed the case of the formal standards setting (i.e. formal standards policy documents and secondary literature). Secondly, to gain insight into what happens in practice with standards from formal and other standards bodies, three case studies of ICT standardization areas have been conducted, i.e., 'standard generalized markup language (SGML)'/'extensible markup language (XML)', 'open systems interconnection (OSI)' standards, and 'unified modelling language (UML)'. From earlier studies these cases were known to highlight different implementation problems.

The third source was an expert panel discussion. The panel members were standardization experts from formal standards bodies, standards consortia and industry.[5] Instead of interviewing each panel member separately, they were asked to discuss and illustrate implementation problems from their personal experience. Compared to interviews, the panel-setting has the advantage that it also allows experts to comment on each other and elicits reactions from the audience, both of which help assess the degree of consensus regarding the topic of discussion.

The structure of the chapter follows the methodologies used. The institutional analysis, which focuses on possible causes in the standard development setting, is discussed in Section 3. The findings from the case studies are discussed in Section 4. The findings of the panel of experts are presented in Section 5. In Section 6, we summarize the causes of incompatibility problems and discuss ways to solve them. In Section 7, we present our conclusions.

INSTITUTIONAL DILEMMAS

In the past, the policy of formal standards bodies such as ISO was to focus on standards development, and on their role in supporting the democratic, voluntary consensus process. Formally, the question of implementation of standards lay outside their framework (Schmidt and Werle 1998, p. 304).[6] In the mid-1990s, there was a rise of standards consortia and other 'grey' standards bodies, which generally speaking prioritized the usability of standards, and treated standards development and implementation as co-evolutionary issues (see Table 3.1). For example, Internet standardization, which at the time had an exemplary status, included demonstrated implementability – i.e. interoperable implementations – in its standards process (Internet Engineering Taskforce/Requests for Comments [IETF/RFC] 2026). More policy recognition of the importance of standards implementability and use by the formal standards bodies was discussed as one of the means to strengthen their position. However, the ideological rationale behind the formal policy made such a change difficult. There were two prominent ideals at stake: the ideal of developing standards in a democratic, consensus-oriented manner, and the ideal of developing implementation-independent standards. Both ideals were and still are highly relevant, and are possible institutional causes of incompatible implementations.

Consensus Decisions

With regard to the former ideal, the emphasis on democratic, consensus-oriented decision-making in committee standardization is more likely to lead to political compromises, which in turn may result in standards containing various options, or in vague formulations behind which opposing parties can rally. Or, to put a more positive spin on it: 'politics helps to achieve an agreement precisely because it does not consider technical details. [...] Terminating a conflict through the adoption of incompatible options [...] keeps the organization viable' (Schmidt and Werle 1998, pp. 270, 271 and 303).

Implementation Independence

The second ideal which sets formal standardization apart from consortium and *de facto* standardization is its concern for implementation-independent standards (see Table 3.1). The formal standards bodies strive for impartial standards solutions, in other words, for solutions that do not favour certain companies, technologies or markets. Keeping these options open is more likely to lead to problems of implementability. Standards that need to cater to different application environments are inherently more complex (e.g. STEP, see Thomas et al., this volume) than standards that cater to a specific implementation environment (e.g. the Internet). More options are needed to address the sometimes irreconcilable standards requirements. The intended generic applicability conflicts with the specificity needed to implement a standard in an unambiguous and consistent manner.

Table 3.1 Typification of three standardization approaches in the mid-1990s

Approach / Aspect	Formal standardization	Consortium standardization	*De facto* standardization
Standards process and implementation	Successive occurences/ implementation outside scope	Parallel occurances	Standards follow implementations/ Standardization is a by-product
Implementation independence	High	Medium	Low

Source: Adapted from Egyedi (1996).

Although the differences between the three standardization approaches can to a large extent still be recognized today (e.g. the ideals of the formal standards bodies have remained the same), the procedures of the formal bodies and the most important consortia are converging. Conformance testing and standards implementation have the attention of a formal body like the European Telecommunications Standards Institute (ETSI) (e.g. ISO 2001 and ETSI 2005a), while impartiality and consensus ideals have become part of the procedures of several consortia (Egyedi 2006).

THREE CASE STUDIES

The following case studies throw light on some additional causes of incompatibility. They concern three clusters of standards, i.e.: SGML and XML, standards belonging to the family of the OSI reference model, and UML, a modelling standard used for system development.

SGML and XML

Drawing from Egyedi and Loeffen (this volume), the initial idea behind XML (W3C 1998) was to bring the 'structured data exchange' functionalities of SGML (ISO 8879:1988) to the web. In the web environment, XML was to succeed SGML. The aim was for XML to remain compatible with SGML.

However, this was only partly achieved because XML documents could not be processed by SGML (1988) tools. The implementation problems we discuss here are set against this background.

Two initiatives were taken to address the incompatibility between XML and SGML. Firstly, an ISO/IEC (International Organization for Standardization/International Electrotechnical Commission) SGML working group drew up 'technical corrigendum 2' (Cor 2: 1999), which:

> remedies defects revealed by the multiple adaptations of SGML for the World Wide Web, intranets, and extranets. The annex corrects errors, resolves ambiguities for which there is a clear resolution that does not cause existing conforming documents to become non-conforming, and provides a choice of alternative resolutions for other ambiguities. Although motivated by the World Wide Web, applicability of this annex extends to all uses of SGML. (SGML 1999, Annex K)

Full implementation of the technical corrigendum was designed to produce an SGML system that was XML-compatible. However, in practice new software providers and standards implementers had no involvement with SGML. Rather than implement the extended SGML, they opted in favour of simply switching to XML.

Secondly, the XML working group included non-binding recommendations in the standard, the implementation of which was to allow XML documents to be processed by SGML (1988) software. However, the standard would not guarantee compatibility (i.e. implementation thereof only 'increases chances' of interworking). In any case, many XML system designers ignored these guidelines.

The emphasis in the SGML standard has always been on its ubiquitous applicability. XML emphasizes simplicity and implementability. Although the SGML standard has been successful in many ways and for a very long time in IT terms, the current wide adoption of XML suggests that in a web-based environment wide standards implementation requires simplicity.

OSI Model

The OSI model is a standard reference framework. It was initiated to rationalize and integrate standards activities in the merging fields of IT and telecommunications in the 1980s. It identifies ICT services as consisting of a set of functions that are mapped onto seven layers (i.e. physical, data link, network, transport, session, presentation and application layer). Within these layers generic building blocks are specified, called base standards. Base standards can contain options. Problems arise when two service implementations are based on different options in base standards. To avoid the interoperability problems involved, the formal standards bodies of 'ISO/IEC joint technical committee 1 (JTC 1)' and International Telecommunication Union's (ITU) CCITT also standardized sets of specified base standards with fixed options for certain application areas (e.g. banking). These are called profiles or functional standards. A functional standard is a 'document which identifies a base standard or group of base standards, together with options and parameters, necessary to accomplish a function or a set of functions' (ECITC 1993).

If we take a closer look at the options in the base standards, we see that a compromise of five different protocol classes was defined for the transport layer protocol. This complicated interworking. To alleviate interworking problems, means were developed to allow a certain amount of negotiation between protocol classes. In addition, profiles were developed that defined a fixed OSI protocol stack for specific applications, including the necessary transport protocol class. For example, the classes of TP0 and TP1 were prescribed for CCITT's message handling recommendation X.400 (Egyedi 1997).

For the session layer, functional units were defined with overlapping functionalities. According to participants in the standards process, this was a political compromise. There was no viable technical reason for the overlap. As a consequence of the overlap, implementers of the session protocol usually implemented one or the other combination of functional units, and not both. That is to say, the session layer, too, gave rise to different OSI stacks (i.e. to fragmentation) – and to interworking problems.

In all, OSI's design objective of standards that would be implementation- and field-independent was ambitious and came at a cost. According to some critics, the costs of implementation were too high. They felt that OSI standards comprised too many overheads, too many options, and complex answers to specific and simple needs. To cut down costs, OSI implementers sometimes omitted functionalities that were part of the standard. This led to products that although in theory were OSI-compatible, in reality complied only in part, which damaged OSI's reputation.

UML

In November 1997, the 'object management group (OMG)' unanimously adopted the 'unified modelling language (UML)' as a standard (OMG 1998). The standard aimed at simplifying and consolidating the large number of 'object-oriented (OO)' software developing methods that had emerged (e.g. Shlaer and Mellor 1988; Booch 1991; Coad and Yourdon 1991); to reduce gratuitous divergence among tools; to encourage a widespread use of OO modelling among developers; and to facilitate the development of a robust market of support tools and training: 'now that neither user nor vendor have to guess which approaches to use and support' (UML reference manual 1998).

However, there are different kinds of inconsistencies in UML modelling. In modelling approaches, consistent naming is a common requirement aimed at avoiding impedance mismatches. Impedance problems occur when a unified naming convention is lacking within and across modelling techniques. UML comprises several complementary and substitutive modelling techniques (e.g. class diagrams, state transition models, activity models and functional models). These modelling techniques use different terminologies to achieve similar results, which (a) leads to misunderstandings between the parties involved in system development (e.g. developers, testers and users); (b) aggravates the problem of integrating information from one model into another during the system design stage – leaving aside the problem that differences in terminology pose during system implementation; and (c) makes components harder to trace and reuse.

Related to the latter point, UML is not intended to be a complete development method, in that it does not include a step-by-step development process. Originally, a companion book for UML-based system development, the 'rational unified process (RUP)' (Jacobson et al. 1999) was proposed. However, according to experts, this work lacks the necessary vigour and freedom of modelling, and has been challenged by UML-based methodologies such as Select Perspective (Allen and Frost 1998), Catalysis (d'Souza and Wills 1999), Uniface (2000), KobrA (Atkinson et al. 2000) and CBD/e (Castek 2000). Again, these methodologies usually produce similar functional solutions. However, they often cannot be exchanged or integrated. Also, they may be completely different in the way they implement the system.

UML is more complicated than some of its predecessors because its aim is to be more comprehensive. It incorporates several kinds of models. Normally, one does not need all the UML modelling techniques in each single project. Because experts know how to combine parts of UML and novices do not, UML profiles are needed that indicate which combinations are useful in certain situations.

Finally, a lack of consistency in and interoperability of UML-based systems also plays a role at the level of the data model. Let us suppose, for example, that 'student' is a class in the UML class diagram. Its real representation in the application area is an instance object with a name (e.g. S. Mohamed) and a number of other instance attributes. In the generic model, the class 'student' represents any student. However, students may come from different countries. Because, for example, the Ethiopian year has 13 rather than the customary 12 months, this makes it harder to represent the date attribute of class 'student'. And if the data model is inconsistent at the instance level, this will obstruct system interoperability (Stojanovic et al. 2001).

PANEL OF EXPERTS

The third important source of information was a panel discussion among experts. Drawing on their personal experience, the experts confirm some of the causes of incompatibility identified in the case studies, but they also identify a number of additional causes.

Complexity of comprehensive, ambitious standards: Some standards include too many details and unnecessary niceties. Moreover, the maturity of the technology under consideration should be taken into account. As standardization literature confirms, if a standard: 'includes too many details at an early stage of the life cycle [of the technology], the wrong aspects may be included. If standardization takes place late in the life cycle but does not respond to specific end-user demands, it may be irrelevant' (Sherif et al. 2005, p. 225).

Ill-structured standards: Writing a standard specification is not a trivial matter. Standards need to be complete, unambiguous, readable, well-structured, etc. It is not easy for people coming from non-standards environments to write standards. Perhaps they need help with what one of the panellists calls 'standards engineering': support for editors and rapporteurs in the application of good standards engineering practices based on experience.

The encryption algorithm for the 'digital enhanced cordless telecommunications (DECT)' standard illustrates what may be at stake. DECT was a voluminous standard. At a certain moment it comprised eight different parts. Although the encryption algorithm itself was well-defined, the information about whether the least significant bit or the most significant bit should be entered into this algorithm first was not easy to find. The answer was included in the standard, but not where one would have expected it to be. European manufacturers misunderstood the standard and implemented it the wrong way in a lot of hardware, whereas Asian implementers may have spent more time reading the standard and interpreted it correctly. There were intense battles between the two camps, which could have been avoided by restructuring the standard and presenting the relevant information together.

Ambiguity of natural language: To cope with the ambiguity of natural language, complex protocol engineering uses formal specification languages (e.g. 'abstract syntax notation one [ASN.1]').[7] Many ETSI standards use ASN.1 successfully (e.g. in the case of 'global system for mobile communications [GSM]'). However, it is not always helpful (e.g. in 'simple mail transfer protocol standardization'). Sometimes the formal technique seems to acquire greater emphasis than the specification itself (e.g. with 'specification and description language [SDL]'). The panellists therefore recommend that formal specification techniques should be used with care, where needed, and in moderation.

Uncertainty about how to handle options: Standards with a narrow range and few options are more likely to be implemented correctly and interoperate. But because they are inherently restrictive in a certain respect they leave less room for product ingenuity – but only in this respect. Standards with a broad range and many options leave more room for product ingenuity, but the chance of non-interoperability increases as a result of picking and mixing options. Although the products then conform to the standard, they do not necessarily interoperate.

There are different kinds of options. There are options with similar functionalities (i.e. there are three ways to do it – specify which way), and options with orthogonal functionalities (if you are going to do 'A', do it this way). Lack of clarity about which type of option is at stake leads to confusion.

Moreover, options are often not fully specified. Although standards usually indicate what to do if one implements an option, they seldom indicate what to do if an option is not implemented. Engineers then make their own decisions.

Complexity by standards overload: Apart from the complexity in standards, lack of interoperability can also result from an overload of standards. For example, the large number of Internet standards (RFCs >100) for 'Internet protocol version 6 (IPv6)' makes it difficult for engineers to pick out the RFCs they need for their products. As ETSI interoperability tests show, IPv6 protocol stacks that have been implemented according to the RFCs still do not interoperate. Although the standards themselves are thought to be of good quality, there are too many of them.

Bugward compatibility: Sometimes standards are implemented incorrectly in order to preserve backward compatibility with a bug-ridden prior version of a product. This phenomenon is referred to as 'bugward compatibility'. For example, Microsoft implemented 'cascading style sheets 1 (CSS1)' incorrectly in its early browsers, but insisted on downward compatibility in later versions to ensure that the content produced for the early browsers would still work.

Missing details, monopoly on tacit knowledge: In DECT the wrong value was awarded to an extension bit in one of the information elements. However, engineers in the field knew what the correct value should be, and widely implemented the standard based on that common understanding – with the exception of one large manufacturer who adhered to the standard. This caused interoperability problems, which were discovered during performance testing of the products. See also Moseley et al. (2003).

There is always a need to rely on the implicit, common understanding of the implementation community. Due to time constraints, not all information can be included in a standard. On the other hand, the panellists feel that one cannot always assume that everyone shares this understanding. Errors should be fed back into the standards body and corrected in the standard.

A slightly different situation arose with regard to a number of router protocols. Here, only a handful of people knew the details that were missing in the specifications. They had a monopoly on knowledge regarding the standard. The companies that were in the routing business had to hire one of these people to get the protocol running.

Interference between standards: New standards sometimes hinder existing standards, that is, standards that were implemented and were interoperable before.

Table 3.2 Causes of incompatibility and their origins

Causes of incompatibility	Locus
Errors, ambiguities, inconsistencies	SP/S
Ambiguity of natural language	SP/S
Missing details, monopoly on tacit knowledge	S/IP
Ill-structured standards	S
Unclear how to handle options	S
Uncertain compatibility of non-binding recommendations	S
Complexity of comprehensive, ambitious standards	C
Too many options and parameters	SP/S/IP
'Bugward compatibility'	C
Unclear official status of standard's companion book	S
Single company pushing for standard, weak specifications	SP
Overload of standards	C/IP
Deviation from and partial implementation of a standard	IP
Interference between standards	C/IP

Note: C = conceptual idea, SP = standards engineering process, S = standard specification, IP = implementation process.

PROBLEMS AND SUGGESTED SOLUTIONS

Table 3.2 summarizes the causes of incompatibility mentioned in the previous sections and assigns them, where possible, to a specific state or process. Most problems are closely linked to what the standard specification (S) looks like; some are caused by a flaw in the design (conceptual idea, C) of the standard; some result from a flaw in the process of drafting the standard (standards engineering process); and some can be traced back to the implementation process. Although there are constraints with regard to time and cost,[8] the standards setting can to a large degree determine whether the above-mentioned problems are likely to occur. Indeed, some standards bodies – and standards committees – already place more emphasis on standards quality than others.[9]

Deliberation: Systematic or Random Causes

What can be done to reduce incompatibility between standard-based products? Some implementation problems would seem to be of a more structural kind (e.g. parallel options and ambiguities resulting from political compromises); while others appear to be of a more random and temporary nature (errors, accidental ambiguities, etc.). For example, the first version of a complex standard may be expected to include some errors. Such errors will be random in the sense that they will differ from those in a different standard and do not contain a systematic bias. However, random errors may also have a structural background. They may be random in the place and manner they are expressed, but systematic in the fact *that* they occur. The challenge here is to find structural solutions for both random and structural problems.

Some structural problems, however, are rooted in fundamental dilemmas. Box 3.1 summarizes the main ones. The difficulty of solving them adequately needs to be recognized.

Recommendations

Different standards bodies have different ways of dealing with causes of incompatibility. For example, ETSI uses a wide range of techniques to improve the standard development process, and to validate and test standards (ETSI 2005a). The procedures followed by the W3C involve wide scrutiny (public comment via Internet), and preferably two interoperable implementations of each feature of the standard.[10] The Internet's IETF requires two independent implementations to progress from proposed standard to draft standard.

Most standardizing bodies both (1) try to *prevent* incompatibility with, for example, interoperability tests (e.g. ETSI), reference implementations (e.g. IETF), and/or by making public the rationale that underlies the decisions of a technical committee (e.g. ISO); and, (2) address the causes of incompatibility retrospectively by means of defect reports, technical corrigenda, etc. during standards maintenance.

Table 3.3 summarizes the solutions discussed in the standardization literature and proposed by the panel experts. Four categories of recommendations are distinguished: drafting of standards, pre-implementation, post-implementation, and standards policy. The most significant category of

BOX 3.1 DILEMMAS REGARDING THE IMPLEMENTABILITY OF STANDARDS

Some incompatibilities derive from a set of fundamental dilemmas, choices regarding standard's design and use that can be summed up in four questions. Design of a standard: 1. Comprehensive or simple standards? 2. Implementation-independent or implementable standards? 3. Consensus on a compromise or implementable standards? Use of a standard: 4. Adapt a standard to one's simpler needs or aim for interoperability with other standard-compliant products? The choice which standards developers and implementers make affects the implementability of the standards.

Table 3.3 Recommendations

Insttitutional measures towards reducing standard-based interoperability problems	
Drafting of standards	• provide institutional support for editors and rapporteurs on standards engineering • involve technical editors • use pseudo-code or formal languages in a focused way • adopt a unified naming convention • clarify the type of options involved • specify how to deal with options (e.g. profiles) • specify the consequences of (not) implementing options • make the rationale that underlies choices in the specification explicit • issue a reference guide with the standard • organize wider scrutiny of the standard • translate the standard also to uncover ambiguities • co-ordinate interrelated standardization of different standards bodies
Pre-implementation	• validate standards before implementation in products ('walk-throughs') • develop a reference implementation/pre-implementation • develop a reference environment • include standard conformance and interoperability testing • organize interoperability events with different vendors (e.g. plug tests) • organize dialogue between standard developers and implementers
Post-implementation	• supply test suites • improve consistent use and integrity of standards with e.g. compliance and interoperabilty conformance statements, compatibility logos, certification programmes
Standards policy	• prioritize implementability as a standard's requirement • reconsider desired level of consensus across all areas

recommendations concerns the drafting of standards. There are many ways to improve the drafting of standards. For example, to deal with the ambiguity of natural language formal specification languages can be used. Translating international standards into other languages often discloses ambiguities as well. In these cases publishing the rationale that underlies a standards committee's decision and reference implementations may help implementers resolve ambiguities.

With regard to standards options, the experts recommend that:

1. standards be very explicit about which options are mandatory and which are optional;
2. optional requirements be fully specified;
3. implementers apply profiles to handle options systematically;
4. the consequences of picking and mixing standard-compliant products be made clear.

For the readability of the standard it may be better to install a technical editor rather than ask a person who has been involved in developing the standard; or, alternatively, to offer more support for the developer-editor. To secure compatibility among interrelated standards, co-ordination between the different standards committees is needed.

Finally, standards policy may want to:

1. reconsider whether consensus is equally desirable in all areas of standardization and/or reflect on other ways to reduce the need for political compromises;
2. prioritize the implementability and validation of standards. This would require the systematic inclusion of standards conformance and interoperability testing in the standards process, and a complementary market-oriented testing and certification programme (including e.g. the availability of test suites and plug test events).

CONCLUSION

Lack of interoperability between 'standard-compliant' implementations is a main source of standards' change. It is caused by different factors. Although the immediate problem usually lies in the way standards are implemented, the underlying causes are often flaws in the scope of standardization, in the standards process or in the specification itself. They increase the need for *post hoc* changes. Improving the drafting process and ensuring the interoperability and implementability of standards would decrease the degree of change.

In conclusion, it is clear that many standards bodies do not address standard implementation issues because they argue that this is best left to the market. However, as far as the impact of standards is concerned, the development and implementation of a standard are intertwined. They cannot be separated in a meaningful way. We would, therefore, recommend that standards bodies shift their emphasis from the development of standards to a more systematic inclusion of implementation concerns.

ACKNOWLEDGEMENTS

I am very much indebted to Sun Microsystems for funding this strain of research, to the NO-REST EU project partners for feeding me with new insights and providing a context in which to pursue writing on the subject, to Ajantha Dahanayake for her knowledgeable input on UML (Egyedi and Dahanayake 2003), and last but not least to the SIIT 2003 panellists and discussants Jim Carlo, Oliver Smoot, Patrick Droz, John Hill, Erik Huizer, Steven Pemberton, Anthony Wiles, Jim Isaak and Mostafa Hashem Sherif for sharing their valuable experience on the subject.

NOTES

1. This chapter is a revision of an article published in *Computer Standards and Interfaces*, **29**, T.M. Egyedi, 'Standard-compliant, but incompatible?!', pp. 605–13, Copyright Elsevier (2007).
2. Egyedi and Hudson (2005) refer to instances where (*de facto*) standards are adapted, extended or selectively implemented as problems of standard integrity – in other words, as a specific subset of compatibility problems.
3. The classic example of market fragmentation is UNIX, the multiuser operating system that became a *de facto* standard in the late 1970s. Different versions were developed, which resulted in a fragmented market.
4. Figure 3.1 aims to help identify and localize causes of implementation problems. In other words, it does not portray a life cycle model for standards. For a discussion of life cycles, see Söderström (2004).
5. Panel discussion, 22 October 2003, 17.00–18.30 hours, 3rd IEEE Conference on 'Standardization and Innovation in IT', 22–24 October 2003, Delft University of Technology, the Netherlands. Panel Discussion 'Problems of Standards Implementation' with Jim Carlo, President-Elect IEEE-SA (Moderator), Oliver Smoot, ISO President (Commentator), and the panel members Patrick Droz, IBM, Manager Networking Software; John Hill, Chairman JTC 1/SC22 Programming Languages, Sun Microsystems; Erik Huizer, IETF trustee of Internet Society, University of Twente; Steven Pemberton, Chair W3C HTML and Forms working groups, CWI/W3C; Anthony Wiles, ETSI Protocol and Testing Competence Centre. In addition, some remarks made by Jim Isaak (IEEE board of directors) and Mostafa Hashem Sherif (AT&T) during the discussion are included in the text.
6. However, on the practical level conformance testing already took place in the 1980s (e.g. in ISO/CCITT on X.25, Linn and Uyar 1994).

7. Additional advantages are that their use makes it easier to test and evaluate these protocols, and that they add value where one can build models that can be validated and simulated.
8. The consequences which the measures suggested in the following section have in terms of costs and delay in standard's delivery are difficult to estimate. They require further study.
9. We use the term 'quality' in a pragmatic sense here, namely in the sense of addressing the problems listed above. Whether quality or opening up a market should be the first priority is subject to debate. Is speed more important than standards quality (i.e. the maturity of a standard)? E.g., a qualitatively more mature Hyperlan standard (ETSI) lost the market to the WLAN standards of IEEE 802.11. Indeed, in the case of Parlay, e.g., the strategy was to develop a standard quickly in order to secure an early market share. At this stage speed was deemed more important than quality. Implementation feedback was then used to improve the standard (ETSI 2005b).
10. http://www.w3.org/Consortium/Process-20010719/tr.html#Recs.

PART TWO

Causes of Change

4. + vs −: Dynamics and Effects of Competing Standards of Recordable DVD-Media

Stephan Gauch

OUTLINE AND FRAMEWORK

Everyone who uses DVD recordable technology will by now have encountered the problem of chosing between different kinds of DVD recordables and devices. Should they buy a device that is compatible with the official DVD−R standard or opt in favour of a (previously cheaper) device that is capable of writing data to DVD+R, or perhaps a device that is able to write both formats but that may be more expensive? And although these are relevant questions in themselves, of course the more fundamental question is: 'Why are there two different standards for DVD recordables at all?' This is a question we will discuss in detail in this chapter. We focus on a specific set of consequences of this 'standards war', namely the way competition and standards dynamics are related, taking into account the constellation of actors involved. There are a number of reasons why standards dynamics may occur. Some of the dynamics can be situated in the environment of the standards, for instance the dynamics of actor constellations or the temporal effects of market entry of the actors involved. Others may be caused by changes in user needs or technological development for a specific artifact. Apart from the dynamics that are linked to certain aspects of products, services or protocols, there are also more fundamental dynamics, like technological change, that is captured in technological trajectories (e.g. Dosi 1982).[1] The relevant distinction is of a temporal nature and can only be uncovered by adopting a historical perspective, observing different technical solutions within a given trajectory. In our case, the products embedded in a technological trajectory are optical storage media, including CDs, CD−Rs, DVDs, the almost obsolete Laser Discs and DivX Discs, and a broad set of recordable DVD technologies. Most of these technologies have been recognized as valuable case studies for standardization, like the DVD vs. DivX standards war (Dranove and Gandal 2000, 2003, 2005), the influence of actor strategies in the creation of the DVD-Video standard using game theory approaches (Lint and Pennings 2000, 2002) or the interaction of market and committee elements in standardization that led to the success story of CD technology (Kretschmer and Muehlfeld 2004). Having said that, there is still a lack of explanation with regard to the subsequent splitting of DVD recordable standards even though differences regarding standardization patterns of 'read' and 'write' standards of DVD have already been recognized in the scientific community (Shapiro and Varian 1999b). According to Besen and Farrell (1991), there are three possible forms of competition in standards, differentiated by the role played by relevant actors in the standardization process: a) the phenomenon of actors competing to determine a standard both in development and in markets is called a 'standards war'; b) the case of mutual negotiation along with a disagreement about certain aspects of a standard is termed 'standard negotiation'; and c) in case one firm already dominates the market and other firms want to make their products interoperable this is referred to as 'standards leader'.

These kinds of insights, which mostly come from game theory, can shed light on specific issues like negotiation, tipping of markets, etc. Unfortunately, such analyses rather fail to capture other important aspects that are relevant to an in-depth analysis of the link between competition and standards dynamics. These aspects relate to the web of interlinkages of actors participating in R&D, market and standardization activities, but also to the technological trajectory in which the standards are embedded. So, rather than taking a rationalist approach by trying to impose certain rationales on the actors we resort to a historical and pragmatic qualitative analsis of structures, interdependencies and consequences, to capture the relevant aspects of competition and dynamic standards. Consequently, we also have to focus on the technical differences and similarities of the technologies and structure and the use of 'intellectual property rights' for the different technical solutions. The overall question we ask in this chapter is in what way the interaction of different forms of competition with regard to standards, the structure of the actors in the standard-setting process and the interaction of formal and informal standardization processes influence the dynamics of the standards in question. We examine the period between 1997 and 2004.

In many ways, DVD recordable technology is very suitable for an analysis of competition and standards dynamics, due to five very interesting conditions. Firstly, the competing standards have a similar technological basis. Secondly, there is a very distinct polarization into two groups of heavily networked actors who are involved in the development of the technology and in setting the standards. Thirdly, the intellectual property right (IPR) structure among those actors has allowed two competing parties to emerge, since both camps were able to develop functional equivalents of optical discs independent from each other, while a dominant design emerged at the level of reading/writing devices that does not reflect this diffused IPR structure. Fourthly, the relevant standards and standard-setting bodies are deeply intertwined, ranging from specifications formed at the level of consortia to international ISO standards. And finally, the differences in time-to-market structures and different paths of standardization reveal different aspects of standards dynamics. In the next section, we elaborate on all of these aspects in detail in order to form a coherent picture of the relationship between standards dynamics and competition.

OVERVIEW OF DVD RECORDABLE STANDARDS

To understand the historical course of the DVD standards war and the dynamics of standards we need to have at least a rudimentary understanding of the technological basis, most notably similarities and differences of the two technologies. Generally, the two DVD recording technologies can be distinguished by two criteria, i.e. the way the data is stored on the medium and the consortium promoting the underlying technology.

The way information is stored on an optical medium can be broadly differentiated in 'write once read many times' (WORM) media, on which data can be stored once, after which it can neither be erased nor changed, and media with 'read–write' capabilities, on which data can be stored, changed or be erased at any given time. WORM media are the DVD−R and the DVD+R and DVD+RDL, where the R stands for recordable and the minus and plus denotes an arbitrary symbol set by the different consortia.[2] DVD recordable media with 'read–write' capacity are the DVD−RAM, the DVD−RW and the DVD+RW.

The other distinction stems from the two consortia backing the different specifications and standards of DVD recordables. One consortium, the DVD Forum, supports the 'official' versions of the DVD recordable standards and in discussions is often referred to as the 'slash'-camp, due to the '−' in the name of the media. The other consortium is the DVD+RW Alliance, which supports the 'unofficial' standard and is referred to as the 'plus'-camp. A schematic overview of the DVD recordable standards that will be considered in the analysis is provided in Table 4.1. In many respects, the various DVD recording technologies are closely related. In most cases the same materials are used to build the discs and the coating of the different layers, while laser diodes of comparable wavelength are used, and the physical appearance is the same for different kinds of discs.[3] However, closer inspection reveals that there are significant differences in terms of the technical approach.[4] This may be of minor importance to the average customer, who will see the technology involved as a black box in which he or she is as interested as in the technology involved in building a car transmission. Nevertheless, the differences involved are important when it comes to understanding the dynamics of standards, as they represent a special distribution of Intellectual Property Rights among a small number of actors and certain aspects of the history of DVD technology itself. These constellations will prove to be important for an explanation of the dynamics of standards under competition, as they are the result of strategic co-operations in the past, present and possibly future.

Table 4.1 Overview of DVD recordable standards and supporting consortia

DVD+RW Alliance		DVD Forum	
Recordable	Rewritable	Recordable	Rewritable
DVD+R	DVD+RW	DVD–R	DVD–RW
DVD+R DL			DVD–RAM

A BRIEF HISTORY OF DVD – A PREREQUISITE

These technological differences originated from the past activities of two groups of actors. When the search began for a CD technology successor that would be suitable for storing high-quality multimedia content in the early 1990s, there were two competing parties who both began developing such a medium, which resulted in two formats: the 'super density (SD)' digital video disc format developed by Matsushita, Toshiba and Time Warner and the 'multimedia compact disc (MMCD)' format supported by Sony and Philips, the developers of CD technology.

While the SD presented a double-side approach with 5 GB of data to be stored per side, the MMCD could store 3.7 GB of data and was single-sided in design. Apart from differences in storage capacity, the technical differences had to do with the use of a single substrate layer with a thickness of 1.2 mm, or two substrate layers with a thickness of 0.6 mm bonded together by an adhesive. As a result, the MMCD format was closer to CD technology than the SD format. Apart from the technical design, the two formats were different in terms of the support from actors that could influence the success or failure of either technology. Whereas the motion picture industry supported SD, due to a foreseeable support by Time Warner and the higher storage capacity, the manufacturing industry favored MMCD, because that technology was closer to established CD technology, which meant that production facilities needed only slight modifications. This posed potential problems to both camps. If the movie industry decided to stick to SD, and the manufacturing industry continued to back MMCD, this could lead to a shortage of playback devices or media. In the alternative scenario, which closely resembles the famous VHS/Betamax dilemma, MMCD devices sales would be low due to a shortage of content. Both situations could lead to effects of excess inertia in the sales of both devices and media (Farrell and Saloner 1986). Both camps were aware of the problems involved, and they initiated a working group consisting of mayor ICT players, such as IBM, Microsoft, Intel and HP, to mediate a solution. By the end of 1995, this working group, known as the Computer Industry Technical Working Group (TWG), proposed to merge the two specifications, to circumvent the problems involved in having two separate standards. The merged standard featured elements of both technologies, adopting the two-substrate approach proposed by SD, while implementing the 8/16 modulation of MMCD. It was called the 'digital versatile disc (DVD)'. This meant that MMCD and SD were combined into a completely new format.

RELEVANT ACTORS IN THE DVD RECORDABLE STANDARD-SETTING PROCESS

Even though merging MMCD and SD settled the issue between the different camps and led to the DVD, which became quite a success story, the conflict remained hidden in the background after it had largely been settled by external forces like the TWG. The fact that there was a split into the two competing recordable clusters of formats, i.e. the 'minus' and 'plus' formats, even though the two underlying technological paths (SD and MMCD) had been merged into the DVD format, draws attention to the network that linked the actors and technology, as well as the connections between the relevant formal and informal standard-setting bodies.

The constellation of the actors in the different consortia shows a distinct pattern that corresponds to structures in the pre-DVD era. The MMCD supporters promote the 'plus'-standards (DVD+R and DVD+RW), while the former SD supporters back the 'slash'-standards (DVD−RAM and DVD−R). Even though there are numerous consortia that are relevant in the context of promotion of optical technology, there are four consortia that are highly relevant to the standard-setting process of DVD recordables: the DVD Forum, the DVD+RW Alliance, the DVD6C and the Technical Committee 31 of the European Computer Manufacturers Association[5] (ECMA TC31). Apart from the vital role these consortia play in the standard-setting process of DVD recordables, their membership structure means that they are an important factor with regard to the dynamics of standards, as they represent the competitive parties in the DVD standards war (DVD6C, DVD Forum and DVD+RW Alliance) and a consortium, the ECMA TC31, which is an

Table 4.2 DVD Forum core members

DVD Forum founding members	
Hitachi	Sony
Matsushita	Thomson
Mitsubishi	Time Warner
Pioneer	Toshiba
Philips	JVC

A-Liaison partner of the ISO JTC 1 and consists of members from both competing parties.

The DVD Forum

The DVD Forum, an industry consortium founded by the IPR-holders of the DVD technology, is responsible for the approval of the official DVD specification called 'books'.[6] The specifications do not refer to writing devices but only to physical or file system specifications or methods concerning storage of certain data representations (i.e. audio recording, video recording and stream recording). Originally founded by the ten companies holding assets in form of 'intellectual property rights', the DVD forum opened up in 1997 for other companies like consumer electronics and computer manufacturers, as well as content developers to extend the acceptance of DVD technology and further legitimize their position as the standard-setting consortium for DVD and DVD-related products.[7] A list of the original founding members is presented in Table 4.2.

All specifications to be included in an official DVD technology format are passed to a 'working group' responsible for developing and ultimately deciding on the specifications and revisions of standards. The 'technical working groups' for the DVD–RAM format specifications are WG 5 (physical specifications for DVD–RAM) and WG 6 (physical specifications for DVD–R[W]) in the case of DVD–R and DVD–RW.

DVD+RW Alliance

When, at the beginning of 1997, the DVD Forum was about to decide on recordable DVD formats, the conflict between SD and MMCD supporters emerged once again. Even though consensus could be reached on DVD–RAM as the official standard for rewritable media, Sony and Philips, the erstwhile supporters of MMCD, together with HP, Mitsubishi, Ricoh and Yamaha, broke ranks and officially announced another specification for a rewritable

Table 4.3 Members of the DVD+RW Alliance

DVD+RW Alliance	
Founding members	Later members
Philips	Dell
Sony	Verbatim
HP	Microsoft
Yamaha	
Ricoh	
Thomson	

disc, which they termed DVD+RW. This specification had been developed without approval of the DVD Forum.[8] A few months later, in June 1998, the DVD+RW Compatibility Alliance, which would later be renamed DVD+RW Alliance, was founded by Philips, Sony, HP, Yamaha, Ricoh and Thomson, while at the same time Philips, Sony and HP started to offer joint licensing of their DVD relevant assets.

To understand the reasons behind the split-off, we need to look at what happened before the DVD was developed. The key players of MMCD are the major IPR-holders of the DVD+RW Alliance. Apart from Sony and Philips, the other members like Thomson or Yamaha did not hold significant IPR, but ranked as very important allies since they could provide a high amount of manufacturing capacity, especially Ricoh and Yamaha, who like Sony and Philips had a reputation for building CD–R devices. The IPR included in the split-off DVD recordable format proposed by the DVD+RW Alliance related significantly to older IPR assets of Philips and Sony – their patents concerning CD–R technology. Relaunching these patents was an interesting proposition for Sony and Philips. With the ongoing diffusion of DVD recordable technology and gradual replacement of CD–RW technology as the main storage solution, Philips and Sony could raise the value of their CD-related IPR which otherwise would have been reduced in the long run, due to the declining relevance of CD–R and declining production. Even if CD–R technology were to become less important over time and manufacturers abandoned the standard, Sony and Philips would continue to reap the revenues from +R(W) technology. Another incentive to split the DVD recordable standard stemmed from the actors who actually held no IPR assets in DVD technology – the manufacturers of blank media – as they could produce at much lower costs since the +R(W) technology was technically closer to CD–R(W) (Spath 2003). Thereby the 'plus' camp would have the chance to challenge the 'slash' camp via the blank media producers entering the market at a lower price which in turn could spur the sales of the recording devices to be produced by Sony and Philips. Moreover, when they founded their own consortium, the content industry was kept out. The content industry, especially the movie industry, had demanded measures regarding copy protection in the DVD Forum, and had slowed down the consensus process involving large capacity DVD WORM.

The DVD 6 C Patent Pool

With the DVD+RW Alliance founded in 1998 and Sony, Philips and HP offering joint licenses, the position of the former SD camp shifted. To counter the position of the DVD+RW Alliance, seven companies applied for a patent pool to simplify the process of licensing. This request was approved in the middle of 1999 (US Department of Justice 2005). As can easily be observed, the DVD+RW Alliance and the DVD 6 C patent pool are completely disjunctive. Another interesting fact is that Pioneer is neither part of the DVD+RW Alliance nor the DVD 6 C , although it was a founding member of the DVD Forum.

This patent pool only covered patents for 'official' formats supported by the DVD Forum and did not cover the IPR assets of Sony, HP and Philips. The license does not include +RW recorder patents, and such patents need to be individually licensed by member companies, although +RW function only recorders that have DVD Player function shall be licensed under DVD–ROM/video essential patents as DVD Players (DVD 6 C 1999). Producers using original DVD Technology therefore had to acquire licenses from both camps, while the patents for recordable DVD technology had to be licensed by either the DVD 6 C in case of the official 'slash'-format or with the DVD+RW Alliance in case of the unofficial 'plus'-format.

The ECMA Technical Committee 31

An important factor for the analysis of the dynamics of DVD recordable standards is the structure of the Technical Committee TC 31 of the ECMA. The ECMA as an industry association dedicated to standardization in ICT tech-

Table 4.4 Members of the DVD 6 C patent pool

DVD 6 C members	
Hitachi	Time Warner
Matsushita	Toshiba
Mitsubishi	IBM
JVC	

nologies plays an important role in the standard-setting processes of DVD recordables. This importance stems from its status as A-Liaison Partner to ISO JTC 1 resulting in specific sequences of standardization processes that follow a unique pattern. In this pattern ECMA acts as an intermediary between the informal and the formal standards setting bodies. The same pattern emerges for all the media types we analysed, regardless of which consortium proposed the standard. The process starts at the basic level of specifications.

When agreement is reached in one of the competing consortia, the standards are proposed to the TC 31 of ECMA, and later to the SC 23 of JTC 1 of ISO. This approach has some strategic reasons since the ECMA is a liaison partner of JTC 1, which implies that standards filed with the ECMA can be put forward by the so-called 'fast-track' using the 'accelerated approval procedure' of the ISO. This procedure allows an ECMA standard to be placed at the 'enquiry stage', leapfrogging early stages of the ISO standard-setting procedure. Taking a closer look at the assemblage of the TC 31, we see that nearly all core members of the DVD 6 C and the DVD+RW Alliance are part of this group. Another striking feature is that all ten founding members of the DVD Forum are represented in the TC 31.

This constellation of members is important, when we consider them in light of certain regularities of the ECMA with regard to a premature termination of a standardization project. The statutes of the ECMA stipulate that an ECMA standardization project cannot be stopped as long as three members of a technical committee keep supporting the project. And because both camps are represented by at least five members, neither camp could stop the other from keeping an ECMA standardization project running till the project is being finished and an ECMA standard established. Once an ECMA standard is agreed upon, the camp can chose to fast-track it to the ISO. This means that both camps are at all times in a position to formally standardize the full range of their technological achievements.

Table 4.5 Structure of the ECMA TC 31 – optical discs and disc cartridges

DVD 6 C	DVD+RW Alliance	Other members
Hitachi	Hewlett Packard	Fujitsu
IBM	Philips	Le Carvennec Consultants
JVC	Ricoh	NEC
Matsushita	Sony	Plasmon
Toshiba	Thomson	Samsung
Mitsubishi	Verbatim	Pioneer
Time Warner		

DYNAMICS OF DVD RECORDABLE STANDARDS

If we summarize the information presented thus far, we can begin to analyse the impact of the conditions we discussed on the dynamics of standards. Using the information regarding the membership structure of the four relevant consortia, the way the actors are connected to the various technologies and the way the technologies are in turn linked to each other, we can now synthesize an overall description of the standardization arena on the basis of three dimensions that are relevant to the dynamics of standards: a) the technology–standards relationship (which technologies are similar and are incorporated into which standard), b) standard–consortia relationship (which standards are supported by which actors) and c) the consortia–actor relationship (how are the actors linked to the consortia). All three levels are represented in Figure 4.1. The level of technology–standards relationship is represented by the arrows connecting the boxes that depict the clusters of standards. The level of standards–consortia interrelationship is indicated by the names of the supporting consortia next to the boxes. Finally, the level of consortia–actor relationship is indicated by the names of the different consortia members and the membership of the actors in the ECMA TC 31 separately indicated.

□ Official DVD 'Forum' standards
→ Paths of Development
● ECMA TC31 Members

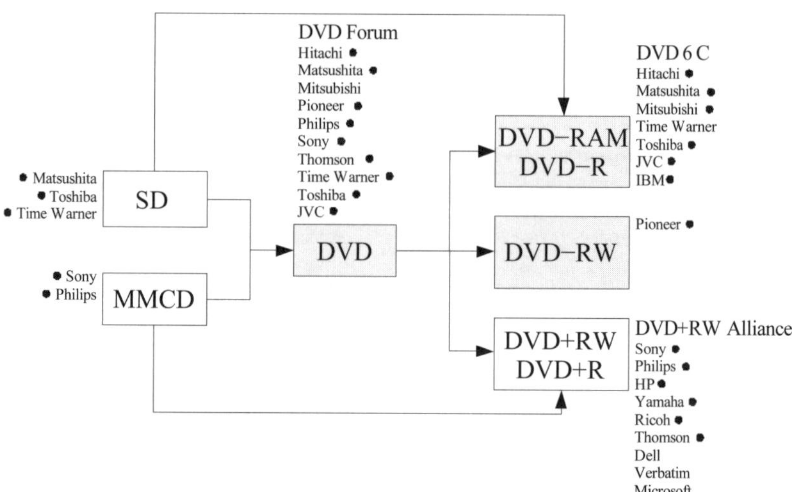

Figure 4.1 Relationship of standards, consortia and actors in the context of DVD recordable standardization

With regard to the relationship between technology and standards, MMCD and the SD technology merged into the DVD standard and then split into the different clusters of standards promoted by the two camps. The split also is an echo of the pre-DVD era, as the SD approach is related to the DVD−RAM and DVD−R technology, while the MMCD technology is implemented using the DVD+R and DVD+RW standards. This merge–split scenario is also reflected in the relationship between standards and consortia, with the DVD Forum supporting DVD−RAM, DVD−R and DVD−RW, and the DVD+RW Alliance supporting DVD+RW and DVD+R. At the level of actors and consortia, we see that the membership structure of the relevant DVD recordable consortia represents the pre-DVD split into actors who either support SD or MMCD, with Sony and Philips, the erstwhile MMCD supporters, forming a separate consortium to promote their own standard of DVD recordables.

Drawing on Besen and Farrell (1991) the 'split' scenario can be interpreted as a consequence of an incomplete standards negotiation process. The differences that were settled in the standardization of DVD did not include the 'write' aspects of DVD technology. It is also reflects a change in strategies of the involved actors from an 'alliance tactics' in the standardization of DVD to a 'going it alone tactics' in DVD recordable standardization (Lea and Hall 2004). The decision to 'go it alone' in standardization is mediated by three factors: a) technological capacity and capability, b) potential availability of network externalities, and c) expected ability to reap the rewards from a standard (Lea and Hall 2004). As we have pointed out, all three factors are provided in DVD recordables, but not in DVD standardization, due to the influence of content providers and media producers. The constellations of actors, standards and technologies help us identify the reasons behind the dynamics of DVD recordable by looking at the historical development of the DVD recordable standards. To analyse the dynamics of standards in this fashion requires a thorough and as complete as possible history of revisions of specifications, as well as revision of standards at the official level. The historical data contains a) the changes of specifications at consortia level, b) specifications that are or are not included in official standards and c) specific differences in timing at all levels of the standardization process. This timeline is presented in Table 4.6.

To account for the above-mentioned patterns in standardization activities, it is useful to distinguish two dimensions of standards dynamics, a horizontal and a vertical dimension. We reserve the term 'horizontal dynamics' to denote straightforward changes to standards (e.g. a new version of a standard). The term 'vertical dynamics' refers to a change in status of a standard (e.g. standardizing a *de facto* standard, or formalizing a consortium standard by a formal standards body). Although horizontal and vertical change may occur in different degrees, the relevance of such a distinction is best illustrated by looking at the extremes of both dimensions – i.e. high and low levels of change on both dimensions.

This results in basically four schematized interrelationship between horizontal and vertical dynamics of standards. The most dynamic circumstance is that of high horizontal and vertical dynamics. As the case illustrates, this is observable in times when competition is at its peak. In the case study high horizontal dynamics and low vertical dynamics typically occurs when continuous technology advancement is combined with a medium to low level of competition. The cost of formalizing the changes outweighs the need to get a competitive edge. The third situation, namely that of low horizontal dynamics and high vertical dynamics, is closely related to the previous one but they differ with respect to timing. Whereas under the previous situation revisions are accumulated before being formalized, in this situation an early implementation of a specification in a standard is followed by ongoing revisions of the specifications without a change to the formal standard. This is also rather typical for a medium to low competition setting. The fourth and final situation, that is, little horizontal and vertical change, describes the consortium approach. Here, vertical dynamics do not exist and only minor changes occur at a horizontal level. Such a lack of dynamics typically occurs in a stable market, one where competition is at its lowest, possibly because a monopoly or oligopoly exists. In such a situation price control is high and the need to introduce innovations is low.

COMPETITION AND DYNAMICS OF STANDARDS

With regard to the horizontal dimension of standards dynamics, two highly active phases can be isolated. The first of these phases occurred between 1997 and early 2000 for the DVD–RAM and DVD–R standard. During that time frame, four major revisions of DVD–RAM and DVD–R took place. This phase was limited to the standards of the 'slash'-camp. Strikingly, another highly active phase started near the end of 2002 and it was limited to DVD–RW, DVD+RW and the two WORM-media types DVD+R and DVD–R. With the market entry of the devices conforming to the competing standards, horizontal dynamics of standards gathered momentum, with the devices of the 'plus'-camp being introduced into the market. This was limited to DVD–RW vs DVD+RW and DVD–R vs DVD+R.[9]

There are some interesting implications with regard to the dynamics of standards, as the horizontal dynamics of standards increase in the light of competition in a market segment. In contrast to the notion of the revision of standards as a reaction to problems regarding implementation, the dynamics of consortia standards is driven by competition between the 'slash'- and the 'plus'-camp. This implies that, in the case of standardization of competing technologies, strategic implications play a major role in the dynamics of standards at a horizontal level. In this case, standards are used with a high focus on competition. This again offers support to the idea that standards play a significant role in stabilizing a competitor's market position (Bonino and Spring 1991). There is also strong evidence suggesting that horizontal dynamics of standards are influenced by competition in the form of technology races between the competing parties, if we consider the standard-setting process as an extension of the development process as has been done by a number of scholars (Blind 2004; Thiard and Pfau 1991; Weiss 1990). From such a point of view, horizontal dynamics of standards should increase rather than be reduced in prolonged technology races and during fierce competition. Accordingly, in phases that are characterized by low levels of competition, revisions serve as instruments to solve implementation issues that occur especially in early stages of less mature standards. This is also reflected in the historical data by the long gaps in DVD−R standardization at the level of specification, which ended when DVD+R entered the standardization arena in 2003. The key issue regarding horizontal dynamics is the need on the part of both camps to distinguish their products from those offered by their competitors, with the aim of acquiring higher market share.

On the whole, two technology races can be identified in the DVD recordable and consequently in horizontal standards dynamics. The first is the race for recordable capacity. This race occurred at the early stages of DVD recordable technology and was limited to the competition between DVD−RAM and DVD+RW in late 1998 and has recently gained momentum with the first specification for DVD+RDL. The other race has to do with recording speed, and it has been a major driver in horizontal dynamics of standards in the second phase of high dynamics since late 2002, as all revisions of specifications included changes in maximum recording speed. Generally speaking, horizontal dynamics of standards increases under competition in a market segment, as aspects of technical superiority become more important for establishing market share. This is basically contrary to the notion that the number of revisions should be higher in the early stages when standards tend to be less mature and revision is needed to solve implementation issues. The effect of competition seems to be much stronger in case of standards wars.

With regard to the vertical dimension of the dynamic of standards, i.e. the number of specifications represented in formal standards, a stable pattern can be observed, whereby the 'slash'-camp tends only to file its basic specifications, while the 'plus'-camp also includes the speed-related aspects of the recording process. The only exception to this pattern is the specification of

Table 4.6 Overview of DVD recordable standardization history

		1997		1998		1999		2000	
DVD–RAM	Spec.	–	July 1.0	–	October 1.9 (4.7 GB)	–	September 2.0	February 2.1	–
	ECMA	–	–	February ECMA-272	–	June ECMA-272/2	–	–	–
	ISO	–	–	April ISO/DIS 16824	–	May ISO 16824	–	–	–
DVD–RW	Spec.	–	–	–	–	–	November 1.0	–	September 1.1
	ECMA	–	–	–	–	–	–	–	–
	ISO	–	–	–	–	–	–	–	–
DVD+RW	Spec.	May 1.0	–	–	–	–	–	–	–
	ECMA	–	–	April ECMA-274	–	June ECMA-274/2	–	–	–
	ISO	–	–	May ISO/DIS 16969	–	–	October ISO 16969	–	–
DVD–R	Spec.	–	July 1.0	–	November 1.9 (4.7 GB)	–	–	February 2.0 (A)	May 2.0 (G)
	ECMA	–	–	–	December ECMA-279	–	–	–	–
	ISO	–	–	–	–	–	–	June ISO/DIS 20563	–
DVD+R	Spec.	–	–	–	–	–	–	–	–
	ECMA	–	–	–	–	–	–	–	–
	ISO	–	–	–	–	–	–	–	–

		2001		2002		2003		2004	
DVD–RAM	Spec.	–	–	–	June 2.1 rev 1 (3 x)	–	–	–	February 2.1 rev 2 (5 x)
	ECMA	–	–	December ECMA-330	June ECMA-330/2 nd	–	–	–	–
	ISO	–	–	–	–	–	March ISO/DIS 17592	–	July ISO 17592
DVD–RW	Spec.	–	–	–	–	August 1.1 rev 1 (2 x)	–	November 1.1 rev 2 (4 x)	–
	ECMA	–	–	–	–	December ECMA-338	–	–	–
	ISO	–	–	–	–		March ISO/DIS 17342	–	July ISO 17342
DVD+RW	Spec.	–	March 1.1	–	–	December 1.2 (4 x)	–	–	October (8 x) 1.3 pre
	ECMA	–	–	–	–	December ECMA-337	–	December ECMA-337/2	–
	ISO	–	–	–	–		–	–	July ISO/DIS 17341 (1 x, 4 x)
DVD–R	Spec.	–	–	–	–	August 2.01 (G) (4 x)	–	November 2.02 (G) (6 x, 8 x)	June 2.1 (G)
	ECMA	–	–	–	–	–	–		–
	ISO	–	July ISO 20563	–	–	–	–	–	–
DVD+R	Spec.	–	–	–	July 1.0	December 1.11 (4 x)	July 1.2 (8 x)	–	July (16 x) 1.3
	ECMA	–	–	–	–	–	–	December ECMA-349 (4 x)	June ECMA-349/2 (8 x)
	ISO	–	–	–	–	–	–		July ISO/DIS 17344 (4 x,8 x)

the DVD–RAM 2.1 rev 1, which was included in the second draft of the ECMA-330 standard, and which included a speed specification of three times the nominal recording speed. In the case of the DVD–R standard, the regularly sold discs with a capacity of 4.7 GB have neither a corresponding ECMA standard nor an ISO standard. This is a stable pattern that applies both to the DVD+R and to the DVD+RW standard. Even though on the whole this observed pattern is stable, there are differences with regard to vertical dynamics, with the ECMA acting as an intermediary between consortia level and formal level. Based on the condition that the ECMA standards propose an intermediary role in the vertical dynamics and all ISO standards stem from fast-forwarded ECMA standards, we can derive the number of specifications that are included in any given ISO standard or draft. Moreover, as described above, both consortia at all times have had the chance to forward their specifications to the ISO level, as both camps could muster the minimum of three members in the ECMA TC 31 to keep a standard-setting project running at the ECMA level and fast-forward the resulting ECMA standard to the ISO JTC 1.

The question that arises from these results is: Why did the 'slash'-camp not forward the specifications including the information on the higher recording speeds while the 'plus'-camp chose to do so? This cannot be explicitly deduced using the available data. Having said that, there are a number of reasonable conclusions that could explain vertical dynamics. One potential explanation is that the 'plus'-camp tried to compensate for the stigma of its standard not being approved as an official DVD standard by the DVD Forum and chose another legitimation strategy by including as much of its specification as possible in an ISO standard. Another hypothesis is that only the winner of the technology race includes the information of higher recording speed in a formal standard. This would also partly explain the exception of the DVD–RAM rev 2.1 rev 1 specification in the revision of the ECMA-330 standard, as at that time DVD–RAM could be recorded at three times nominal recording speed, whereas the other rewritable specifications supported only single speed recording. On the whole, the vertical dynamics of standards were high at the beginning of the standard war (DVD–RAM vs. DVD+RW), between 1997 and 1999. During this timeframe the only WORM medium (DVD–R) shows very little vertical dynamics, and no vertical dynamics after the first basic specification was published as an ISO standard. This leads us to the conclusion that vertical dynamics are generally higher at the beginning of a standard-setting process, when competition is high and competitors have an incentive to be the first to produce a full-grown formal standard. This could be another explanation for the high vertical dynamics of the DVD+R standard between 2002 and the present, as the DVD+R standard arrived on the market comparably late, in the spring of 2002.

MULTIPLE IMPLEMENTATION AND DYNAMICS OF STANDARDS

Another factor that could influence the dynamics of standards at horizontal and vertical levels has to do with the possibility of implementing competing standards in a single device by what we choose to refer to as 'multiple implementation'. The concept of multiple implementation is similar to the concept of multiprotocol stacks found, for example, in 'multiprotocol label switching' (Table 6.1, Egyedi and Loeffen, this volume). We distinguish between multiple implementation and multiprotocol stacks, since we consider the latter to be a special case of the former as multiple implementation is not necessarily limited to protocols, but can also encompass technical artifacts. Unlike the concept of adaptors, which is more of an add-on technology solution to the problem of competing standards, the concept of multiple implementation describes a different solution to the problem of competing standards: it is a technical solution that represents the transition from the rival evolution of standards (Shapiro and Varian 1999a) towards a stable duopoly in which competing standards can coexist. Thereby the chance of the market tipping towards one or the other of the two standards is reduced. In the case of DVD recordables the situation is even more complex than in the case of the infamous VHS vs Betamax war where only two formats competed. This complexity arises from the fact that each camp does not hold only one format but rather a mix of different formats that in most cases have functional equivalents in the other camps portfolio. So for instance the 'plus'-camp represents DVD+R while the 'slash'-camp represents DVD−R, both being functional equivalents but both having different technological aspects. Multiple implementation can therefore occur in two distinct ways relative to the implementation of technologies from either camp's format portfolio. A polarized implementation strategy would therefore comprise the implementation of at least two formats from the portfolio of only one of the camps. This attempt is most likely to happen if the perception of hardware manufacturers expect a tipping of the market to one of the camp's portfolios. A diffused strategy would represent the implementation of rival functional equivalents from both camps portfolios. This strategy is likely to occur if manufacturers want to spread risk and expecting the market not to tip to either format or as a way to capture a greater share of the market where a first-mover has already begun to introduce products.

The polarized strategy is evident in the implementation of both DVD−RAM and DVD−R in early devices built by Panasonic (the LF-D321U) and introduced to the market in 2001. The diffused strategy was first adopted by Sony in late 2002, a member of the 'plus'-camp, with the DRU-500A supporting both DVD+RW and DVD−RW. The diffused implementation strategy proves to be a dominant strategy in standards war with low chances of tipping due to equally strong camps. This also shows in the sales figures, as '[n]early 50% of the DVD writers market is already for the models from the likes of Sony, Pioneer & NEC which are the dual drives (+/− R)' (Optical Disc Systems 2004). Drawing on Anderson and Tushman the option of multiple implementation is therefore the dominant design, as the 'most strict selection mode is one in which one design emerges that accounts, over time, for over 50 per cent of new implementations of the breakthrough technology. Only one design can meet this criterion' (Anderson and Tushman 1990, p. 614). This means that the dominant design in this case applies not to a single standard, but to a set of whole cluster of standards, with some of the standards actually competing for market share.

The concept of multiple implementation offers some interesting insights into the dynamics of standards at a horizontal as well as a vertical level, by providing an answer to the question why there is an ongoing technology race and why the market does not show a preference for either standard. As Kortum and Lerner (1997) have argued, technology races should not be seen as races with a definite finish, but rather as an ongoing process that spurs innovation. Having said that, Kortum and Lerner are unable to explain why those races actually keep their momentum. In the case of standards wars, a diffused implementation strategy offers an answer to this question, as it leads to a stable structure of coexistence. This stability exists because neither of the actors engaged is able to abandon its strategy without running the risk of losing market share once a reliable multiple implementation device that integrates competing formats is introduced at a price reflecting the willingness to pay of risk averse customers. One explanation for this can be derived from diffusion theory, as consumers tend to be more risk-averse in later stages in the diffusion process (the late majority and the laggards) than they are in the early stages of that process (the innovators, early adopters and early majority) (Rogers 1995). Assuming that risk aversion increases with adoption rate, the strategy of a diffused implementation strategy becomes the dominant strategy, as it helps reduce the risk of choosing the unsuccessful solution. This option also reduces the risk for the customer and will be especially be attractive to risk averse customers in the later stages of the diffusion process given that the higher price of the devices does reflect the willingness to pay for the reduced risk. This is consistent with the argument presented by Farrell and Saloner, that customers will try to avoid taking the risk of buying the 'wrong' standard, for fear that the market may end up choosing competing standards (Farrell and Saloner 1985; Vercoulen and van Wegberg 1998). There is one element of competition that remains, as DVD recordable technology is a networked product. This means that, apart from the revenues derived by the sales of devices, there are also revenues involved in the sale of media content.

This component keeps the competition alive and prevents competing parties from terminating their R&D activities, and as such it accounts for the ongoing technology races. As far as the dynamics of standards are concerned, this leads to a stable structure, as the chance of tipping markets is reduced, while at the same time technology races are kept running, which accounts for dynamics standards at the horizontal and vertical level.

CONCLUSIONS AND DISCUSSION

Standards are not static, nor do they exist and evolve in isolation. Instead, they exist and evolve in a dynamic environment characterized by competition among networking organizations, some of which are bound together in consortia. We have shown that in light of competition, some proportion of the dynamics of standards can be explained by the diffused IPR structure, which led two competing parties to engage in technology races. Different from studies that focus standards' change in answer to implementation problems, we focus on standards' dynamics that stems from the competition between rival consortia. Competition leads to a high amount of horizontal and vertical standards dynamics. With the market entry of late-movers, technology races and standards wars lead to a high degree of horizontal dynamics, with a distinct pattern of vertical dynamics applying only in cases of substantial technical advantage of one of the competing parties' solution over the other. The effect of competition on standards dynamics is likely to be higher in sectors or technologies where IPR holders have a strong incentive to co-ordinate with other actors, especially when economies of scale are important and production can be outsourced, as is the case in the production of blank media. Keeping the specifications fixed for a long period of time can prove to be a disadvantage for a firm, as this will strengthen the competitors' position to include their newest technical developments in their standard and in turn provide a good that appears to be superior to customers, leading to higher sales and higher market share. However, such a hypothesis cannot be tested using the available data.

Finally, we ask the question whether or not the effect of standards dynamics induced by competition and innovation poses a problem? An answer to this question digs deep into the fundamentals of the relationship between innovation and standards. On the one hand a standard that does not keep pace with innovation may become redundant, and even have negative effects due to lock-ins. On the other hand, a standard that changes too often may lose its co-ordinative benefits, with a plethora of incompatible implementations floating around and producers and users unable to adapt to new versions. Dynamic standards are a trade-off between continuity and discontinuity. This raises some crucial issues. First, are the improvements introduced through innovations, the costs of adapting to newer versions of a standard and the positive effects of timely and flexible standards in balance? Second, are there ways to reduce the potential cost introduced by dynamic standards? The former issue is hard to grasp in a thorough empirical fashion and is almost impervious to quantitative measurement, but there clearly are options when it comes to addressing the latter issue. Using the insights from this case study we will elaborate on some of the potential solutions to reduce or internalize the potential switching costs involved. The three solutions for reducing the switching costs between dynamic standards are backward compatibility, 'patching' the implementations to conform to newer standards and introducing multiple implementation of standards in light of competition and standards wars.

In some cases, high standards dynamics introduced through competition may reduce the value of long-term investments, in our case the DVD recorders, since the network goods (blank media) required to harness the value of the recorder are no longer available or suitable. If blank media conforming to a newer and incompatible version of a standard become available and drive blank media that conform to earlier standards out of the market, old devices are rendered useless.[10] In the case of networked information technology goods, this negative effect of standards dynamics can largely be reduced in three ways. One option is downward compatibility, which helps retain the value of the long-term investment. This option solves both the problem of information retrieval from legacy media, an issue addressed in great detail by van der Meer (this volume), as well as using old recorders with newer media. The second option, which is also common in DVD recordable technology, refers to firmware patching, i.e. adapting older implementations to the newer version of a standard.[11] However, this largely shifts control from the user side to the producer side. If producers choose to discontinue support for older devices, there is little customers can do. The third option caters to the needs of risk-averse customers who want to buy devices that can deal with both competing standards (multiple implementation). In this case, users of such devices can choose freely between blank media conforming to either of the competing standards. The likely result is that such devices become the dominant design, a design which may also have to reconcile the standards war between HD DVD and the Blu-Ray Disc which is raging at the time of writing.

NOTES

1. The fact that standards are not only embedded in but have similar effects to trajectories by constituting rules of permanence has been highlighted by Schmidt (1998).

2. The suffix DL in the case of DVD+RDL refers to the specification of recording data on two storage layers thereby achieving roughly twice the capacity of the single layer discs. Since the specification of DVD+RDL is relatively new, it does not provide much good insight into the dynamics of standards. The specification reached version 1.0 in early 2003, and to a large extent it is not included in this analysis. It is listed here for the sake of completeness.
3. Even though DVD−RAM, especially older versions of discs, are sometimes packaged in a case.
4. The actual technical differences will not be discussed in this chapter since they do not provide greater insight into the mechanisms that lead to a forking of the DVD recordable standards and dynamics of the standards.
5. By now, the European Computer Manufacturers Association has been renamed Ecma International. However, because its older name was still being used at the time the events described here took place, we have decided to use the older name rather than the current one.
6. The term book in this represents a technical term like 'red book', 'yellow book' or 'orange book' in CD technology.
7. By now approximately 250 companies have joined the DVD Forum.
8. As a reaction, the DVD Forum announced that the format proposed by those firms would not be supported by the DVD Forum. They even added that the proposed format must not hold the prefix 'DVD' since it was not supported by the DVD Forum and hence should be called 'phase change rewritable (PC−RW)'. This position has not changed since then as a notice on the DVD Forum website proves: 'Please note that the "+RW" format, also known as DVD+RW was neither developed nor approved by the DVD Forum. The approved recordable formats are DVD−R, DVD−RW and DVD−RAM'.
9. It should be noted that the influence of DVD−RAM for the broad consumer market has decreased over time, with DVD−RAM being used mainly in a professional context.
10. This can, in an abstract way, be compared to blank VHS cassettes being driven out of the market by DVD recordables. The difference here is that blank media conforming to newer versions of a standard drive out older versions of the same standard, rather than one product replacing a completely different kind of product.
11. Concepts like firmware patching also highlight the co-evolutionary character of the dynamics in the implementation/standard, or, more precisely, the standard/environment relationship. Instead of simply assuming a one-way causality between problems of implementation and changes in standards, options like firmware patching also allow the implementations to be adapted to newer standards.

5. Internet Addressing Standards: A Case Study in Standards Dynamics Driven by Bottom-up Adoption

Jos Vrancken, Marnix Kaart and Michel Soares

INTRODUCTION

The looming crisis in Internet addressing, by the depletion of IPv4 addresses within the coming three to six years (Huston 2007), offers an interesting case in standards dynamics. It involves two competing standards, IPv6 and NAT, each of which can solve the crisis. It is the way they behave in the adoption process that will determine the future of Internet addressing for decades to come.

Traditionally, Internet addresses are arranged via the IPv4 standard, which was developed between 1974 and 1979. Within this standard, Internet addresses consist of four bytes, allowing some 4 billion host machines to be addressed, when used as a flat namespace. In the past, this approach has proven very useful, and it has made the emergence of the Internet possible. But due to the exponential growth of the Internet, we have come to a point where the available address space is no longer enough. For instance, although these days Internet access can almost be seen as a basic human right, there is no way that every person on the planet can have an IPv4 address. By the same token, in this day and age it is virtually impossible to run a business without being present on the Internet.

In addition, there is an important technological development which will stretch the IPv4 scheme even further. As a result of the increase in computing power and storage capacity per cubic millimetre, and the reduction in computer chip prices, within a few years the number of devices per person will increase enormously. Not only mobile phones, 'personal digital assistants (PDA)' and desktop-PC's, but virtually any appliance or utensil will contain computing and (wireless) communication devices: cars, vacuum cleaners, refrigerators, clothes, etc. (Lu et al. 2008; Meloan 2003). All of these devices will communicate and therefore need identification. Metcalfe's law (Durand

2001) dictates that the majority of these devices will be connected to the Internet, offering unrivalled information access, reachability and visibility. This development is referred to by various names, such as 'ambient intelligence', 'ubiquitous computing' or 'pervasive computing' (Imperial College London, Distributed Software Engineering Section 23).

It is safe to assume that an address space of 10^{12} will be the minimally required space in the coming two decades, and an additional extension by several orders of magnitude would be welcome.

IPv4, used as a flat address space, will not be sufficient, so a new approach will have to be adopted. In this chapter we consider and compare the two most likely candidates for this new addressing scheme: IPv6, the 'official' successor to IPv4 (Deering and Hinden 1995 and 1998), defined by the IETF, and NAT, a bottom-up emerging solution to the shortage of address space (Egevang and Francis 1994; Srisuresh and Egevang 2001; Tsirtsis and Srisuresh 2000; Tsuchiya and Eng 1993).

We begin by discussing the general technicalities involved in addressing and routing, followed by a technical description of the two alternative approaches. After that, we take a look at the properties of bottom-up processes, complexity, emergence and network effects that can be applied to the adoption process of each of the two schemes involved. This results in the criteria for the bottom-up adoption or emergence of standards. Using these criteria we can then compare the strengths and weaknesses of the two standards and assess their chances for adoption. From this, lessons can be drawn about the required suitability criteria of envisaged standards in terms of their bottom-up adoption. It is these lessons that are the contribution to standards research provided in this chapter.

ADDRESSING AND ROUTING IN FLAT AND HIERARCHICAL NAME SPACES

The real problem concerning Internet addressing is not so much unique identification (which is in fact fairly easy, see for instance Ethernet addresses) but routing: finding a certain device by its address and finding a reasonably efficient path through the network to reach that device. The simplest form of addressing is a flat address space or name space, of which IPv4 and IPv6 are examples. The address of a device in a flat space is a single identifier, which is network-wide unique. When assigning an address to a new device, the uniqueness has to be guaranteed. In the Internet this is done by instances such as 'Internet corporation for assigned names and numbers (ICANN)' and the regional Internet registries. In principle, when searching a specific device by its address, the whole address space has to be searched. It is obvious that this becomes unwieldy when the space is too large, in which case a name space can be divided into subspaces or domains. If the subdomains are still too large, this process can be repeated as often as necessary. This results in a tree-structure or 'hierarchy' of subdomains. Only the lowest domains in the hierarchy are flat spaces. The addresses of devices now become paths, i.e. series of identifiers denoting the device, then the lowest domain to which it belongs, then the next enclosing domain, etc. Moreover, the path by which device A denotes device B is dependent on their relative position. This is best illustrated by telephony, which offers a fine example of hierarchical addressing. For telephony, the hierarchy has, in many countries, three levels: the international level distinguishing countries, the national level distinguishing regions within a country and the local level. When calling a number in the same local domain, the short local number suffices. When calling a number in a different country, the so-called 'absolute' path (complete up to and including the top of the hierarchy) is used, starting with a code identifying absolute paths (two zeros in many countries), the country code, the regional code and then the subscriber's local number. Another well-known example of a hierarchical address space is a file system in Unix or Windows.

From a manageability point of view, hierarchical name spaces have a strong advantage: one can easily start a new domain in any of the existing domains in the tree. Only the name of the domain has to be unique within its parent domain. Within the new domain one has complete freedom (apart from local uniqueness) in defining names for the devices in that domain. A hierarchical addressing scheme can cover many different local addressing schemes.

The strongest advantage of hierarchical systems lies, however, in the scalability of the routing. In a flat space, routing scales linearly with the size of the network. Hierarchically, routing is hardly an issue: you only need to follow the path. It is only in the lowest domain, which can be as big or small as appropriate for the purpose of routing, that one has to resort to straight searching. Paths do not need to be very long: path length is logarithmic in network size (size measured in number of nodes). This means that routing is logarithmic in hierarchical spaces, whereas it is linear or worse than linear in flat spaces. Considering the current size of the Internet and its expected growth in the near as well as the more distant future, this makes the adoption of a hierarchy simply unavoidable.

It is, therefore, no surprise that, within the flat IPv4 system, a limited form of hierarchy has been introduced, for reasons of manageability and routing. Addresses are divided into two parts: the subnetwork and the host. This means that an internet protocol (IP) address is actually a two-step path. However, this primitive form of hierarchy does not represent the capabilities of a genuinely hierarchical system, in which new domains can be introduced

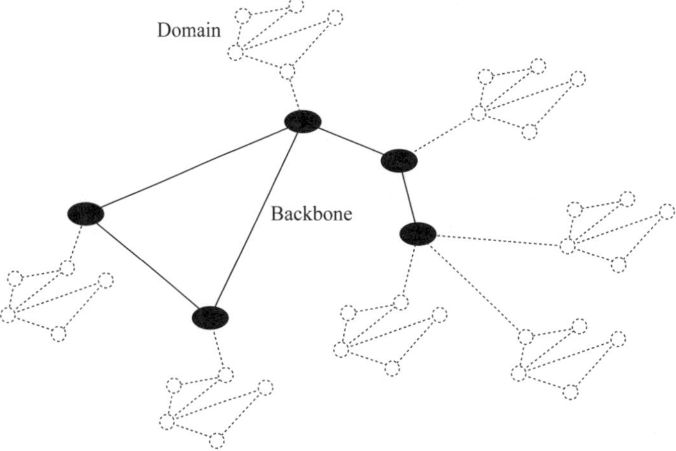

Figure 5.1 Network structure

at will and in which paths can have arbitrary lengths and can cover different local addressing schemes.

Figure 5.1 portrays the Internet structure in a schematic way. Although the Internet clearly has a hierarchical structure, it also has lots of direct shortcuts between domains. The Internet's hierarchy covers three levels: so-called autonomous systems at the highest level (van Beijnum 2002), then the domains and finally NAT-areas behind a single IP-number (to be explained below). The structure of IPv4 addresses reflects this network structure, although not in an obvious way. The mapping between domains and addresses has evolved over time (A, B, and C classes and 'classless interdomain routing [CIDR]': classes are just domains of different sizes, Fuller and Li 2006), and leaves much to be desired.

Apart from the complexities introduced by evolutionary growth, the real problem with Internet hierarchy seems to be that there are too few levels and that the partitioning into levels is far from optimal. In addition, there is no accepted, common way of introducing new levels and repartitioning the network.

Other Alternative Addressing Schemes

Are there any other addressing schemes imaginable for the Internet? In light of the effort needed to introduce a new addressing scheme, it is highly unlikely that any other schemes will become viable alternatives, simply because such a development would already have taken place by now. Most likely, it is going to be a combination of the NAT, IPv4 and IPv6 schemes.

IPV6

IPv6 was defined by the IETF in 1995, when the shortage of IPv4 address space was recognized as a future problem (van Beijnum 2005). Apart from a 128-bit address space, it differs from IPv4 especially in the header format, which is optimized towards efficient handling in the routing process. On the other hand, IPv6 has not tackled the routing problem. Because the Internet currently has a very shallow hierarchical structure with only two levels (see above) in the public area, routing tables become oversized and the routing process tends to become too expensive. Another problem that IPv6 has left unsolved is the so-called multi-homing problem. This problem is about having more than one Internet access provider while using different providers at different times. Organizations that do not want to depend on a single 'Internet service provider (ISP)' would like to use multi-homing.

Actual use of IPv6 is still very limited. A symposium in November 2006, organized by the Dutch IPv6 task force in the Netherlands, offered detailed information about the status of IPv6 in a western, industrialized country in 2006. Although there is a certain amount of IPv6 traffic, it only represents 0.1 per cent of the total traffic. In addition, most IPv6 traffic has to do with the illegal exchange of information. Apparently, people engaging in this kind of activity have come to appreciate the stealth properties of IPv6, which come with its relatively esoteric use (Hania 2006).

A large ISP (XS4All) announced it was working on the introduction of IPv6, but the problems were huge, not so much in terms of networking equipment but mainly with regard to the applications involved. Real business opportunities were hard to find for IPv6, both for subscribers and for the ISP itself (van Eijk 2007; Hania 2006). Actually, this ISP was quite happy with NAT, which offered many advantages, in terms of security, network modularity, address space, etc. For subscribers, NAT also offered significant advantages such as security and multi-homing (Hania 2006).

'Réseaux IP Européens (RIPE)', the European Internet Registry, located in the Netherlands, distributor for both IPv4 and IPv6 addresses, had seen a decrease in interest in IPv6 in the past two years, instead of an increase (Karrenberg 2006).

Predictions as to when IPv4 will really be depleted still varied strongly (Huston). Worldwide, the distribution rate is about 165 million IP-numbers per year, at which rate all the available space will have been used up in about four years time. However, there are several effects that may play a role in the final stage of IPv4 distribution, such as a rush for the last available numbers, which would accelerate depletion, as well as a trade in IPv4 numbers. With an increasing shortage, several speakers (Hania 2006; Karrenberg 2006) predicted that IPv4 address space would become a valuable marketable asset.

We can add the conclusion that this will undoubtedly stimulate the use of NAT and that it is likely to set free a considerable amount of IPv4 address space, possibly extending the IPv4 era by several decades.

A very serious drawback of IPv6 from a migration point of view is that it is not compatible with IPv4. An IPv4 machine cannot see IPv6 sites and vice versa, unless gateways are installed. But in most cases, these gateways are application-specific 'application level gateways (ALGs)' that require an effort on both sides. This means that it is not a good idea to try to do business worldwide using an IPv6-only site (unless there is a special reason why only IPv6 sites are used within the target group). To maintain worldwide visibility, some of the many migration strategies from IPv4 to IPv6 (van Beijnum 2005) include dual stacks, which means that a site is equipped with both an IPv4 and an IPv6 address. A dual stack strategy obviously cannot be a solution to address space shortage, and it is therefore not a strategy for migrating towards IPv6.

NAT

A very different solution to IPv4 address space shortage is offered by NAT (Egevang and Francis 1994; Srisuresh and Egevang 2001; Tsirtsis and Srisuresh 2000; Tsuchiya and Eng 1993). This approach was also defined by the IETF, in 1994, as a short-term solution to address space shortage, while waiting for the next generation of IP. NAT can be seen as adding an extra level to the Internet hierarchy, at the lower end.

In Figure 5.2, the local area network (LAN) nodes do not have a worldwide unique (or 'real') IP address but only a locally unique IP address. Only the NAT router has a real IP address. From the point of view of the rest of the Internet, it looks as if all requests come from this node. In reality, requests from any host within the LAN are translated into requests from the NAT router and marked by means of the 'transport control protocol (TCP)' port number field ('Internet assigned numbers authority [IANA]') in the packet. When the answer returns, this packet is assembled into a packet with the right local IP address and TCP port number. In this way, a host within the LAN initiating requests (a 'client') experiences no limitations. A host who is waiting for requests from others (a 'server') currently does experience limitations. This is because port numbers are now globally assigned to specific applications (80 to web servers, 25 to mail servers, etc.), so currently one cannot have two port 25 mail servers within a LAN behind a NAT router, both accessible from the Internet. But this can be remedied and this remedy can emerge in an evolutionary fashion, as will be detailed below. The address space of port numbers (16 bits) then adds to the address space of IPv4

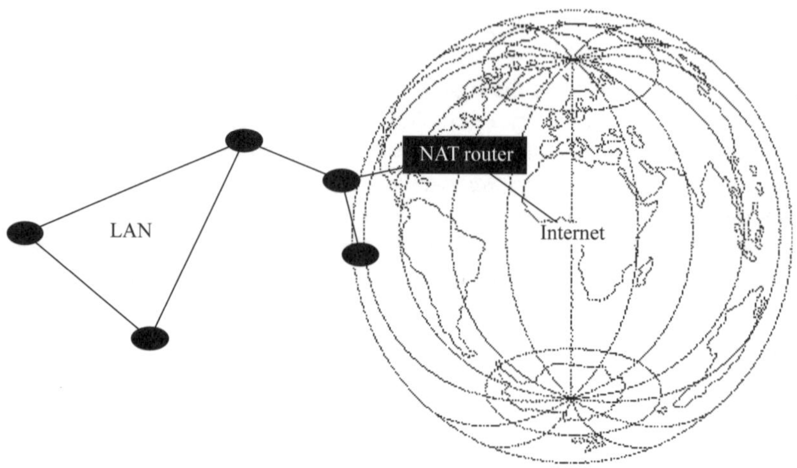

Figure 5.2 Connecting a LAN via a NAT gateway

numbers (32 bits), resulting in 48 bit addressing for servers. The address space for clients, that do not need to be visible on the Internet, is even bigger. There can be millions of clients behind a NAT gateway, using a single public IP address. At the moment, NAT is being used very frequently. Internet access by 'small office or home office (SOHO)' users are virtually always implemented via a NAT gateway.

MAKING NAT INTO A REAL ADDRESSING SCHEME

To turn NAT into a genuine addressing scheme, the coupling between port numbers and types of applications (the so-called 'well-known port number', for instance port 25 for mail servers or 80 for web servers) has to be abolished (there are more reasons to do this; Kohler et al. 2006; Lear 2006). When publishing a mail server for instance, the IP address (of the NAT router) is no longer sufficient: the port number, which then is no longer automatically 25, has to be added as well. This is already technically possible and often done, for various reasons. This way of addressing and publishing servers can be introduced in an evolutionary way. Any LAN administration team can do this on its own. Firewalls could present a complication here, as they are often port-sensitive, but a LAN's firewall is controlled by the same LAN administration team, so it is possible to make the necessary adaptations.

Even 'domaine name system (DNS)' translation of mnemonic names into address numbers can be extended to include port numbers, as is currently already done in the case of the SIP protocol for Internet telephony (session initiation protocol [SIP] 2002) by means of the 'service (SRV)' record (DNS SRV).

NAT and IPv6 have a problem in common. Applications and addressing became mixed up in the IPv4 era. Applications are referring directly to IP addresses and put IP addresses in the data they exchange with other applications, sometimes even encrypted, so there is no way to make the NAT gateway transparent for such applications. A number of applications have to be adapted or an 'application-specific' gateway (ALG) has to be developed. For a large group of applications, variants of NAT and NAT traversal techniques have already been developed, due to the omnipresence of NAT-gateways (Ford and Srisuresh 2005; Huston 2004; Raz et al. 2000).

NAT does allow recursive repetition (that is, several nested networks behind NAT routers). This does extend the address space for clients but not for servers.

THE END-TO-END PRINCIPLE

The end-to-end principle is often mentioned as the primary objection to NAT-like solutions. The principle expresses the assumption that the network should only transmit packets from one application to the other, without any changes being made to the packets: all intelligence resides in the end points. NAT is said to hamper the free communication between applications, which is indeed true. NAT makes the network less transparent. Whether this is a disadvantage is a matter of debate. From the perspective of network people concerned with the proper functioning of the Internet's infrastructure, NAT is a complicating factor that makes the network and the applications using it more complex. Users and individual organizations, however, would like to be in control of who can access their machines. In that case, the NAT box (managed by local administrators close to the users) is an excellent way of controlling visibility and of monitoring all traffic to and from the organization. This means that the end-to-end argument is not likely to affect their behaviour. As far as they are concerned, the additional complexity caused by NAT is not a real disadvantage. To a large part, it is hidden within applications and network equipment.

At this point we wish to emphasize that IPv6 will not restore end-to-end communication. Firewalls are very similar to NAT gateways and they are often combined in a single box. They both tamper with all packets to and from an organization. Many of the traversal techniques apply to firewalls and NAT simultaneously. Security mandates the presence of firewalls as much with IPv6 as it does with IPv4 (van Beijnum 2007; Ford and Srisuresh 2005).

BOTTOM-UP PROCESSES AND COMPLEXITY

The bottom-up adoption of standards is an example of a so-called bottom-up process. Bottom-up processes consist of the unco-ordinated initiatives of large groups of actors, either individuals or organizations (Johnson 1992, 2001; Vrancken 1994). They contrast with so-called top-down processes that can be encountered in highly hierarchical organizations, where only the top has the right to take initiatives. Both types are theoretical extremes; in practice all processes are found somewhere in between the two extremes.

In a bottom-up process, each actor considers his environment and takes decisions based on his own interests. In this sense one may argue that there is some form of co-ordination, as each actor looks at other actors and his decisions are often influenced by what others are doing. In the case of standardization, where the value of a standard is strongly dependent on the extent of its use, this effect is particularly important. This is the reason why bottom-up processes, without any explicit co-ordinating instance, can still produce structured, coherent results. Any *de facto* standard is an example of such a coherent result from a bottom-up process. The Internet has made this self-organizing co-ordination effect in bottom-up processes stronger. Different actors can find each other and exchange information far easier than before the Internet age. In addition, a successful solution that is made or chosen by one of the actors in the process can easily spread to other users.

The content of the Internet is one big bottom-up process. Other examples of bottom-up processes are science and art. The latter example illustrates that even without clear criteria or clear goals, a bottom-up process can achieve useful results.

An important difference between top-down and bottom-up processes has to do with their relationship with complexity. In a top-down process, the top necessarily has to deal with the whole, and therefore with the complexity of the whole, the global complexity. In addition, solutions to problems have to be understood by the top. The top does not like to take risks, it wants to be sure. In a bottom-up process, actors are only confronted with the local complexity in their immediate environment. The bottom-up approach is much more of a trial and error approach. A bottom-up approach offers the possibility to produce and try many different possible solutions. It does not require a thorough understanding of a solution and the effects it will have, especially not with regard to the global effects. However, a successful solution can spread quickly and become the solution used by many actors. Because nobody in a bottom-up process feels responsible for the global effects, the global effects of bottom-up emergent solutions may vary from highly beneficial to highly detrimental.

The distinction between top-down and bottom-up is sometimes presented as the difference between user optimum and system optimum. In a bottom-up process actors strive for user optimum, which is often different from the system optimum, i.e. the optimum averaged over all users. The top-down approach is often associated with striving for the system optimum.

Both top-down and bottom-up have their specific pros and cons, summarized in Table 5.1. A proper understanding of these pros and cons is essential to understanding the future prospects of the different addressing schemes for the Internet.

Top-down processes are started and managed by a single person or a small group of people (the 'top'), which favours the efficiency and goal-orientation of the process and the predictability of the outcome. A small group of people, on the other hand, has a limited work capacity, a limited intelligence and a limited capability of idea creation. Therefore top-down processes have difficulties in handling complexity and in generating and trying large numbers of different options. Moreover, responsibilities are often clearly defined in a small group, with the effect that top-down processes are often characterized by a fear of taking risks.

Bottom-up processes include many actors, and as a result they are very creative and highly intelligent (leveraged by today's communication facilities), and they have the work capacity needed to try many different options. Because efficiency, especially overall efficiency of the process, goal-orientation and predictability of results is nobody's responsibility, bottom-up processes are not strong in these aspects. On the other hand, badly defined responsibilities make bottom-up approaches strong when it comes to taking risks.

CRITERIA FOR BOTTOM-UP ADOPTION

The above-mentioned considerations lead to the following criteria for the bottom-up adoption of a standard. First of all, a standard must be attractive from the viewpoint of single actors. This attractiveness is the sum of one or more of the following effects:

1. the standard has an official status, being defined and supported by an official or well-known standards defining institute (ISO, W3C, IETF, etc.);
2. the standard has local, short-term beneficial effects, independent of whether or not the standard is adopted by others. In other words, it solves a local problem for the actor; this is especially important when the standard is not yet widely used;
3. the standard is already widely used;
4. the standard is compatible with existing solutions;
5. the standard has a good chance of becoming the dominant standard in the near future and solves many existing problems;

6. the standard has few viable competitors;
7. in case of competing standards, the standard is, or can be, implemented in such a way that it becomes compatible with its competitors;
8. the standard has low local complexity: it is easy to introduce it locally.

Table 5.1 Pros and cons of top-down and bottom-up

	Top-down	Bottom-up
Efficiency	+	–
Predictability	+	–
Goal-oriented	+	–
Can handle global complexity	–	+
Can produce results in the absence of clear criteria (e.g. art)	–	+
Can try many different possible solutions	–	+
Daring to take risks	–	+
Creativity and group intelligence effects	–	+

Secondly, the global complexity caused by the standard is much less of a problem in bottom-up adoption. Single actors do not see or care about this global complexity. The same can be said of the predictability of the global effects. A third factor that makes a standard's position stronger is that it should allow for a gradual adoption (its advantages should be proportional to its degree of adoption and they should become available before it is widely adopted). A fourth factor is that the standard should allow gradual 'functional'extension. It should not limit the creativity in a bottom-up process.

COMPARING IPV6 AND NAT

Using the criteria outlined above, the positions of the two competing addressing schemes in the adoption process can be evaluated. IPv6 is attractive mainly because of its official status. As far as the other attractiveness-enhancing effects are concerned, it scores less than or equal to NAT. It has no local, short-term benefits. Its benefits depend on whether or not the whole world will move to IPv6. If such a development does not take place, one may as well stick to NAT. It has low compatibility with IPv4. As a matter of fact, its compatibility is fully dependent on NAT: there is a form of NAT (NAT-PT [Tsirtsis and Srisuresh 2000] where PT stands for protocol translation) with the purpose of connecting IPv6 and IPv4 domains, but this form has recently been deprecated for being overly complex (Aoun and Davies

2007). IPv6 does not solve any of the existing problems in routing, multi-homing, mobile IP, real-time traffic, multi-casting, etc., or the solution can be implemented just as well in IPv4 (Karrenberg 2006). It is not being widely used. IPv6 and NAT have only each other as competitors. The local complexity of IPv6 and NAT is probably equal, whereby IPv6 still suffers from teething problems although there are clear improvements (Zhou et al. 2007). The main complexity is in the development of ALGs, which is more or less the same for IPv6 and NAT (Ford and Srisuresh 2005; Hania 2006; Huston 2004). The global simplicity of IPv6 only applies to identification. As far as routing is concerned, IPv6 offers no improvement over IPv4. Its gradual introduction is dependent on NAT and the development of appropriate ALGs. Ironically, these are exactly the measures that make its introduction superfluous: once NAT and the required ALGs are installed, the question as to what addressing system one has in the private space becomes totally irrelevant. Finally, with regard to the functional extensibility, IPv6 has some extensibility because of the so-called extension headers. However, in essence it is more of the same in comparison with IPv4, which means that virtually anything that can be done in IPv6 can also be done in IPv4.

Although NAT was originally also defined by the IETF, since it was developed it has been rather neglected because of the threat it poses to the introduction of IPv6, which means that NAT will have to make do without official support. Having said that, it has local, short-term benefits, it is compatible with IPv4 and it is already widely used, in fact it is omnipresent. If the IETF were to stop neglecting it and show a willingness to develop it into a full hierarchical approach to Internet addressing, it would be capable of offering scalable routing. Which of the two alternatives will lead to the lowest global complexity is still not clear: routing under a flat system will remain complex and IPv6 will not restore end-to-end connectivity. Anyway, global complexity is not very influential in bottom-up adoption. Gradual introduction is what actually took place with NAT, the possibility of which was already noted in its very first defining document (Tsuchiya and Eng 1993).

WHAT WILL HAPPEN WITH ADDRESSING IN THE INTERNET?

Given the pros and cons of the two alternatives outlined in this chapter, we may conclude that it is unlikely that homogeneous addressing in the Internet will be realized within the foreseeable future. Although both alternatives solve or sufficiently alleviate the shortage of address space, neither user community has a decisive incentive to change. NAT continues to offer many options for further functional extension, while retaining compatibility with the existing

Internet. The existing communities of IPv6 users have no reason to switch either. Worldwide visibility makes little sense to them, as their target group is limited by linguistic and cultural barriers.

Actually, a decade of unsuccessful attempts to introduce IPv6 casts serious doubt on its underlying philosophy. Although having a very large homogeneous address space may seem advantageous due to its simplicity, the hierarchical philosophy, of which NAT is just one example, has very appealing properties as well. Addressing is about more than address space only. The modularity, independence and distributed management created by a hierarchical scheme, the variety of different addressing systems it can combine, and last but not least its ability to emerge bottom-up could make the hierarchical philosophy the most viable approach to addressing, making IPv6 just one of the many domains in the future Internet.

CONCLUSIONS

In the absence of an authority that can direct the adoption of a proposed standard, this adoption depends on the unco-ordinated initiatives of large numbers of actors (individuals and organizations). This process is known as 'bottom-up adoption'. It is an example of a so-called bottom-up process, which contrasts with top-down processes, in which all initiatives are taken by a single body (the 'top'). Properties of bottom-up processes can be translated into criteria that determine the suitability of a standard for bottom-up adoption. Important criteria are that the standard should be compatible with existing systems, that the standard should offer local, short-term benefits to the actor adopting it, that it should be easy to introduce locally and that it should allow gradual introduction and gradual functional extension.

This can be illustrated by the case of future Internet addressing schemes. The current addressing scheme of the Internet, known as IPv4, will run out of address space within three to six years. There are currently two alternatives aimed at solving this problem: IPv6, the official solution to address space shortage defined by the IETF, and NAT, which was also defined by the IETF at about the same time, but which is not supported officially as a solution to address space shortage. The adoption rate of IPv6 is still only marginal, whereas NAT has proved very successful and is currently being used everywhere. IPv6 fails to meet most of the criteria for bottom-up adoption, while NAT has a much closer fit with the criteria. With the exception of having an official status, NAT scores better or equal on all of the criteria. In addition, IPv6 will depend on NAT for its adoption. The very measures needed for the migration to IPv6 are also the measures that make its migration unnecessary.

NAT is a primitive form of hierarchical addressing. This kind of addressing, already applied in many environments for many different purposes, varying from telephony to XML namespaces, would be a fundamental step forward. Most notably, it would lead to a distributed management of addressing in the Internet, something that is highly necessary if the Internet will keep growing, in size and in diversity, in the way it has done over the past two decades. The expected increase in the number of communicating devices per person makes this growth more than likely. We would recommend the IETF to stop neglecting NAT, and instead to start developing it further into a full hierarchical addressing approach. Improved versions of NAT will be needed for the migration to IPv6 anyway.

The most probable outcome for addressing in the Internet, in our view, will be a combination of different schemes, with IPv4, IPv6 and NAT all playing a role. In the future Internet there will be a large variety of different namespaces in different domains, based on a hierarchical addressing philosophy rather than an underlying homogeneous addressing scheme. As a practical consequence, we can recommend any organization, in the absence of a specific incentive to move to IPv6 (see for instance Durand 2006), to wait and see what will happen. Early adoption will confront organizations with the teething problems of IPv6, most notably in applications, due to its current marginal use (Hania 2006; Zhou et al. 2007).

The history of IPv6 and NAT shows how important it is to consider carefully the type of adoption process needed for a proposed standard. A standard's success will to a large extent depend on its suitability for a feasible adoption process. Standards with a large intended scope of applicability, such as standards intended for worldwide use, will virtually always depend on bottom-up adoption. Standards that do not meet the criteria for this way of adoption will have a hard time gaining any degree of adoption, especially when there are alternatives that score better.

ACKNOWLEDGEMENTS

This chapter is based on research sponsored by EU project NO-REST, the Next Generation Infrastructures Research Centre at Delft University of Technology and the Next Generation Infrastructures Foundation. We thank the following people for useful discussions and/or comments: Hendrik Rood, Paul Allen, Karst Koymans, Wim Vree, Piet van Mieghem, Egbert-Jan Sol, Henk Uijterwaal and three reviewers of draft versions of this chapter.

6. Incompatible Successors: The Failure to Graft XML onto SGML

Tineke M. Egyedi and Arjan Loeffen

INTRODUCTION[1]

Priorities in standardization change. Rules for developing standards are revised. Standards are updated or become obsolete. This is part of the dynamics of standardization, irrespective of the area of interest. For example, a number of pressing problems in the field of ICT, the focus in this chapter, show an interesting similarity with those in Esperanto, the *neutrala lingva fundamento* created by Ludwik Lejzer Zamenhof. Zamenhof addressed these problems in his foreword to the Fundamento Krestomatio, an anthology of Esperanto texts, and specifically in the foreword to the first (1903) and the fifth (1907) editions (Esperantista Centra Librejo, Paris 1931). The aim of the anthology was to supply models and encourage the development of a common style in the use of Esperanto. Zamenhof feared that without such models different dialects would develop (1903). After rereading the anthology in 1907, Zamenhof noted that Esperanto authors spelt words differently (e.g. *jesuo* and *jeso*). In addition, his taste for Esperanto had evolved. He ached to make some improvements but restrained himself because he felt that continuity should take precedence over perfection (Egyedi 1996, p. 7).

In the software sector, this dilemma is also felt strongly. At stake is the choice between stable standards or up-to-date – but possibly incompatible – standard revisions. In 1988, for example, the X.400 series (message handling protocols) was updated and expanded in order to meet new needs. Standardizers discussed whether to maintain backward compatibility with the 1984 version, or make a clean start with a new standard. They could not reach complete agreement. Of course, backward compatibility would safeguard earlier investments in R&D, training and equipment. But of what value is a standard if it is compatible with earlier versions but unworkable or not up-to-date?

Incompatibility between successive standards lays a heavy burden on IT users and developers. In this chapter we try to understand under what circumstances and for what reasons standardizers, despite having different initial intentions, may sacrifice backward compatibility. We focus on the case of XML, the extensible markup language standard. Initially XML was to be backward compatible with SGML, to allow reuse of large parts of SGML software.

CONCEPTUAL FRAMEWORK

Many standards have 'functional equivalents'. In other words, they address the same problem and offer similar functionalities. A recent example concerns two standards which describe an XML-based file format for office applications, 'open document format (ODF)'[2] and 'office open XML (OOXML)'.[3] Competition between such standards often leads to standards wars. Examples are the wars between standards for DVD recordables (see Chapter 4), 'wideband code division multiple access (W-CDMA)' *versus* 'code division multiple access 2000 (CDMA2000)' in mobile telecommunications (Grindley et al. 1999), and OSI versus Internet standards (Hanseth et al. 1996). Innovation literature has however paid very little attention to the sequential relationships between standards, that is to say, to the way standards (predecessors) are revised and succeeded by new standards (successors). Succession in standardization – whether with regard to company, *de facto*, consortium or formal standards – implies change and renewal. Renewal comes in various shapes: new editions, revisions (new versions, technical corrigenda, amendments, annexes etc.) and new standards. The successor addresses the same area but tries to improve on its predecessor. Therefore, new entrants in the market (standards users) will usually implement the successor. Vrancken et al. (Chapter 5) show with the example IPv4 and IPv6 that some form of rivalry may also exist between standard versions.

As the previous chapters show, where compatibility between standards is at stake, there is a difference between standards that improve on other standards and are thus related (e.g. Chapter 2), and competing standards with equivalent functionalities, which are in principle unrelated and the subject of standards wars (e.g. Chapter 4, see Table 6.1). In the former case, those who standardize the successor will usually seek compatibility with its predecessor to preserve the installed base – unless there are good reasons not to (e.g. technically impossible or a change in the product). The preferred way to do so is to create a backward compatible successor. For example, WordPerfect 5.1 software, a *de facto* standard at the time, could handle WordPerfect 4.2 documents. The reverse also occurs. Where companies only need a subset of the standard's options, they may want to specify a standards profile[4] to which to conform, rather than comply with the more elaborate original standard.

Table 6.1 Characterization of relationships between standards based on the dimensions of functionality and compatibility, and examples of associated phenomena

Compatibility relation / Functionality relation	Compatible standards	Incompatible standards
Related successor standards (improved functionality)	Stability, continuity grafting (e.g. update)	Discontinuous, disruptive, rivalry, reengineering, e.g. embrace-and-extend
Unrelated standards (equivalent functionality)	Co-operation e.g. bridges, multi-protocol stacks, routers	Competition e.g. fragmented market, tipping, multiple implementation[a]

Note: [a] For 'multiple implementation', see Gauch (Chapter 4).

If the successor standard is compatible, compliant technologies should be able to work together with products that were able to interoperate with its predecessor. This is typically the aim when the successor is a new edition or a minor revision of a standard. The innovations involved are incremental in nature: the improvements being made are part of normal problem solving (Kuhn 1970). The problem addressed by the old standard has not changed and – in essence – neither has the means to solve it. Both standards are part of the same 'technological paradigm'[5] (Dosi 1982). Because the new standard supports earlier developments, the development is said to proceed along a 'standards trajectory' (i.e. analogous to the meaning of 'technological trajectory', Nelson and Winter 1977). The new standard exploits its predecessor's installed user base. It brings continuity to technology development.

Evolutionary innovation theory distinguishes between incremental and radical innovations, but not between different kinds of incremental innovation (Christensen 1997).[6] To analyse heritage relationships between standards, however, this distinction is relevant, because different kinds of incremental relationships have a different impact on the market. A new vocabulary is needed to distinguish and identify different types of heritage relationships. We draw an analogy with the process of grafting in horticulture, where a scion (added, improved functionalities of a new standard) is grafted onto a stock (prior standards functionalities). Scion and stock need to be closely related if the desired plant part is to survive (Encyclopedia Britannica). With regard to standardization, we use the term grafting to refer to the process of developing a standard (successor) based on another standard (predecessor) with the intention to improve the latter's functionality and/or usefulness in other respects while preserving compatibility[7] with its predecessor's context of use.

In other words, grafting refers here to a specific type of heritage relationship: compatible succession. It may include a simple standards' update (main-

Table 6.2 Taxonomy of successor standards

Successor categories / Dimensions	Type I: Graft	Type II: Shift	Type III: Revolution
Paradigm change	incremental	incremental	radical
Trajectory	continuous	discontinuous	disruptive
Compatibility outcome	compatible	incompatible	incompatible

tenance) as well as novel functionality (e.g. the concept of message store, which was included in the downward compatible X.400 [1988] standard of the Comité Consultatif International Télégraphique et Téléphonique [CCITT], was innovative).

This chapter focuses on compatibility issues in standards' succession, that is to say, on the first row in Table 6.1. In this area grafting is one of the possible outcomes, while incompatible succession is another. We use the three characteristic dimensions that were addressed earlier to identify different types of succession and analyse their impact: firstly, whether its technology represents a paradigm shift; secondly, whether or not the successor is part of a technological trajectory; and thirdly, whether or not the successor standard is compatible with its predecessor. As noted, the first two dimensions allow us to distinguish levels of incremental change. The three dimensions are listed in Table 6.2, which identifies three 'ideal' types of standards' succession. The Type I succession refers to a 'grafting' relation between successors, which is characterized by incremental improvements and trajectory-compliant developments, and which maintains compatibility (for examples, see above).

The two other 'ideal' types describe incompatible successor standards. The Type II successor represents an incremental shift. It is paradigm-compliant but incompatible with its predecessor (discontinuous standards development). For example, the IPv6 is not compatible with IPv4 (see Chapter 5). To re-create compatibility, for example, a separate standard on 'transition mechanisms for IPv6 hosts and routers' (IETF RFC 2893) has been developed. As it is, IPv6 is a Type II successor, incompatible and discontinuous, but paradigm-compliant (see Table 6.2).

The Type III successor represents a revolution. It introduces improvements to a standard that signify a radical paradigm shift (disruptive standards development). It is not backward compatible with its predecessor. In Telefax standardization (CCITT 1989–92), for example, the succession of Group 3 for analogue networks by Group 4 for digital networks illustrates a Type III succession (Schmidt and Werle 1998). In these situations, the rivalry that ensues between successors is no different from that which exists between unrelated standards with equivalent functionality.

According to the XML standard of W3C, XML is a case of grafting (Bosak 1996b). It is positioned as a Type I successor, in other words, one that is compatible with its predecessor, the 1988 SGML standard. As the next sections demonstrate, it is compatible in many respects, but not in all.

MARKUP LANGUAGES

When XML was launched, it was well received by the IT community. Although the popular press mostly hailed it as a functionally rich sequel to the HTML, those involved described XML as a welcome leaner version of the SGML. In the following sections, we examine the history of these standards, their technology, and their market. We cover the period up to the year 2000, the period in which XML emerged as a successor to SGML (Chapter 2).

SGML

Work on SGML started in 1969 with the development of a language called the 'generalized markup language (GML)' at IBM (Goldfarb 1990). It was used to manage the large amount of complex industrial documents at IBM. GML was designed to record document structures independent of how these structures would subsequently be processed. For example, GML documents recorded headings, paragraphs, lists and figures – in other words, information that is useful for editorial applications – but no formatting instructions. In this manner, GML separated the document description from the formatting languages (IBM used several such languages for printing). Also, because GML identified document structures, fragments of documents could be addressed and reused in different contexts.

In 1978, the American National Standards Institute (ANSI) took an interest in IBM's work on GML. By the efforts of Charles Goldfarb, one of the three inventors of the language, work started on a more generic version: SGML. A major addition to the original design was made. In order to determine the validity of the document structure, and to support a wide variety of lexically different languages (e.g. different signs for start-tag), a formal description, or 'grammar', would accompany each document. Firstly, this grammar identified the type of components ('elements') and their interrelations ('content model'). It was defined separately in what was called a DTD. Secondly, the DTD included a descriptive lexical and syntactical model that defined how the data was to be recorded, archived and distributed.

Working drafts were published between 1980 and 1983. In 1983, the Graphic Communications Association (GCA) produced the first SGML recommendation. It was adopted by the US International Revenue Services

Table 6.3 Aims of the SGML and XML standardizers

SGML Objectives	Design goals for XML
1. Documents 'marked up' with the language must be processable by a wide range of text processing and word processing systems.	1. XML shall be straightforwardly usable over the Internet.
2. The millions of existing text entry devices must be supported.	2. XML shall support a wide variety of applications.
3. There must be no character set dependency, as documents might be keyed on a variety of devices.	3. XML shall be compatible with SGML.
4. There must be no processing, system, or device dependencies.	4. It shall be easy to write programmes which process XML documents.
5. There must be no national language bias.	5. The number of optional features in XML is to be kept to the absolute minimum, ideally zero.
6. The language must accommodate familiar typewriter and word processor conventions.	6. XML documents should be human-legible and reasonably clear.
7. The language must not depend on a particular data stream or physical file organization.	7. The XML design should be prepared quickly.
8. 'Marked up' text must coexist with other data.	8. The design of XML shall be formal and concise.
9. The markup must be usable by both humans and programmes.	9. XML documents shall be easy to create.
	10. Terseness in XML markup is of minimal importance.

Sources: SGML: ISO 8879:1986, Clause 0.2; XML: XML 1.0, 2nd edition 2000.

and the US Department of Defense (DoD). The ISO also became interested. It started a working group on SGML (ISO/IEC JTC 1/SC 18/WG 8, now equivalent to ISO/IEC JTC 1/SC 34). This led to an international standard in 1986 (ISO 8879:1986). An amendment was issued in 1988 (ISO 8879:1988).

The 1988 version remained stable for eight years. In that period, ISO also published a number of SGML-related, supplementary standards. We mention two important ones (see Table 6.4 for other examples). The first was the HyTime (ISO/IEC 1997), a standard that addresses hypermedia relationships. It offered a rich model for addressing and linking SGML documents as well as other type of information objects. Another important standard, called the DSSSL (ISO/IEC 1996) addressed styling. It specified rules for transforming and formatting SGML documents. Furthermore, various tools and applications were created. Because the SGML concept was based on process-independent document structures, the same data in SGML documents could be understood by, for example, database and text processing tools. The range of SGML supporting tools included word processors, parsers, transformers, publishing engines, browsers, document management systems, and even dedicated programming languages and libraries. Areas of application included publishing (e.g. as used by the American Association of Publishers, IBM, and the US DoD in the 'continuous acquisition and life cycle support [CALS]' initiative), text research ('text encoding initiative'),

Table 6.4 Overview of some of the main aspects of SGML and XML

Aspects \ Standards	SGML	XML
Standard	ISO 8879:1986	XML 1.0 (1998)
Adaptions	ISO 8879:1986/Amd 1:1988 ISO 8879:1986/Cor 1:1996 ISO 8879:1986/Cor 2:1999	XML 1.0 2nd edition (Bray et al. 2000)
Standards committee	ISO/IEC JTC 1/SC 18/WG 8 (later: ISO/IEC JTC 1/SC 34)	W3C XML WG
Initiators	IBM, GCA, AAP, DoD etc.	Microsoft, Netscape, Sun etc.
Primary goal	Publishing and document management	Web-based information interchange
Supplementary standards e.g.		
• addressing and linking	Linking: HyTime	Xlink/Xpointer/Xpath
• transformation and rendition	DSSSL	XSL and XSLT
• architecture binding	Architectural forms	Namespaces
• document model	Property sets	DOM

and the exchange of product information (Society of Automotive Engineering J 2008).

One of the important uses made of SGML was the HTML. It was developed by Tim Berners-Lee (CERN) for the World Wide Web, and first standardized by the IETF in 1995 (Berners-Lee and Connolly 1995; Raggett et al. 1999; W3C 2000). HTML did not start out as a fully SGML-compliant application. It complied from the second version onwards. Many of the rules imposed on SGML documents were not – and are still not – enforced by browsers for HTML documents. Most browsers even accept and process invalid HTML documents.

XML

The W3C installed the SGML Editorial Review Board (ERB) in 1996 to develop XML (Connolly 1997). Its members all had SGML expertise. Many also participated in SGML(-allied) ISO working groups. Apart from bringing the power of SGML to the web (XML), the ERB aimed at developing specifications for 'XML hypertext link types' and for DSSSL use in an Internet context (Bosak 1996a).

The review board became a regular XML working group (XML WG) a year later. Microsoft, one of the three active members of the XML WG, was an early adopter of XML for Internet Explorer. Netscape, likewise an active member, started supporting XML at a later stage. Together, these two companies covered a large share of the HTML market, which is of interest because at the time web-browsers were the main platform for XML document exchange. The W3C recommendation for XML 1.0 was published in February 1998 (Bray et al. 1998).

A wide range of XML applications, tools and standards emerged in the period leading up to the year 2000. The applications addressed very different areas: publishing, electronic data interchange (XML/EDI), data modelling (UML/XMI), workflow management (WfMC), software engineering (SOAP), and so on. The functionality offered by XML-based software tools was equivalent to that which was provided by SGML. However, the advent of web content delivery, and the emergence of XML servers and middleware led to additional XML functionality. In addition, many libraries and XML extensions to existing programming environments became available. Also, the number of W3C XML-based specifications and standards by far exceeded those for SGML. W3C produced additional recommendations on naming (namespaces), normalization (XML information set), transformation (XSLT), publication (XSL, Associating style sheets), implementation (DOM), addressing (Xpath) and linking (Xlink) of XML documents.

GRAFTING EFFORTS

Because many large companies and associations had put a lot of effort into SGML (AAP, DoD, Air Transport Association [ATA], etc.) and SGML initiatives (e.g. Text Encoding Initiative [TEI]), the intent was to create backward compatibility and graft XML onto SGML. Also the application domain of the new XML 'dialect' was expected to remain the same. Therefore the SGML encoding tools, knowledge and data were to be preserved as much as possible.

The participants in XML development were SGML experts. They partly were or had been active in SGML or SGML-allied standards developments (e.g. DSSSL-O), and often knew each other from, for example, GCA conferences. Because there was overlap in the membership of W3C's working group and JTC 1's WG 8, there was reciprocal influence. However, there was also a degree of group identification (us-them)[8] and standards politics (e.g. personal differences and the 'not-invented-here' syndrome).

Compatibility Intent

When the W3C's working group started, it was clear that: 'the ultimate goal of this effort is the creation of a form of SGML that can be used to transmit documents (or document fragments) to a future generation of Web browsers and similar Internet client applications' (Bosak 1996b). But whether this

XML would be an SGML subset, a derivative, a conformance level, or an application profile was not yet decided and, as the chair of the working group wrote: 'our uncertainty has two levels: we're not sure where the optimum balance is between SGML compatibility and ease of implementation as a general goal, and we're not sure which specific features of SGML should be retained in XML' (Bosak 1996b). The starting point was that XML would be compatible with SGML. That is, existing SGML tools should be able to read and write XML data, and XML instances were to be SGML documents without changes to the instance.

Overlap between the constituents of the W3C and the JTC 1 working groups kept the intention to ensure compatibility alive. In September 1996, soon after the electronic discussion list of the W3C working group started, Eve Maler posted a contribution which illustrates some of the compatibility concerns at stake (Maler 1996), i.e.:

> Who is the customer/audience for XML – existing robust-SGML users, existing Web/HTML users who are not SGML-aware, or both? [...] I'd rather think of XML as an effort to define a cohesive SGML 'application profile' that benefits both tool creators and document creators, rather than a set of unrelated cool hacks that make it easier to write parsers. [...] What should happen when existing SGML documents (including valid HTML) are processed by XML tools? Should a 'round trip' between the two forms be possible, or is only XML to SGML or SGML to XML okay?

These issues were partly resolved. Some were impossible to resolve satisfactorily (Durand 1996). The result was an XML specification that was largely, though not fully, aligned with SGML (1988).

Technical Relationship Between SGML and XML

XML had the following properties: it was a profile, a subset and an adaptation of that SGML version (Clark 1997). Firstly, XML was a 'profile' of SGML, and, thus, it complied with a predefined set of SGML options. These options addressed, for example, character set (XML applies ISO/IEC 10646; ISO/IEC 1993), name case sensitivity (in XML all names are case sensitive), lexical form of the markup (in XML form of the start- and endcodes, processing instructions etc. are fixed), and minimization[9] (not allowed in XML; other so-called 'SGML features' are also not supported). So, if XML had been purely a profile of SGML, an XML application would automatically have been an SGML application, and XML documents would automatically have been processable by SGML tools.

However, XML was also a 'subset' of SGML. That is to say, some SGML constructs were no longer accepted in XML (e.g. so-called 'exceptions' and the 'and'-connector in content models were dropped, and elements with mixed content required a fixed content model structure). In order to enforce additional constraints, extra validation was required. SGML compliant software did not impose these constraints.

Had XML only been a profile and subset of SGML, all XML documents would have been processable by SGML-based systems. However, XML was also an 'extension' of SGML. It allowed for additional constructs. These represented a genuine breach with the SGML tradition: XML documents that used these constructs were not processable by SGML (1988) systems. An important example is the 'well-formed' document. In XML, the DTD is optional, which allows for a very flexible use of XML. But it requires that the document has a predictable lexical form, and explicitly encodes every element, attribute and data character. Conversely, DTD use was mandatory in SGML. SGML included no such concept as 'well-formedness'. The optionality of DTDs in XML documents is but one – important – example of an extension.[10]

To make XML compatible with SGML, design compromises were made. There were features in XML 1.0 that almost nobody used ('notation', 'entities', attributes with 'entity' values), and features that a minority thought was superfluous (see the 'simple markup language' initiative) and merely meant to confirm the relation with SGML. Although XML was grafted onto the SGML trunk,[11] the process did not lead to full compatibility with the SGML (1988) standard. As Charles Goldfarb remarked in response to an XML claim to SGML compatibility 'in spirit and in fact':

> If XML is a subset of SGML 'in fact', why should existing 'compliant' SGML tools require any adjustments? One can argue [...] whether a DTD-less markup language is a subset of SGML in spirit, but to be one in fact means that conforming XML documents must conform to 8879. At present, they don't. (Goldfarb 1996a)

To become compatible, the SGML (1988) standard needed to be adapted.

Re-forging Compatibility

There were two initiatives to address incompatibility between XML and SGML. They focused on how XML documents could be processed by 1988 SGML tools in spite of the existing incompatibility. Firstly, WG 8 developed a 'technical corrigendum 2 (cor 2, 1999) to re-establish compatibility with XML. It contained two annexes, the normative Annex K on 'web SGML adaptations' and the informative Annex L for 'added requirements for XML'. Annex K was an optional extension of SGML (N 1929).[12] Together, the two annexes corrected a range of incompatibilities. The draft second corrigendum was finalized in December 1997, a year after the XML draft. It was formally

Table 6.5 Overview of the state of compatibility between the most relevant combinations of documents and software that conform to SGML to XML 1.0

Documents \ Processable by	SGML (1988) software?	SGML (1999) software?	XML (1998) software?
SGML document (1988)	Yes	Yes	No
XML document (1998), normative part only	No	Yes	Yes
XML document (1998), also recommended parts ('Interoperability')	'increases chances'	Yes	Yes

Notes:
SGML (1999) with, SGML (1988) without technical corrigenda.
XML 1.0 with and without the recommended part.

published in 1999, a year after the XML 1.0 recommendation. Full implementation of both technical corrigenda, which we refer to as SGML (1999) in Table 6.5, would make an SGML system XML compatible.

Secondly, as part of the standards process in W3C, the XML working group included non-binding recommendations into the standard. Their implementation should allow XML documents to be processed by SGML (1988) software. The standard, however, would give no guarantee (i.e. it 'increases chances').

Table 6.5 summarizes the compatibility status for different combinations of SGML and XML standard versions. The outcome of the compatibility efforts was that normative XML documents were not processable by SGML (1988) compliant software, but that SGML (1999) compliant software would handle XML documents. In a sense, SGML (1999) was made 'upward compatible' to its successor, XML.

ANALYSIS OF GRAFTING OUTCOME

According to our taxonomy (Table 6.2), the XML standards effort started out as a Type I grafting process. However, XML did not maintain backward compatibility with SGML. It developed into a different type of succession. Should we speak of a 'shift' or of a 'revolution'? Although XML represents a clear discontinuity in the SGML standards trajectory, we would argue that XML development has remained SGML-paradigm compliant.

Briefly recapitulating, a paradigm is a set of shared views, heuristics, exemplars, etc. that guide and structure the way a practitioners' community normally solves its problems. In the case of SGML, several features structure the way SGML practitioners (i.e. standards developers and implementers) work. For example, the problem that lay at the origin of SGML was the need to reuse information fragments and share documents across publication systems in a future-proof way. IBM addressed the problem by separating the syntactical and the logical document structure. It determined – as it were – the sort of answers with which to solve the puzzle and laid the foundations for the SGML approach. XML developers were raised with the principles of SGML. SGML was a technical exemplar. It facilitated the identification, exchange and reuse of information fragments in different contexts. XML, too, was initially document-oriented. Furthermore, in discussions XML was called a 'lean-and-mean dialect of SGML' (Goldfarb 1996b). It was to become a simpler version of SGML. Increased simplicity was possible, for example, because XML could in the mean time refer to Unicode and the ISO 10646 standard for character sets. Simplifications like these confirm rather than deny the importance of SGML for XML. Except for the DTD-less document, which we would typify as a shift 'within' the SGML paradigm, the general SGML mindset and strategies also apply to XML. In other words, the succession relationship between the SGML and XML standards is that of a shift rather than a revolution.

Turning to our research question, due to which circumstances and for what reasons was the aim of backward compatibility sacrificed? Firstly, XML's web-based user context had little in common with the SGML user context in the 1980s. The computer and communication technologies of the 1990s obviously offered many new opportunities and posed different constraints. Moreover, XML was applied in new domains (see Figure 6.1) and for different purposes. Although the information modelling approaches of SGML and XML were in principle identical, the SGML problem was foremost how to manage the 'company-internal', complex flow of documents. XML, on the other hand, developed as a solution to the limitations of HTML in respect to 'company-external, web-oriented' document exchange (see Table 6.6).

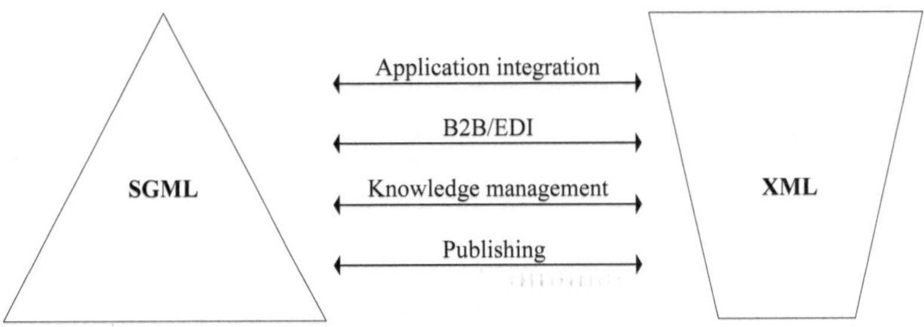

Figure 6.1 The relative importance of domains of use in SGML and XML

Table 6.6 Causes for discontinuity: differences between the problems, context of use, and standardization setting of SGML and XML

Causes for discontinuity \ Standards	SGML	XML
Information problem		
• Orientation	Company-internal	Company-external
Context of use		
• Technology	1980s (mainframes etc.)	1990s (Internet, chips etc.)
• Domains	Publishing	B2B, application integration
Standardization		
• Frame of reference	GML	SGML, HTML
• Standards body: culture	ISO (formal standards body): stability, accountability	W3C (standards consortium): pragmatism, speed
• Problem, emphasis on	Ubiquitous applicability	Simplicity, implementability

At the time some people thought the XML market would only be of interest to SGML users (Goldfarb 1996c). Others hoped to target the huge, well-funded, energetic Web population (Bray 1996). There would be an important marketing advantage in being able to say: 'XML processors can read HTML' (Bray 1997). Therefore compromises to XML compatibility with SGML were considered that left the installed base of HTML untouched. The deliberations are illustrated by the following quotation, which partly explains the discontinuity in the SGML trajectory.

> For the 99% of the world that doesn't care a bit about SGML [...]. They know HTML, so we must make things look like HTML. But when it comes to adding the important things that HTML doesn't have, we should make them as attractive as possible. [...] The SGML folks need a standard, as well as capability so they will continue to need SGML. But for the rest of the world, clean extendible markup is the biggest need, not SGML compatibility. (Durand 1996)

The successful uptake of HTML was also influential. It was an exemplary achievement. The message for XML standardization was: aim for simplicity. If we compare the SGML aims with the design goals of XML, the latter's emphasis on ease of implementation and usability was salient (see Table 6.3). Simplicity was difficult to align with compliance to SGML: in addition to bringing SGML to the Web, the XML initiators also aimed at including HTML-related issues like styling and linking as part of the XML working group charter. This underscores the relevance of HTML as a second frame of reference for XML development.

Finally, XML standardization did not take place in the ISO, the formal standards setting. It took place in the W3C environment, a standards consortium. This was a salient decision, because at the time these standards setting environments were seen as competitors (Egyedi 2006). The non-ISO environment made it easier for XML developers to deviate from standard SGML solutions. As other cases testify, a change of standards setting facilitates taking decisions that might lead to incompatibility (i.e. a by-product of the 'not-invented-here' syndrome).

CONCLUSION

The XML and SGML standards committees set high value on maintaining compatibility between the two standards, as the considerable grafting efforts illustrate. Nonetheless, the W3C committee failed to graft XML onto SGML. It could not resolve satisfactorily the tension between the required new functionalities and vested interests in the well-established SGML standard.

Why was compatibility between XML and SGML not maintained? There were external pressures, developments and demands that made compromises difficult. Most importantly, since the early 1980s the IT environment had radically changed. The web provided new and unexpected possibilities. Markup languages were being used in new domains and for different purposes. Moreover, the success of HTML provided a new frame of reference for standardizing markup languages, one that prioritized simplicity. In addition, there were internal, standardization-related circumstances, such as the change of standards setting (i.e. from ISO to W3C), which made it easier for XML developers to drop the more stringent compatibility requirements.

In this chapter we argued that to understand the impact of standards' succession on the market a threefold distinction in types of succession is required. We used the succession metaphors of graft, shift and revolution. Grafting involves the smoothest transition to a new standard and has the least disruptive impact on the market. The succession revolution is most disruptive for the market. Because on the one hand XML follows the SGML paradigm in many respects, but on the other is incompatible with SGML, SGML-XML succession is to be characterized as a succession shift. Its impact on the market is mixed. In many respects XML builds forth on SGML principles, therefore earlier SGML training and experience remain valuable. However, incompatibility hinders easy re-use of software and threatens the sustainability of SGML documents. Moreover, incompatibility increases rivalry between successors: it forces newcomers to choose between standards, and choosing in favor of one standard more or less rules out the other. The outcome of rivalry between successors may well be comparable to that of standards wars.

Whether competition among successors and among functional equivalents lead to different wars and outcomes is a matter for further research.

All in all, the lesson that can be drawn from this study is that even in cases where, in principle, standard developers actively support the aim of backward compatibility, the latter is not an easy solution to the disruptive impact of standards' change.

NOTES

1. We are very grateful to Pim van der Eijk, Charles Goldfarb, Diederik Gerth van Wijk, and Willem Wakker for their insightful comments on an earlier version of the original publication. This chapter is a revision of an article published in Egyedi and Loeffen (2002), copyright Elsevier.
2. OASIS OpenDocument v 1.0, 2nd edition, was adopted under the PAS procedure by the ISO/IEC JTC 1 as open document format for office applications (ISO/IEC 26300:2006).
3. ECMA-376: Office Open XML, which at the time of writing is being fast-tracked as ISO/IEC DIS 29500 – whether the fast-track succeeds is as yet unclear (ISO 2007).
4. 'Profiles [...] define conforming subsets or combinations of base standards [...] to provide specific functions. [They] identify the use of particular options available in the base standards' (ISO/IEC JTC 1 N 5154, 1998.01.05).
5. 'The term "technological paradigm" refers to the set of technology-related cognitions which structure and focus the behavior of practitioners in a field of technology. Shared methods, heuristics and rules develop. Exemplars, that is exemplary achievements in the practitioner field further focus activities' (adaptation of Dosi [1982, p. 152] to applied sciences in Egyedi 1999, p. 356).
6. An exception is Christensen, who distinguishes between sustaining and disruptive technologies to explain why many exemplary, successful firms fail (1997, XV). However, his focus colours his terminology, which diverges unnecessarily from Kuhn and Dosi (e.g. 1997, p. 27, footnote 7).
7. The ISO defines compatibility as the 'suitability of products, processes or services for use together under specific conditions to fulfill relevant requirements without causing unacceptable interactions' (ISO/IEC 1991). The term has a general use and is therefore preferred here. It includes upward and downward compatibility, and interoperability – a term sometimes preferred by information technology practitioners.
8. Tim Bray quoted in Goldfarb (1996d).
9. Minimization is the technique of omitting or reducing markup, for example, the omission of end-tags.
10. For more detail and other examples we refer to Egyedi and Loeffen (2002).
11. XML should be 'a lightweight, lean, mean, easy-to-learn on-ramp for SGML' (Bray 1996).
12. Annex L, an informative annex, is explicitly XML-oriented. The final text of Annex K (N 1955) is above all presented as the outcome of the ongoing review – largely independent of XML. 'This annex remedies defects revealed by the multiple adaptations of SGML for the World Wide Web (WWW), intranets, and extranets. The annex corrects errors, resolves ambiguities for which there is a clear resolution that does not cause existing conforming documents to become non-conforming, and provides a choice of alternative resolutions for other ambiguities. Although motivated by the World Wide Web, applicability of this annex extends to all uses of SGML' (Goldfarb 1997).

PART THREE

Change in an Implementation Context

7. The IEEE 802.11 WLAN Installation at RWTH Aachen University: A Case of Voluntary Vendor Lock-In

Kai Jakobs

BACKGROUND

Despite popular belief to the contrary, standards are by no means static. In fact, there are dynamic aspects involved during standards setting and maintenance, during their subsequent implementation into a system, during the installation of such a system at a customer's premises, and finally during its appropriation and adaptation to local needs. This chapter focuses on the latter.

More specifically, a closer look at the installation of a WLAN at RWTH Aachen University revealed a phenomenon that warrants some closer attention. RWTH voluntarily relinquished a major benefit customers are usually keen to obtain from the use of standards-based systems – the independence from one particular vendor. In this chapter we analyse the motivation behind this surprising move.

The remainder of this section starts with a brief discussion of the benefits to be gained from the use of standards-based ICT systems by companies and organizations. It then describes the environment of the case study. This is followed by an equally brief description of the technology that was implemented in this case. Subsequently, Section 2 describes the case study and the role standards played with regard to the installation of the WLAN. Section 3 analyses the various dimensions of 'dynamics' that played a role in this context. In Section 4, finally, I provide some concluding remarks.

Why Implement Standards-based ICT at all?

After all – why not leave it all to the market? Let us imagine what might happen if it were solely up to the market to decide upon a winning technology. Consider, for example, a situation where different technologies with roughly the same functionality are available. None of them command sufficient support to establish themselves as 'the standard'. This may lead to a situation of uncertainty in which potential buyers postpone their purchases so as not to run the risk of investing in a loosing technology. As a consequence, innovation in that technical domain would almost come to a standstill. Clearly, nobody would benefit from this kind of situation.

On the other hand, organizations wishing to implement new ICT systems stand to benefit from various aspects associated with standards, each of which may yield major savings, including (Jakobs 2006):

1. Avoiding technological dead-ends
   Users want to avoid purchasing products that eventually leave them stranded with an incompatible technology. A number of issues need to be considered in this context. It has to be decided, for instance, if and when a new technology should be purchased, and which one should be selected. Companies that adopt a specific technology too soon may end up with an unsuccessful technology, as well as having spent considerable time and money on backing what is in the end the wrong horse. It has to be decided if and when to switch from a well-established technology to a new one.
2. Less dependency on vendors
   Being locked-in to a vendor-specific environment is increasingly becoming a major risk for a user, despite the advantages associated with integrated proprietary solutions. In particular, problems occur if a vendor misses an emerging development, and its users are forced to switch to completely new systems; a very costly exercise (Ferné 1995). Accordingly, standard compliant products from a choice of vendors appeal to the users, who can pursue a pick-and-mix purchasing strategy, and who also stand to benefit from price cuts due to increased competition.
3. Promotion of universality
   Ultimately, users would like to have seamless interoperability between all hardware and software, both internally and externally. In an increasingly globalized marketplace, this can only be achieved through international standards. Clearly, this holds especially for communications products. Ideally, it should not matter at all which vendor or service provider has been selected; interoperability should always be guaranteed. This implies that user needs and requirements are met by the standards (and the implementations). There is, however, another major economic benefit: the costs of incompatibility may be tremendous. For instance, in the 1980s half of General Motor's annual automation budget (i.e. hundreds of millions of dollars) went into the design of specific interfaces between incompatible machines, a situation that would not have occurred if adequate standards had been available in the first place (Dankbaar and van Tulder 1992).

Obviously, the issues described above are important for universities as well. Before turning to RWTH's approach towards the installation of standards based systems, let us first have a brief look at the environment within which the WLAN was to be installed.

RWTH Aachen

Founded in 1870, RWTH Aachen is one of the largest and most highly regarded technical universities in Europe. Its nine faculties include Mathematics, Computer Science and Natural Science; Architecture; Civil Engineering; Mechanical Engineering; Mining Engineering, Metallurgy and Geo Sciences; Electrical Engineering and Information Technology; Humanities; Business and Economics; and Medicine. Traditionally, engineering has been RWTH's major strength. More recently, its computer science department has been ranked among the top three in Germany on a regular basis.

In 2007, the university had around 30 000 students and a staff of over 10 000, including over 400 professors and over 3500 academic and research staff. Its overall annual budget amounts to over €500 million.

RWTH is not a campus university – its buildings are scattered throughout the town and the surrounding area. In recent years, a consolidation process has led to the formation of three main centres. However, a considerable number of individual buildings throughout the city are still occupied by university institutes, chairs and labs. Also, there are twenty halls of residence, most of them located outside the main central areas.

Today, virtually all RWTH buildings are connected to the university's 'gigabit-ethernet backbone network'. In contrast to this backbone, which is centrally managed by the university's Computing and Communication Centre (CCC), internal LANs are managed almost exclusively by the individual institutes.

By now, all major lecture halls have also been equipped with LAN access, providing access to internal services and to the Internet. However, fixed, wire-based networks have the obvious disadvantage of offering only fixed 'access points (APs)', thus severely limiting the flexibility of the network infrastructure. Moreover, they are not normally accessible from outside buildings, which means there are many 'black spot' areas without network access. On top of this, extensions to fixed networks are expensive and their construction is time-consuming (new cabling).

To overcome these limitations, to allow wider access to services and information, and to provide greater flexibility, the idea for the installation of a 'wireless LAN (WLAN)' was born.

The MoPS Project

'Mobile professors and students (MoPS)' was a project that was jointly managed by RWTH's computer science department's chair Informatik 4 and RWTH's Computing and Communication Centre. Its aim was to set up a university-wide WLAN to complement and extend the fixed network infrastructure.

The MoPS-network currently comprises more than 450 access points, covering some 60 buildings. Many of RWTH's central areas, such as the library, the main refectory, and the major lecture-hall buildings, are covered by MoPS, and the network is still expanding. Furthermore, the WLAN now also covers some central areas of the city outside RWTH. MoPS is based on the IEEE 802.11b/g standard, offering a bandwidth of up to 54 Mbps per cell.

The IEEE 802.11 Standard

This section provides a brief account of the developments until 2000–01, i.e., until the start of the WLAN installation at RWTH. Later developments (in particular, 802.n) are not addressed, as they are not relevant to the events discussed here.

The initial standard

As a 'mobile extension' of the almost ubiquitous 802.3 ethernet standard, the IEEE started work on the first WLAN standard in 1990. The first specification, IEEE 802.11, which was published in 1997, uses the 'industrial scientific medical frequency band' at 2.4 GHz, or infrared (IR[1]). In both variations it supports a data rate of up to 2 Mbps.

The original purpose of the standard (back in the early 1990s) was to 'provide wireless connectivity to automatic machinery, equipment or, stations that require rapid deployment, which are portable, or hand-held or which are mounted on moving vehicles within a local area' (IEEE 1991). This originally envisaged application environment is quite different from the actual deployment of the WLAN standards adopted in the late 1990s. This shift with regard to the intended use is probably one of the reasons for the follow-up work.

Moreover, when the 802.11 standard was adopted in 1997, wired ethernet LANs were capable of transmission speeds of up to 10 Mbps (as opposed to 2 Mbps). Also, early 802.11 products were relatively costly. As a consequence, the original 802.11 standard enjoyed only very limited success in the market.

802.11 a/b

Work on two follow-up standards commenced in 1997. Both standards were published in 1999. The 802.11b standard was released first. This version is a supplement to the original 802.11 standard, and offers a net bandwidth of up to 11 Mbps, comparable to the 'original' 10 Mbps ethernet. However, because of communication overhead, the maximum throughput in practice is about 5.5 Mbps, with a range of about 50 metres indoors. CSMA/CA[2] is used for medium access. Like the original 802.11 standard, 802.11b also uses the 2.4 GHz radio signalling frequency. 802.11b subdivides the spectrum into 14 overlapping channels. Three or four channels may be used simultaneously in the same area, with little or no overlap. Today, this version is widely used, as it offers the lowest production cost, an acceptable signal range, and cannot be easily obstructed (provided it is not installed near other appliances that use the same frequency band, such as microwave ovens and cordless phones).

Several extensions have been made to the 802.11b protocol in order to increase bandwidth up to 44 Mbit/s. However, these extensions are proprietary and have not been endorsed by the IEEE. Many companies refer to such enhanced versions '802.11b+'.

Another version, 802.11a, was released in 1999, almost in parallel with 802.11b. This standard uses the 5 GHz frequency band, which was regulated at that time. It supports a raw transmission rate of up to 54 Mbps, yielding a net rate of some 20 Mbps. Using this higher frequency band implies a lower transmission range of this version, and increased difficulties penetrating walls and other obstructions. Also, production costs are higher than they are for 802.11b. The fact that the frequency band was regulated also imposed limitations on the use of this version.[3] On the other hand, the 802.11a maximum speed is much higher compared to 802.11b, it supports more simultaneous users, and does not interfere with other appliances. Because 802.11a and 802.11b utilize different frequency bands they are not compatible.

Comparing 802.11a and 802.11b

Table 7.1 shows the respective scope and purpose of the 802.11 a/b standards projects. The major difference in terms of the purposes of the projects is the inclusion of imaging and, particularly, voice transmission that was foreseen for 802.11a. This is one of the possible reasons for the development of different standards.

Another reason is the fact that, in 1997, the 5 MHz frequency band was still regulated in many parts of the world. Thus, 802.11b 'played it safe' in terms of restrictions of usage due to regulations, whereas a certain risk was associated with the development of the 802.11a standard.

802.11g

The 802.11g standard represented an attempt to combine the best aspects of 802.11a and 802.11b. Released in 2003, 802.11g offers a raw data rate of up to 54 Mbps, which results in a net data rate of around 25 Mbps. Like 802.11b,

Table 7.1 Purpose of the 802.11a/b standards projects

802.11a	802.11b
According to the 1997 'project authorization request form', the scope of the 802.11a project was: *To develop a high speed (about 20 Mbit/s) PHY for use in fixed, moving or portable wireless local area networks. The PHY will be used in conjunction with the 802.11 'medium access control (MAC)'. The 802.11 MAC will be reviewed to assure its capability to operate at the speeds targeted by the project.*	According to the 1997 'project authorization request form', the scope of the 802.11b project was: *To develop a higher speed PHY extension to 802.11 operating in the 2.4 GHz band.*
The purpose of the proposed 802.11a project was: *To create a high speed wireless access technology suitable for data, voice and image information services. This technology should be beneficial for improved access to fixed network LAN and internetwork infrastructure (including access to other wireless LANs) via a network of base stations, as well as creation of high performance ad hoc networks. The project will focus on communication techniques which use the spectrum efficiently and enable a high aggregate throughput, as well as high speed for an individual network.*	The purpose of the proposed 802.11b project was: *To extend the performance and the range of applications of the 802.11 compatible networks in the 2.4 GHz band by increasing the data rate achievable by such devices. This technology will be beneficial for improved access to fixed network LAN and internetwork infrastructure (including access to other wireless LANs) via a network of access points, as well as creation of high performance ad-hoc networks.*

Table 7.2 Characteristics of 802.11 and 802.11a/b/g

Logical link control (LLC) Media access control (MAC)			*Data link layer*
Frequency hopping spread spectrum	Direct sequence spread spectrum	Orthogonal frequency division multiplexing	*Physical layer*
802.11	802.11b/g	802.11a	
2.4 GHz	2.4 GHz	5 GHz	
2 Mbps	11 Mbps	54 Mbps	

it uses the 2.4 GHz frequency for greater transmission range. 802.11g is backwards compatible with 802.11b; that is to say, 802.11g access points work with 802.11b wireless network adapters and vice versa. Table 7.2 summarizes the main characteristics of the different versions.

THE CASE STUDY

The original goal of the case study was to analyse aspects, and the impact, of 'dynamics' in the installation (and maintenance) of a large standards-based system. While this purpose is retained in this chapter, some of the focus has shifted toward the phenomenon of a voluntary vendor lock-in.

Material Compilation

The relevant information was compiled from several sources, including project proposals, (technical) reports, presentations and papers. In addition, information was retrieved from relevant websites (most notably those of RWTH's CCC and of the chair Informatik 4).

Most importantly, interviews were conducted with the heads of the units in charge of RWTH's WLAN project, including 1) the head of 'communication systems – operations' at the CCC, in charge of running the system, 2) the head of 'planning, development and controlling – information management' at the university administration, and the administration's project liaison, 3) the two leaders of the MoPS and 'ubiquitous RWTH for mobile E-learning (URMEL)' projects, chair Informatik 4.

Additional information was provided by the head of the 'communication networks' department at the CCC.

Project Development

The actors

Three entities, plus a somewhat unspecified group of 'users', have been the main actors in the development of the university's WLAN. These include:

1. RWTH's Computing and Communication Centre (CCC)
   CCC is in charge of RWTH's central supercomputing facilities and a number of other central computing and communication services. The latter includes, for instance, installation and maintenance of the university's high-speed data network infrastructure and RWTH's connection to the Internet.
2. The chair Informatik 4 (i4)
   The chair is one of the largest groups at the computer science department, focusing on communication networks and distributed systems.
3. The university administration
   Without their consent the RWTH's WLAN would never have materialized.

As far as technical issues are concerned, CCC and i4 have been the important players. It should be noted, however, that officially CCC is the one entity in charge of all university network infrastructure activities. In particular, individual chairs, institutes or departments may well run their own internal LANs, but they have nothing whatsoever to do with, or any say in, the university's central infrastructure.

General

The project saw the light of day in early 2001, when Professor Spaniol (chair i4, and Associate Director of the CCC) recognized the need to install a WLAN for RWTH, to complement the fixed university network.

Following some internal discussions, and after winning a contract from the German Ministry of Science and Technology,[4] the project was launched in 2001, with an additional contribution from the university (as a central entity, as opposed to its individual entities, such as institutes and chairs).

Although the project was very much pushed by i4, the CCC eventually took over responsibility and most of the project management. However, much of the actual current installation work was carried out by i4 staff, mostly in conjunction with staff from the respective user entities.

Because RWTH is anything but a campus university, the project had to adopt an incremental approach, initially installing access points only at the most important central buildings and institutes. The network is still expanding, and it now also covers some of the city's central areas. At the time of writing (January 2007), the network consists of 453 APs, roughly 90 per cent of which are operational at any given time. According to current estimates, another 500–600 APs will be needed to ensure a 100 per cent coverage. In addition, an upgrading process has been under way, moving from the mainly 802.11b based network toward an 802.11g based system.

Technical development

In 2001, specifications providing for a functionality similar to that offered by the 802.11 standards were available. These included the 'high performance radio local area network standard 2 (HIPERLAN/2)' from the ETSI and, albeit with a different functionality, Bluetooth. Moreover, proprietary systems were available.

However, none of the above-mentioned solutions ever were real options – no products were available for either of the standards-based solutions,[5] and RWTH's IT policy requires the use of standard-based products whenever possible. Also – like HIPERLAN/2 – the available proprietary solutions utilized the 5 GHz frequency band, which in 2001 was still regulated in Germany. Other technologies, discussed very briefly and dismissed very soon, included:

1. Satellite networks
   very expensive, no coverage inside buildings, low data rate;

2. Cellular systems
   GSM,[6] very good coverage, but expensive and offering only a low data rate;
3. Infrared Data Association (IrDA)
   inexpensive, but requires line-of-sight between communicating partners and provides only low data rates;
4. Digital enhanced cordless telecommunications (DECT)
   easy to build infrastructure, inexpensive, but very low data rate.

In fact, the only standard that was seriously considered was IEEE 802.11b: 'anything else than 802.11b was never debated [...] as HIPERLAN and Bluetooth were not available at the time (HIPERLAN never will be) and proprietary solutions offered no benefit especially when thinking about the heterogeneous user group' (RWTH source).

The original 802 standard did not offer any advantages over the 802.11b version, while in particular the lower transmission rate was a genuine disadvantage. The 802.11a standard, while technically attractive in some instances, suffered from the same problem as the proprietary solution – it is based on the 5 GHz band. The project has been developed in parallel with much of the development of the 802.11 standards (see Figure 7.1). At the time, products based on the 802.11b standard had been available for about two years, and were state-of-the-art. In contrast, the products implementing the 802.11a standard were first marketed around the time the project was started. This delay was due both to the success of the 802.11b-based products and to the fact that the 5 GHz frequency band was still regulated in large parts of the world.

As technical development continued, the 802.b version was succeeded by the 802.11g standard while the project was still ongoing. In fact, early products based on a draft 802.11g version had already been available at the start of the project. However, the large suppliers did not release any products

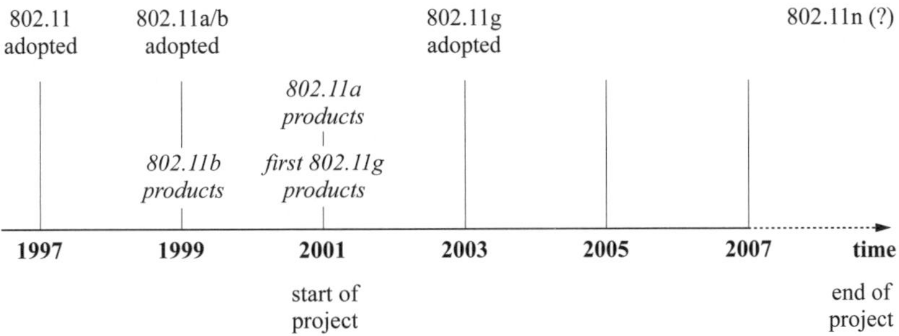

Figure 7.1 Timeline of the project and of availability of 802.11-based product

prior to the final approval of the standard by the IEEE (in 2003). Therefore, 802.11g was not considered at the start of the project.

Standards

Impact

The availability of an accepted standard for WLANs was seen as a major enabler of the actual implementation of the WLAN. However, this was not so much due to a desire to establish an open environment, but largely to the fact that it would have been next to impossible to impose a proprietary system on a heterogeneous environment like the RWTH (unless, of course, it was fully funded and maintained by a central entity, which was not really an option). Moreover, as one interviewee put it:

> The network would probably not exist without the standard, as it was clear from the beginning that students would receive no funding for their WLAN equipment; with most students being 'financially challenged' it would have been hard to motivate them to buy (back then expensive) proprietary equipment which could only be used at RWTH Aachen (and during the first year basically only in the computer science buildings).

On the other hand, installing a system like a WLAN also depends on the demand. If there had been a considerable level of demand, in the absence of a standard RWTH might have opted in favour of a proprietary system. In such a case, the need for a working WLAN system would have carried more weight than any considerations about vendor lock-in and fear of technological dead-ends (but this is, obviously, hypothetical).

Implementation

RWTH is not only a geographically dispersed institution, it is also highly decentralized in terms of responsibilities. For instance, while the CCC is in charge of RWTH's high-speed backbone network, of managing of the university's intranet and of providing the connection to the outside world, they are not in direct control of all networking activities. In fact, many LANs have been installed and are maintained by individual chairs or institutes. In such an environment it is crucially important to use standards-based systems to ensure a reasonable level of interoperability. To this end, the CCC has to approve all procurements in the networking sector, and uses this influence to push for standards-based systems throughout the university.

Thus far, this approach has worked reasonably well. RWTH has been quite successful using standards-compliant systems. However, for various reasons the CCC has adopted a general policy of purchasing network equipment from one vendor only, at least for the network infrastructure (including, for instance, routers and switches for LAN interconnection, but also APs for the WLAN). The CCC is also trying to make other university entities (institutes, chairs, etc.) follow this approach.

Over time, one recurring experience has triggered this 'single-vendor' philosophy: elements of the networking infrastructure have always been a major source of interoperability problems.

> Routers and switches from different vendors continuously cause compatibility problems, even for standard-features. This is partly due to throughput problems caused by the use of cheap 'standard-based' systems within a departmental LAN. The same holds for firewalls.

In fact, installation and maintenance of a network can be very much simplified if all equipment has been provided by a single vendor. This is particularly important in the light of scarce human resources.

The WLAN is another case in point here. Interoperability problems could frequently be traced back to different implementations of the standards by different vendors which could not inter-operate. Moreover, numerous upgrades of the AP software were necessitated by increasingly standards-compliant releases of this software. The same is true for end-systems (primarily laptops), where equally frequent SW/driver updates became necessary. While this was not a major technical problem, it did cause considerable additional workload, as the software had to be uploaded manually for many APs. In such cases, proprietary management tools can frequently be used to support maintenance and thus reduce the additional workload caused by software updates. This further reinforced the CCC's view with regard to the advantages of purchasing products from only one vendor.

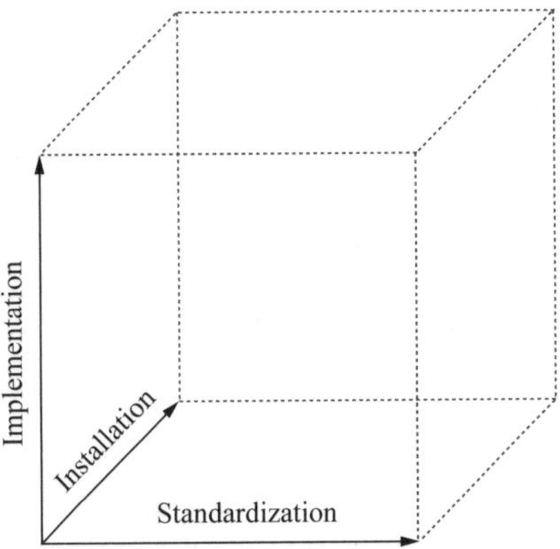

Figure 7.2 The dimensions of dynamics

'Improved' implementations of a standard (i.e., those with additional, proprietary features) represent a different, yet related issue that was also encountered during WLAN installation. Typically, they are added with the goal of establishing a customer base that is locked into this 'improved' technology. This happened during the initial installation phase of the WLAN. A vendor's APs supported 128 bit link layer encryption. This had been identified as a central requirement by the CCC.

> The main reason that the particular product was chosen, was that it has a proprietary extension of the weak link layer encryption WEP [wired equivalent privacy] and supports 128 bit asymmetric encryption. It's ironic that this feature was *never* used neither standard WEP nor the proprietary variant are configured in the MoPS network. The reason is that the WLAN security concept was not finalized at the time the initial AP lot was purchased – the concept is based on VPN [virtual private network] technology and hence there is no need for link layer encryption.

However, it turned out that this resulted in a lock-in situation, as this vendor's APs could only interoperate with its own WLAN cards. Eventually, the APs were phased out.

> Our first WLAN access points used a proprietary encryption technology in addition to the standard features. If you wanted to use this you also had to buy the PC cards from this vendor, which were of rather poor quality. The product wasn't successful, and the access points were gradually replaced over time.

The staff at the CCC is aware of the risk of a lock-in associated with the 'one vendor' strategy. However, it appears that the perceived benefits outweigh this risk. 'We are aware that vendor-specific features may come to fruition, and we accept that.'

Dynamics of standards

As can be seen from Figure 7.1 above, the development of RWTH's WLAN overlapped with the standardization activities of the IEEE 802.11 group. As a result, the system was initially based on the 802.11b standard. With the availability of the 802.11g version APs based on this standard were bought and installed. However, as the latter was designed to be backward-compatible to the former, this did not cause major problems (as far as the standard was concerned).

The one problem that did occur was caused by a vendor who prematurely claimed to be compliant with the 802.11g standard, which at the time had not yet been formally passed. In fact, his implementation was based on a draft standard, which changed subsequently. However, this phase lasted only for a few months; the number of users with pre-802.11g cards was relatively small, and there were no complaints.

ANALYSIS – THE ASPECTS OF DYNAMICS

Three different dimensions of dynamics are relevant to this case. These include the dynamics of (see also Figure 7.2):

1. Standardization: This refers to the process of standards setting, where successive versions of standards (or new ones), corrigenda, addenda, etc. create a dynamically – albeit comparably slowly[7] – changing environment.
2. Standard implementation
   Vendors incorporate standards into the systems they offer. Here, dynamics occur, for instance, through inadequate implementations (which need to be improved at a later stage), but also through 'improved' ones (which may incorporate proprietary enhancements, with the potential of causing incompatibilities with the original standard).
3. System installation
   Users install the (standards-based) systems on their premises. Aspects of dynamics may, for example, occur through adaptation to local needs, or through a lengthy installation process (during which, e.g., new requirements may emerge, which then need to be addressed as well; see, e.g., Fleck 1994 or Jakobs et al. 1996).

These dimensions are mutually independent. After all, it is perfectly feasible to produce different, incompatible implementations of a very 'static' standard, as well as install perfectly standards-compliant systems in a way rendering them incompatible. It should also be noted that users potentially contribute to incompatibilities through the adaptation of standards-based systems to local particularities. This holds despite the fact that ultimately they are the ones who stand to suffer the most from any incompatibilities that result from dynamics.

The aspects of dynamics that can be identified with regard to the individual dimensions will be discussed below, together with the effects they had on the installation of the WLAN at RWTH.

Standardization

The most obvious aspect here is the succession of versions of the 802.11 standard, most notably the move from 802.b (completed 1999) to 802.g (completed 2002). However, despite some potential fairness issues (802.11g is said to grab more than its fair share of bandwidth in a mixed 802.11b/g environment, see e.g. Tan and Guttag 2004) no interoperability issues have thus far been identified.[8] Neither did this aspect of dynamics play any major role in the installation of the RWTH WLAN.

Another, related aspect is the speed of the succession of technology 'generations'. Whereas it took ten years (1985–95) to move from the original 802.3 standard (Ethernet) to 802.3u 'fast ethernet', this was reduced to about two years in the case of 802.11–802.11b, and to about another four years for 802.11b–802.11g. While it is clearly desirable to standardize on the basis of the best technical solution, this fairly quick succession may create considerable problems on the part of the users. They have to decide whether to install an existing version or wait for an improved standard. At this rate of succession, the third alternative, i.e. to go for an existing standard and to update the installation when a new version is released, will typically be out of the question for most, as the resulting costs would be prohibitive. However, RWTH faced exactly this problem, as the system needs to be upgraded from 802.11b to 802.11g – a costly exercise. Alternatively, they could decide to wait for the future 802.11n version. Of course, this would also imply a number of open questions, including, for example: 'Will the standard ever materialize? And if so, when?' and 'Will backward compatible implementations become available?'

Finally, an aspect that is at least related to the 'dynamics' problem is the parallel development of similar standards. In the WLAN case, IEEE and European Telecommunication Standards Institute (ETSI, HIPERLAN/2) have been producing (incompatible) standards covering virtually the same areas. Such parallel activities may pose considerable problems for users (similar to those caused by a quick succession of new versions of a standard). For the RWTH WLAN, this was only a marginal problem, as 802.11b products were readily available on the market in 2001, whereas nothing comparable was in sight for HIPERLAN/2. Nevertheless, it would certainly be beneficial for users if standard bodies agreed up-front on developing common standards, rather than competing ones.

Implementation

In almost all cases, a standards setting process produces a series of drafts that will ultimately lead to the final standard. While in most cases the 'final draft' is almost identical to the standard,[9] this is not necessarily always the case (X.500/88 is a particularly memorable case in point, see e.g. Jakobs 1989). In such cases, premature implementations of a draft standard may cause problems. This happened in the 802.11g case, where RWTH purchased APs based on a draft standard. In fact, it was fairly common at the time for smaller vendors in particular to offer systems based on draft standards. This did not represent a major problem for the RWTH system, however, and could be solved by upgrading the AP firmware after a couple of months. However, such premature implementations are risky – being the first on the market at all costs may become an expensive exercise, not only for the vendor but also for any early adopters.

Another, similar, implementation-related issue surfaced when it was found that AP software releases converged to the original standards specification only over a period of time, necessitating numerous software updates in the APs. Similar problems were observed for the end-systems software. Apparently, vendors shipped early versions of their systems with software that was not 100 per cent standard-compliant (probably in order to hit the market at the earliest possible stage), and only later moved towards standards-compliance through a series of software updates.

Installation

Aspects relating to the dynamics of system installation may also be identified. For one (although this was probably not really that important), the project's starting date and, particularly, its duration meant that a number of new standards emerged during installation. This, in turn, necessitated decisions in the initial stage of the project on which standard to install, and if and when to update at later stages.

The most interesting aspect in the context of the WLAN installation is RWTH's voluntary vendor lock-in. In the WLAN case, this could be observed in two variations:

1. Proprietary extensions
   In the case of the non-standard APs with 'improved' software (128-bit link layer encryption), the importance of the underlying requirement for adequate data security was the overriding point. Apparently, this requirement even outweighed the time-tested policy of using only standards-based systems. The lesson to be learned here would be that users should carefully consider the real importance of each individual requirement, and weigh it against that of other requirements (in this particular case, there was a contradiction between the requirements 'secure data transmission' and 'interoperability').
2. Interoperability and maintenance
   Here, everyday experience in running a fairly large and heterogeneous private network indicates that interoperability problems are likely to occur if systems from different vendors are deployed. This holds even if standards compliance is claimed for all implemented systems. From a practical point of view, it is more than understandable that solutions are sought to achieve and maintain interoperability. If this has to be done with the proviso to use standards-based systems, there is hardly any alternative to selecting one vendor, sticking to its products, and hoping for the best.

In the face of incompatible implementations of standards the approach of a voluntary vendor lock-in is one solution to a potential dilemma facing many providers of private network infrastructures. Other solutions would be to use proprietary systems or to make enough resources available to overcome maintenance and interoperability problems locally. The latter, i.e. trying to solve problems locally, is likely to be next to impossible for most organizations (it certainly was for RWTH). Not unlike the process of the adaptation of standards-based systems to local needs it would also run the risk of compromising standards compliance of the system (see also e.g. Jakobs 2006). Indeed, standards are supposed to offer both maintainability and interoperability across different vendor platforms, not to necessitate finding the lesser evil, i.e. a lower degree of interoperability and maintainability or dependency on a single vendor.

Also, the situation outlined above favours large and powerful vendors (who may be assumed to stay in business long enough). Organizations following RWTH's approach will primarily turn to such suppliers when buying equipment. This, in turn, will reduce the flexibility that could be achieved by using smaller, local vendors.[10]

SOME FINAL REMARKS

RWTH's 'one vendor' philosophy, i.e. to try and use only one vendor for standards-based systems, is interesting, not least as it makes nonsense of one of the very fundamental ideas underlying any standardization activity – to reduce the user's dependency on a particular vendor. It is, therefore, in some respects not too different from installing proprietary systems. Yet, this policy is the result of continuing frustrating experiences with incompatible systems from different manufacturers all of which were supposed to comply with the respective relevant standard (RWTH's experience with such problems goes back for decades). In the particular case of the WLAN installation, these earlier experiences were further re-enforced (problems with other vendors' proprietary extensions, ease of installation and maintenance; see above). Clearly, the very practical benefits offered by the approach adopted in this case (no interoperability problems, simplified maintenance and installation) took precedence over more abstract (during the time of installation) deliberations regarding potential drawbacks (vendor lock-in).

There is no doubt that standards are an indispensable prerequisite of interoperability. However, the very fact that a large technical university sees the necessity to adopt a one-vendor approach suggests that standardization and its processes need to be complemented by additional mechanisms to ensure interoperability of standards-based systems. These mechanisms include:

1. testing whether or not an implementation conforms to a standard,
2. testing the interoperability of different implementations of the same standard.

Both services are offered by some standards setting bodies (e.g. ETSI); other bodies are involved in the development of appropriate test suites (e.g. the OpenGroup). However, the fact that such tests are voluntary somewhat reduces their practical value.

To make passing such tests mandatory for any software that implements a standard (not unlike the requirement for 'conformité Européenne [CE]' marking for e.g. electromagnetic compatibility) would be a potential solution to the conformance problem. This approach would be less suitable for interoperability testing, however, simply because each vendor's product would need to be certified for interoperability with all other products, leading to n*(n−1)/2 tests per product. Having said that, such certificates to guarantee interoperability with at least selected other products (by large vendors) would be a great help to users.

Moving one step further: the availability of interoperable implementations could be made a prerequisite for a specification to become a standard (not unlike the approach adopted by the IETF). While this does not completely solve the problem of implementations that do not interoperate, it helps make sure that the number of ambiguities, unclear wordings, unnecessary and under-specified optional elements etc. in the standards could be minimized (see also Jakobs 2002b).

In any case, there are still major obstacles on the route from a standard to interoperable systems that need to be overcome. The voluntary vendor lock-in discussed above represents one option open to users. However, a solution without the need for such (or other) comparably drastic action by users would definitely be preferable. Standards bodies, certification agencies, users, and other stakeholders may need to join forces here to provide a sustainable working solution.

NOTES

1. IR was dropped from later revisions of the standard, because it could not compete with the well-established IrDA protocol, and because of a lack of actual implementations.
2. Carrier sense multiple access with collision avoidance.
3. In Germany, for instance, permission to use this frequency band was granted only in late 2002. Worldwide, a decision of the 2003 'World Radiotelecommunciations Conference' to grant its use made worldwide use easier.
4. At the time, the ministry had launched a programme to support universities wishing to build a wireless infrastructure.

5. To the best of my knowledge, HIPERLAN/2 products have still not hit the market, and it is most likely that they will never.
6. 'Global system for mobile communications', formerly 'groupe special mobil'.
7. Compared to, for instance, the frequency with which updated implementations or new S/W releases may occur (e.g. patches for the Windows operating system). It may be more appropriate to speak of a 'quasi-static' situation here.
8. As can be seen from Table 7.2, these changes only affected the physical layer of the protocol stack. Such changes are typically unproblematic; the virtually problem-free move from one version of ethernet to its successor (10 Mbps to 100 Mbps to Gigabit-Ethernet) is a case in point.
9. The directives for the technical work of JTC 1 state that: 'A FCD [final committe document] shall be advanced to FDIS [final draft international standard] only if the text has been stabilized, consensus has been demonstrated, and the substantial support of the P-members of the SC has been obtained.'
10. In RWTH's case, an academic entity (i4) got in contact with such a local supplier (not necessarily with the consent of the CCC). This contact offered the opportunity to take part in future product development, and to implement add-ons that would support local research activities. 'Informatik 4 [...] has established relations to a local vendor. The products of that vendor are technically on the same level as the products of the well-known vendor but at a lower price. Additionally the local vendor offers the possibility to take part at the further development of its products.' This activity is a clear example of an adaptation of a standards-based systems to local needs (in this case, research needs). In this particular case the functionality of the standard was not effected (just some management functionality was added to the AP software). Yet, this is nevertheless a double-edged sword; as such added functionality may well compromise standards compliance, and thus further reduce interoperability.

8. A Case Study of the Adoption and Implementation of STEP

Josephine W. Thomas, Steve Probets, Ray Dawson and Tim King

INTRODUCTION[1]

The widespread adoption and implementation of a standard is not always as successful as originally anticipated. Academics and practitioners who have devoted themselves to the development of these standards are often left asking why adoption and implementation falls short of expectations, despite evidence of the benefits of the standards. For example, a study commissioned by the US National Institute of Standards and Technology (NIST) found that STEP, the 'standard for the exchange of product model data' (ISO 10303), has the potential to save the automotive, aerospace and shipbuilding industries in the United States approximately \$1 billion per year in interoperability costs (Brunnermeier and Martin 1999). A further study commissioned by NIST in 2002 found that STEP is conservatively estimated to be saving the transportation equipment manufacturing community over \$150 million per year in mitigation and avoidance of interoperability costs, with the figure expected to rise to \$700 million by 2010 (Gallaher et al. 2002). Despite these findings, Meister (2004), in his study of the development and implementation of STEP over 20 years, notes that, 'while STEP is in use in companies around the world, its adoption has not been as widespread as initially expected'.

An extensive review of the literature revealed that only two specific studies (Meister 2004 and Dreverman 2005) have assessed the factors that affect the adoption of ISO data-exchange standards like STEP. Meister's research sought to answer two questions: 'Why were organizations not adopting STEP, even if they were participating in its development through the standards writing process?', and 'Why has STEP adoption been so slow or, at least, why is it perceived to have been slow?' Meister (2004) answered these questions using a single-site interpretive case study approach, based on three theoretical lenses, namely: economic-based literature, diffusion of innovation theory and institutional theory. Meister's study offered insight into the developmental and organizational factors that impact the adoption of data-exchange standards from the perspective of members of the ISO/TC184/SC4[2] subcommittee responsible for the development of STEP.

Dreverman (2005) carried out a study, sponsored by the Dutch process and power industry association (USPI-NL), into the adoption of three product model data standards in the process industry supply chain. The three standards studied were ISO 10303 (STEP), ISO 15926 and ISO 13584, all of which have been developed by the ISO subcommittee ISO/TC184/SC4. The initial problem statement for his research was: The speed of adoption of product model data standards in process industries seems to be lower than in other industry sectors. Consequently, Dreverman (2005) sought to identify the factors that impede or slow the adoption of these standards within the process industry. Dreverman used factor analysis and actor analysis to establish the issues surrounding the three named standards. The factor analysis was based mainly around 'diffusion of innovation (DOI)' theory, and the actor analysis described how the motives, power and actions of the various actors in the process industry affected the adoption of the standards. Dreverman also offered insight into the developmental and organizational factors that impact the adoption of standards like STEP.

Dreverman (2005) and Meister's (2004) research are the only two studies that focused on the adoption of standards produced by the subcommittee ISO/TC184/SC4, despite the fact that to date the subcommittee has published 367 standards, including STEP (ISO 2006). This lack of published studies on the adoption of data-exchange standards like STEP underlines the need for the research presented in this chapter, and reinforces Swann's (2000) assertion in his report for the Department of Trade and Industry in the United Kingdom, that 'the literature concerning the factors that influence the rate of uptake (diffusion) of standards is limited'. Swann's assertion is further confirmed by Byrne and Golder (2002), who explicitly state that the literature surrounding IT standards adoption is limited and that there is a need for more empirical studies.

In this chapter, we examine the issues surrounding the adoption and implementation of STEP more closely through an empirical study of the adoption and implementation of a specific STEP Application Protocol,[3] AP224 (ISO 10303-224) within the UK Ministry of Defence. The aim of this empirical study is to provide insight into the actions that can be taken to facilitate and improve the adoption and implementation of standards like STEP.

RESEARCH THEORIES AND APPROACHES

The goal of this research is to further our understanding of the factors and barriers that are critical to the adoption and implementation of data-exchange standards like STEP and identify what actions can be taken to address these issues. Due to the limited body of work into the adoption of STEP, a broader review of the literature was carried out into the factors that impact the adoption of other IT-related standards. What emerged from this review was that most diffusion-related research was based on two theories: DOI theory and a theory that is often referred to as the 'economics of standards'.

Most DOI studies build on the sociology model of Rogers (2003) for the adoption and diffusion of technology innovations. This model captures the characteristics of the innovation, communication channels and social system as they interact over time. Rogers (2003) lists five innovation attributes that influence the adoption decision, these include: relative advantage, compatibility, complexity, trialability and observability. The social system characteristics can be further divided into characteristics of the individual, group, organization, decision-makers, and the roles of opinion leaders and change agents like champions. Communication channels are important to the adopting community for learning about the existence and substance of an innovation. These channels may be internal or external to the organization and may transmit either formal or informal communications (Prescott and Conger 1995). Mustonen-Ollila and Lyytinen (2003) go on to list 28 DOI-related attributes in their meta-analysis of over 200 information-system adoption decisions. DOI theory provides a rich explanation of how new innovations are adopted, and how adoption decisions are affected by perceptions of the standard itself as well as the characteristics of the adopters and their environment.

In addition to classical diffusion of innovation theory, the adoption of standards has been studied from an economic perspective (Fichman and Kemerer 1993; Katz and Shapiro 1986). This approach is often labelled the 'economics of standards', and focuses on an innovation's inherent economic value to potential adopters. Two main theories have been used within this economic stream. The first related theory is network effects. Network analysis is often based on the theory of positive network effects, or network externalities, which describes a positive correlation between the number of users and the utility of a product (Katz and Shapiro 1986). A second factor that is often classed under 'economics of standards' is switching costs. In the current context it refers to a standard specific investment that makes organizations hesitant to change a supported standard.

Other authors have used game theory to understand the adoption of IT-related standards (Belleflamme 1999; Xia et al. 2003). Fichman and Kemerer (1993) argue that there is so much variety among potential scenarios that no single theory of innovation adoption and diffusion is likely to emerge. They propose that innovations are most likely to be dominant when they score highly on both diffusion of innovation and economics of standards criteria (ibid.). The main factors that emerged within this research were linked to DOI theory and the economics of standards.

West (2003) contends that a more robust and influential framework for understanding technology adoption in an organizational context has been developed by DePietro et al. (1990, cited in Dedrick and West 2003). Their model defines a 'context for change' that consists of three elements:

1. Technology
   The model subsumes the five innovation attributes that, according to Rogers (2003), influence the likelihood of adoption.
2. Organization
   The propensity to adopt is influenced by formal and informal intraorganizational mechanisms for communication and control. The resources and innovativeness of the organization also play a role.
3. Environment
   Organizational adoption of new technologies depends on having the prerequisite skills for effective deployment, which means that, as Attewell (1992) found, the availability of external skills (such as through integrators or consultants) is essential for adoption by some organizations.

These three elements, which are often referred to as 'TOE', are posited to interact with each other and to influence technology adoption decisions (West 2003). However, the TOE framework is simply a taxonomy for categorizing variables, and does not represent an integrated conceptual framework or well-developed theory. Therefore, the TOE taxonomy is used simply to categorize some of the findings detailed later in this chapter.

In relation to approaches to research on IT standards adoption, West (1999) notes that most research on innovation adoption focuses on a single innovation and the people adopting that innovation. This is an innovation-centric approach that focuses on the general adoption and diffusion of a standard or standards across their target population or organizations. Another approach examines individual adopters, usually organizations, and the innovations they adopt. This is referred to as an adopter-centric approach, and it examines the adoption of standards within organizations from a decision-making perspective. West (1999) contends that innovation-centric diffusion research tends to have a pro-adoption bias, with late adopters labelled 'laggards'. This bias is weaker in the study of adopting organizations, which instead demonstrate a bias towards the ability to adopt any innovation rather than any particular innovation. Meister (2004) took an innovation-centric approach that looks at the adoption of STEP over 20 years. Dreverman took a more combined approached that leaned slightly more to the adopter-centric approach. However, neither study looked at the issues surrounding the adoption of standards like STEP within a specific organization. In this chapter we address this by presenting the results of an adopter-centric study of the factors and barriers critical to the adoption of STEP within the UK Ministry of Defence (MoD). The UK defence community was chosen because the two cited STEP-related studies have not looked at data-exchange standards adoption in a defence environment.

METHODOLOGY

Dedrick and West (2003) suggest that a richer framework for understanding IT adoption decisions can be developed through a qualitative study of a specific standards adoption case. Using the case study approach, this research sought to confirm existing factors surrounding the adoption of IT-related standards like STEP, and explore whether there are any as yet unidentified factors that may influence the adoption of these standards, specifically in the UK MoD.

Case studies can be used to collect both quantitative and qualitative data (Yin 2002); for the purpose of this study only qualitative data was collected. Different methods were used to collect data, including semi-structured interviews, informal discussions, and the study of archival material and existing documentation. The hour-long interviews were carried out with implementers and end-users involved in a STEP project called 'rapid acquisition of manufactured parts (RAMP)'. 'Implementers' refers to the individuals both within the MoD and in industry, such as consultants and software vendors, who are responsible for the practical implementation of RAMP. The term 'end-users' refers to MoD and industry employees who will be working with information systems based on RAMP. Additional interviews were carried out with MoD employees who had had exposure to STEP and two defence standards linked to STEP, namely the NATO codification system and defence standard 'Def Stan 00-60'. In the end a total of 15 interviews were carried out.

CASE BACKGROUND

UK Ministry of Defence

Few commercial organizations or government departments in the UK can compare in sheer size and sophistication to the MoD, which has an annual budget exceeding thirty billion pounds and over 300 000 service and civilian personnel (MoD 2005). Procurement and logistics are handled by two main agencies, the Defence Procurement Agency and the Defence Logistics Organization. Both agencies are made up of what are known as 'integrated project teams (IPTs)'. The MoD also works closely with a vast number of prime and sub-contractors or industry partners to achieve its goals, and according to the MoD policy, standardization is the key to ensuring the interoperability, quality, safety, reliability, maintainability, effectiveness and efficiency of the equipment used by the UK Armed Forces (MoD 'Support Solutions Envelope [SSE]' 2005). The MoD 'acquisition management systems (AMS)' standardization authoritative encourages the application of what they term 'smart standardization' principles at all stages of the acquisition life cycle of a product (MoD AMS 2003). Consequently, in order to ensure that this concept of 'smart standardization' is realized, the choices of standards to be used in the various missions or projects within the MoD are selected against a standardization hierarchy. Within this hierarchy, European standards are the first choice of standards in the MoD, followed by international, national, commercial and finally military standards (Stirling 2001), and UK Government policy is that civil standards are used wherever possible in preference to military standards. This national policy resonates with NATO policy, which states that 'NATO standards will only be developed when the requirements are not covered by existing international, civil or military standards' (MoD 2002).

RAMP Project – ISO 10303-224

The main STEP project currently running within the MoD is the 'rapid acquisition of manufactured parts (RAMP)' project, which is based on ISO 10303-224 – 'mechanical parts definition for process planning using machining features'. The RAMP process was originally conceived to enable the US Department of Defense (DoD) to overcome difficulties in obtaining small batches of spare parts, particularly those nearing obsolescence. The UK Navy saw the use of RAMP, which is based on an international standard and used in the US Navy, as an opportunity to deal with these same issues. Consequently, in 1998 the UK Navy mechanical RAMP pilot project was conducted to prove that the system worked in the UK operational environment. Following on from that, in 2001, a second study was carried out by a large prime contractor to further test the extent of RAMP applicability across a wider range of products. These two projects concluded that RAMP using ISO 10303-224 could significantly reduce lead times involved in the procurement of mechanical spares and consequently, cost savings could be realized by an elimination or reduction of stockholding (LSC Group 2002). In December 2003, a prime contractor involved in the 2001 study embarked on the implementation of the UK's first production application of RAMP within an MoD IPT.

FINDINGS AND ANALYSIS

The adopter-centric approach looks at the diffusion of an innovation within an organization. Zaltman et al. (1973) examined innovation adoption within organizations and determined that the adoption process frequently occurs in two stages, an organization-level decision to adopt an innovation (primary adoption), followed by actual implementation, which includes departmental or individual adoption (secondary adoption).

Some authors, such as Chen (2003), focus on the primary adoption decision process, while others, for instance Gallivan (2001), focus on secondary adoption. Indeed, the frequently cited 'technology acceptance model (TAM)', proposed by Bagozzi et al. (1992) and Davis et al. (1989), is used to address secondary adoption. Details of many of the technology acceptance models went beyond the scope of this research. The findings presented in this chapter focus on both the primary and secondary adoption of data-exchange standards within the UK MoD.

Primary Adoption – The Decision to Adopt the RAMP Project Within the MoD

This section details the factors and barriers that have been critical to the primary adoption of the STEP-based RAMP application within the MoD. A variety of factors influenced the primary adoption of RAMP within the MoD. These factors are discussed using the TOE framework.

Standard (technology)-related factors

The standard (technology)-related factors subsume the five innovation attributes that Rogers (2003) argues influence the likelihood of adoption. These factors include: relative advantage, compatibility, complexity, trialability and observability. At a primary adoption level, four of these attributes directly impacted the adoption decision.

The first was the relative advantage of STEP over other standards. One interviewee who has worked in the MoD for over 30 years explained this point by stating that:

> STEP seemed the logical way to go and the STEP-based approach [RAMP] was the best way. It gave us that degree of neutrality that we did not have to rely on single source supplier and [it] gave us a capability of holding a file neutrally that we could exchange. We did not feel a need to try any other standards.

The RAMP project had no competing standards. The trialability of the standard through numerous pilots, demonstrations and seminars positively impacted the adoption of RAMP. These actions were beneficial in promoting the standard, gaining interest and proving the standard and supporting technologies worked, and could offer benefit. These pilots were also able to show the benefits that could be achieved from using the standard. This finding is confirmed by Byrne and Golder (2002) who ascertain that anticipatory standards should have an example installation, which can be used to guide possible implementers and help in the diffusion of a standard.

Complexity was raised as one of the main barriers to the adoption of the RAMP project and had a negative impact on primary adoption. Apparently as a result of this complexity, some decision-makers found it difficult to understand the standard and how it worked. Two of the implementers confirmed this, and one of them stated: 'When you talk about STEP [decision-makers] think there is some "black magic" [...] and they say "absolutely no way are we going to understand that"'. This argument around complexity of STEP is confirmed by Meister (2004) who postulates that: 'STEP is a complex standard because of its scope and requisite details, not because of a fundamental design or development problem'. Complexity is one of the main factors that has emerged within other IT standards adoption research (Mustonen-Ollila and Lyytinen 2003; Rogers 2003; Dreverman 2005). Inevitably the main impact of this complexity was in the implementation stages during secondary adoption because having a complex standard puts more pressure on implementers.

Studies conducted by Rogers (2003) and others (Meister 2004; Dreverman 2005) show that observability is a critical factor in supporting the adoption decision of an innovation. Many of the interviewees revealed that there was a challenge establishing the observability of STEP. This was due to the lack of information regarding other success stories, case studies and implementations of the standard. One of the AP224 implementers explained the reason for this by stating that: 'there are some [AP224] implementations being done. They are company implementations, but they are keeping [the details] within the company, so you are really not sure what is going on. They are not being informative of their work. That makes it very hard'. The voluntary flow of information between existing and potential adopters is important for creating positive expectations. The general availability of information about a standard has a positive impact on the diffusion of an innovation (Nilakanta and Scamell 1990). The importance of communication and information channels has been found in other adoption and diffusion of innovations studies (West 1999; Mustonen-Ollila and Lyytinen 2003; Rogers 2003).

The technology-related factors that impacted the primary adoption of STEP within the MoD correspond with the factors that have emerged in other IT standards adoption studies, confirming Rogers' (2003) assertion that: 'standards that are perceived by organizations as having greater relative advantage, compatibility, trialability, observability and less complexity will be adopted more readily than other standards'.

Organization-related factors

The organizational factors that affected the primary adoption of AP224 related to six key issues:

Organization size and type

Chen (2003) argues that: 'large government agencies are traditionally said to be strong supporters of standardization efforts'. This was found to be true in the case of the MoD. As was previously mentioned, the MoD SSE emphasizes that standardization is key to ensuring the interoperability, quality, safety, reliability, maintainability, effectiveness and efficiency of the equipment used by the Armed Forces (MoD SSE 2005). As one interviewee who has worked in the MoD for over 25 years stated: 'I have a business to run. It is called the Royal Navy. The best way for me to run my business is by applying standards. That is my corporate rule'. This strong support for standards is driven by the fact that the MoD is a large organization at the top of a supply chain made up of hundreds of contractors and industry partners, and an effective exchange and sharing of information and the management of equipment is greatly enhanced by the use of standards. This confirms Meister's (2004) finding that the adoption of these data-exchange standards needs to be thought of in terms of supply chains rather than individual organizations.

Drivers (motivation)

Themistocleous (2002), when looking at the adoption of enterprise integration technologies within two large organizations, found that the internal and external drivers and pressures were key factors in the adoption of technology within an organization. The RAMP project leader explained that the main internal driver (motivation) behind the project was that: 'There is a lot of cost [associated with storing parts] and whilst big warehouses full of spare parts can be absorbed in some form of government bureaucracy [...] you cannot afford to have this asset that is appreciating at 6% per year. And our shareholders are taxpayers'. Therefore, there were clear economic drivers behind the use of RAMP, which helped facilitate its adoption.

Managerial influence

There were managers within the MoD and several consultants who were vital in championing the benefits of the standard, and who were responsible for getting the standard to its current level of implementation. As one MoD user noted: 'once some key managers saw the business benefit and were able to see the changes required in light of these benefits, support for the adoption of the standard grew'. Meister (2004) found that having a strong visionary leader or champion was a common element of every successful STEP adoption story. This confirms work by Rogers (2003) and Prescott and Conger (1995), who conducted a longitudinal study into the factors that affect the adoption of innovations, and they explain that champion support for an innovation means that someone within the organization becomes a special advocate for the innovation, taking actions to increase the probability of successful adoption and implementation and this was demonstrated in the study. This is further affirmed by Fichman (1999), who explains that the actions of certain kinds of individuals (opinion leaders and change agents) can accelerate adoption.

Organization culture

This issue relates to organizational culture towards change. Indeed, resistance to change was the most commonly cited primary adoption barrier. The source of this resistance varied among the different MoD representatives. The main sources included:

1. reluctance to change current ways of working,
2. switching costs,
3. fear of loss of power, control and jobs.

These findings are consistent with the commonly cited resistance-to-change factors identified by Kotter et al. (1998) in the *Harvard Business Review*. All the factors point to personal characteristics, which show that some potential adopters are more innovative than others (Fichman 1999). A second issue relating to organization culture was user attitudes towards standards and standard bodies. Some of the common attitudes and perceptions of end-users were:

1. standards are very complex and are very costly to implement,
2. standards restrict the way people work and bring no real benefit,
3. the ISO standards development community is a group of academics who are not connected to reality,
4. standards like STEP are simply ideas that software vendors and consultants are trying to market.

Many of these views emerged as a result of the end-users' experience with other standards. Some have emerged in other studies; for example, an ISO/TC184/SC4 member interviewed by Meister (2004) found that in some countries the term standard meant constriction and a change in current ways of working to match someone else. As a result, some end-users involved in the RAMP project were reluctant to adopt the standard. However, one implementer explained how to get around this challenge by stating that: 'Standards, I believe, are necessary. What we have to be able to do is not frighten people by their implementation and also stress to people that they are not there as a restraint, they are there as a business enabler'.

Existing infrastructure
The existing infrastructure factor is linked to an organization's attitude towards change, and was particularly demonstrated in the RAMP project. Some stakeholders, who had investments in technology and software that would be lost with the introduction of the standard, were reluctant to adopt the standard due to the additional switching costs they would incur. This was particularly the case for the prime contractor involved in the adoption decision. Therefore, this had a negative impact on the adoption decision process. This is in keeping with findings by authors such as Hovav et al. (2004) who explain that even if an innovation is considered to be superior on the basis of objective criteria, a potential adopter may still not adopt the innovation due to the presence of a large installed base of existing innovation, leading to the presence of sunk costs through irreversible investments, which can introduce a drag on the adoption of a new standard.

Resource availability
Resource availability within the MoD is greatly affected by restructuring and review initiatives. This was particularly the case in the RAMP project. After the 1998 pilot there was a major reorganization of the MoD, in addition, the associated changes that resulted from the 'smart procurement initiative' started in 1997 (LSC Group 2002). These activities may explain some of the reasons for the delays that occurred between the first successful pilot in 1998 and the subsequent pilot project in 2001. In addition to the reviews and restructuring initiatives that take place in the MoD, the other challenge to resource availability is the regularly changing of position of employees within the MoD. This reorganization and general moving of people has an impact on the financial and human resources available to support the RAMP project. To further compound resource availability challenges, the influence and consequences of urgent operational requirements (e.g. wars) may require people to be reassigned to different projects without notice or warning, again making continuity on a project very difficult.

Environmental-related factors
The key factor within the environmental characteristics is the impact of network effects on the adoption decision. There was a positive network effect on the adoption of RAMP in the UK Navy, based on the fact that this project was first established in the US Navy. As one implementer said: 'It was quite a sensible choice to a use an existing standard that did have some support and use.' These findings point to results found in research on network externalities. In network externalities, each buyer of a technology receives greater benefits as the user network increases in size. Examples of this include the telephone service and fax machines (Warner 2003). These benefits include

an increase in support and resources surrounding an innovation. Though this RAMP example is slightly narrow, there was an acknowledgment that by using an international standard there would be an increased benefit as more people work to the standard, and one MoD decision-maker noted: 'In the case of an international standard, there is a hope that as more organizations outside the MoD and contractor sector work to the standard, there will be benefit in working with the standard'. This confirms another hypothesized factor in the economics of standards regarding the role of positive network effects that accrue to all adopters of a popular standard (von Weizsacker 1984). Therefore, the MoD is positioning itself for greater network benefits as the adoption of AP224 increases.

There were additional positive network effects from the related implementation technologies surrounding the RAMP project, particularly with regards to the use of XML to implement STEP. The use of XML for data exchange into and out of MoD systems is being encouraged wherever appropriate. Hence, the use of XML to implement RAMP encouraged the uptake of RAMP because there was compliance with MoD policy, which states: 'XML must be used to exchange information between systems within the MoD and between MoD systems and external partners' (MoD Central Data Management Authority [CDMA] 2004).

Primary adoption conclusion

These factors are all the issues that impacted the primary adoption of the STEP-based RAMP project within the MoD. There were two main negative impacts on the adoption decision. The first was the complexity of the standard. The main source of complexity was attributed to the conceptual idea and scope of the standard. One STEP developer explained that, if dealing with a large industry group with numerous stakeholders and data: 'simplification does not work, so the common denominator is usually the more complex picture'. This confirms Jakobs' (2002a) assertion that 'official' standards bodies (e.g. ISO) have a strong tendency for 'all-embracing', over-arching solutions that solve all problems at once. Jakobs goes on to explain that this sometimes leads to extremely complex specifications, that even large companies can be hesitant to implement, because of their complexity and because they tend to solve problems that nobody has ever encountered. The second main negative impact was related to organizational culture, more specifically user attitudes towards change and the standards. An MoD end-user pointed out that the traditional military way to overcome resistance to change was a 'you just do it' attitude. However, the interviewee went on to point out that, even in a military environment, employees will not work with the system whole heartedly and that will frustrate what needs to be done on a project and lead to project overruns.

Despite these challenges, in the end the relative advantage, trialability and managerial intervention from champions within the MoD were the key drivers behind the primary adoption of the standard. However, once the MoD had agreed to adopt the standard, there was still a challenge convincing contractors to adopt the standard. This is because as you travel down the defence community supply chain, the response of prime contractors to the decision to use a standard is not always positive. This was particularly true in the case of the primary adoption decision process between a MoD IPT and a prime defence contractor involved in this RAMP project. The contractor was reluctant to take on the use of an open neutral standard like AP224 because the company believed that this would empower the MoD to take business to any contractor who was willing to comply with the standard, which could result in a loss of their business with the MoD. So it was important that a balance was reached so that benefit could be realized by both the MoD and prime contactor, and this was accomplished through a gain-share contractual arrangement. One interviewee explained that the essence of the arrangement was that: 'If the MoD says we need 100 spares, the team within this organization look at the electronic STEP-based stock holding and would say you do not need 100 you need ten and they would have saved the MoD 90 spares, so half of the cost that they saved goes back to the contractor'. This contractual arrangement means that both the MoD and contractor share the benefits and risks associated with the project. Indeed some of ISO/TC184/SC4 members interviewed by Meister (2004) suggested that customers, like the MoD, should promote STEP 'by writing it into contracts', which was the case in this project. Once both parties were happy with the contractual arrangement, in December 2003, the prime contractor embarked on the implementation of the UK's first production application of RAMP within an MoD IPT.

Secondary Adoption – the Implementation of the RAMP Project Within the MoD

All interviewees involved in the adoption and implementation of the RAMP project were asked to give their view on the current rate of uptake of the standard within the MoD. The head of the RAMP project within the MoD when asked the question stated: 'I do not believe the uptake in the Royal Navy has been as great as it could be. We are starting to do some business but it is not been taken up as quick as we had hoped'. Another interviewee described the rate of uptake as, 'fair to middling'. All RAMP project interviewees in the end expressed some disappointment at the current rate of uptake or diffusion of the standard within the organization. The factors and barriers surrounding the secondary adoption of the STEP-based RAMP project are also discussed using the familiar 'technological, organizational and environmental (TOE)' framework.

Standard (technology)-related factors

The main innovation attributes again related directly to Rogers' (2003) DOI theory of innovation characteristics. The main characteristic that emerged was complexity. The complexity of the standard had a negative knock-on effect on the cost of implementation and on understanding and learning costs. Some of the issues of complexity were a result of end-user perceptions that standards are complex, but most of the complexity debate centered around the conceptual idea and scope of ISO 10303-224. The implementers particularly emphasized the complexity of the ISO 10303-224 during secondary adoption because they faced direct implementation challenges, as one interviewee noted: 'the concept of the AIM and ARM[4] is preposterous. It's a real impediment to working with the standard'.

The secondary adoption RAMP project also highlighted another of Rogers' (2003) characteristics, compatibility. Compatibility was an issue at two levels, the first was the legacy technologies around RAMP were not compatible with some of the systems used by the end-users. As one implementer pointed out: 'the design end was stuck on a UNIX machine; no one is interested in using UNIX machines'. The use of UNIX was a legacy that was inherited from the original implementations of RAMP carried out in the US. Dealing with this problem caused delays and had a negative impact on the time taken to implement the standard. The second issue related to the compatibility of different versions of the standard. The second edition of AP224 was published in April 2001, and the projected publication date of edition three was June 2006. The head of the development team explained that they made a conscious decision to avoid compatibility issues during revisions but the downside was that they had a standard that was very similar to the original version, despite a lot of effort going into the revision process. Consequently, some of the stakeholders involved in the standard argued whether these revisions were necessary. As one interviewee put it: 'What real benefits have we had from the different editions other than a lot of work and a rewrite of everything?' However, one of the implementers, who was also a developer of AP224, pointed out that the revisions were a key bargaining tool:

> [Doing revisions] has been important. As an example, people wanted to vote down certain standards but we persuaded them not to do that because the new requirements they wanted we could put in later editions and that enabled us to keep moving on. That was an important negotiating process.

Nonetheless, some implementers still found that newer versions lacked backward compatibility with earlier versions of the standard; this caused a certain amount of rework to be done, causing delays in implementation of the standard. The case study of AP224 highlights some of the conflicting challenges of standards succession, and confirms Egyedi and Loeffen's (2002) view that succession in standardization is often a problem, and that the advantages of improvements must be weighed against those of compatibility.

A final challenge with regard to standard factors relates to the fees required to access the ISO data-exchange standards. There is an ongoing debate with regards to the fees associated with the purchase of completed standards. Although some interviewees believed that the fees relating to the standard were minimal relative to the project costs, other implementers disagreed with this view. They argued that having to justify the cost of purchasing a copy of the standard was not always easy on a day-to-day basis when dealing with managers who could not necessarily see the need for the extra cost. The implementers interviewed believed that having freely available standards would make life easier for them and result in increased interest and use of the standard in general. In the end, a licence was purchased which dealt with the issue surrounding the fee in this specific case. Nonetheless, a number of commentators agree that providing standards documents at no charge expands the dissemination of the document (Krechmer 1998; Swann 2000). Oksala et al. (1996) take this view one step further and declare that: 'standards whose dissemination are controlled for the purposes or garnering additional revenue sow the seeds of their own demise'. However, Krechmer (1998) explains that accredited standards bodies like the ISO often use document charges to avoid increasing members' dues. This highlights the importance of finding ways to have innovative pricing schemes for standards that help facilitate the adoption and implementation of the standards.

Organization-related factors

The organizational factors that impacted secondary adoption related to attitudes towards change and standards at two levels. The first is at a departmental level. Some MoD departments or IPTs are unwilling to engage in the use of standards due to their narrow view of their own department costs and benefits and not on the benefits the use of standards would bring to the whole organization. Therefore departments that do not perceive the implementation of a standard will offer them direct benefit tend to be reluctant to adopt a new standard. This confirms findings by Weitzel (2003) who explained that independent business units perceive no incentive to invest in compatibility when the benefits from standardization are accredited to the 'entire' firm or any other entity different from the investing unit. This shows the importance of internal promotion and marketing within the organization to garner support for a standard.

The second level is at an individual level. In primary adoption the attitudes to change and standards at an individual level was related to the managers and decision-makers. During secondary adoption more emphasis is placed on individual end-users' decisions whether to use the RAMP software or not. The two main reasons for resistance at an individual level were, firstly, end-users not wanting to change from using proprietary systems they were familiar with. Secondly, some end-users were resistant to outsiders and consultants coming in. This was noted by one of the consultant implementers who explained that: 'There is massive resistance to anything [consultants] do, and it is connected to politics'. Some perceptions identified in primary adoption relating to the complexity of standards and the ISO community also emerged within secondary adoption.

Environmental-related factors

The main environmental factor identified during secondary adoption was the remoteness of the standards community. Two implementers who were interviewed expressed that they felt the standards community was very remote, resulting in a sense of isolation and a lack of a support network. One of the implementers stated: 'The only real mechanism for engaging with the ISO community is to attend their thrice-yearly meetings'. The implementers went on to state that: 'There is no community out there that people can turn to and have user group meetings and swap ideas around and get suggestions. It can be pretty lonely'. In their view: 'Developers do not do anything for the standard except propagate it and do not support it'. Another implementer who had more input and engagement with developers agreed that: 'One barrier is the remoteness of the standards community, the complete lack of anybody to support the implementation process which clearly you would get if you were paying for a proprietary system. So it is the underlying marketing and support that you would expect to receive for starting on any of these processes which is transparently absent when you adopt a standard'. There appears to be a disconnect between the two communities in this case and a need for better communication channels, which are a key element for successful diffusion of an innovation (Rogers 2003; Hovav et al. 2004). Available communication channels can also facilitate accessibility to information by organizations regarding a new standard (Nilakanta and Scamell 1990). Therefore, communication between the standards community and implementers is vital to ensure successful implementation of a standard in order to facilitate secondary adoption. This finding reinforces the importance of effective and clear communication between the stakeholders involved in the development, use and implementation of these standards.

Secondary-adoption summary

These factors are the key issues that impacted the secondary-adoption implementation of the STEP-based RAMP project within the MoD. Despite these challenges, work continues on the project. The first phase is now complete and tangible benefits have been realized. One report states that, to date, £60 000 of stock reduction has been realized (Dobson 2005). With these kinds of results, one of the key stakeholders expressed a belief that if this pilot project is completed and successful, then other IPTs within the MoD could become interested, which would cause the standard to diffuse throughout the organization. This is in agreement with a secondary-adoption strategy described by Gallivan (2001) as the advocacy strategy. Within this strategy an organization targets specific pilot projects within the firm and the outcomes are observed and used to determine continued adoption of the innovation.

CONCLUSION

This chapter has highlighted the cross-section of factors that have impacted the adoption and implementation of a STEP standard within the UK MoD. Most factors relate to DOI theory, the economics of standards, and elements of organizational theory. In addition, these findings have revealed that the issues surrounding the adoption and implementation of a standard are not limited to the characteristics of the adopting organization, some factors are related to the idea that lies behind the standard and the characteristics of the standard development organization.

In this example, the idea to develop an overarching product data exchange standard like STEP has, in many people's view, resulted in a complex standard that is challenging to implement. Regarding the standard development setting, in this case ISO, the way standards are revised, promoted and supported had an impact on the implementation of the standard. The revision process was viewed by some interviewees as being too long, which can cause delays in the implementation process and compatibility challenges. In relation to promotion of the standard, marketing and promoting the standards from a centralized team could help raise the profile of the standards and encourage adoption and implementation. The ISO/TC184/SC4 subcommittee has established an education and outreach programme; however, priority needs to be given to resourcing this outreach programme with people and finance. Finally, a number of implementers expressed the view that they felt the standards committee was often very remote, and they felt they had no support. This then impacted the effectiveness of the implementation of the standard within the organization. Steps should be taken to get an implementers' forum up and running using an online forum and arranging annual meetings. What these results indicate is that the adoption and implementation of a standard like STEP within an organization is impacted by all phases leading up to a standard's implementation.

NOTES

1. Any comments attributable to UK Ministry of Defence (MoD) employees (as part of the interview process) reflect the thoughts of the individuals and not necessarily those of the UK MoD.
2. ISO/TC184/SC4 – ISO (International Organization for Standardization), Technical Committee 184 (Industrial Automation Systems and Integration), and Sub-Committee 4 (Industrial Data).
3. STEP is built as a series of parts to support the development of standards for product data exchange, sharing and archiving. Parts 201 to 240 detail the implementable data specifications of STEP known as application protocols.
4. An Application Protocol (ISO 10303-2xx) is in principle first written independently of STEP using the terminology of the application or industry area, the result is an 'application reference model (ARM)'. This model is then mapped to STEP concepts using the EXPRESS data modelling language. The result is an 'application interpreted model (AIM)', which is the actual data model of the application protocol in STEP (Männistö et al. 1998). EXPRESS is a data modelling language that was developed specifically for STEP made up of entities, attributes and type hierarchies (Kahn et al. 2001).

PART FOUR

Scale of Change

9. How stable are IT standards?

Tineke M. Egyedi and Petra Heijnen[1]

INTRODUCTION

One might assume that committee standards are stable and that they are not changed easily. Indeed, 'stability' would seem to be an intrinsic, defining characteristic of standards. It is usually a precondition for interoperability between IT products and services. Standards are signposts (Mansell and Hawkins 1992). They are a point of reference for producers, suppliers and consumers, and reduce transaction costs[2] (Kindleberger 1983). They co-ordinate technology and market development (Farrell and Saloner 1988). To be effective, they need to be stable.

However, as we know intuitively, standards are not static entities. In practice they are being revised, split and merged, withdrawn, succeeded, reinstated, etc. We use the term 'standards dynamics' to describe the changes a standard undergoes after it has been developed and published, including its withdrawal, replacement and possible after-life.

The chapters in this volume provide several examples of standards dynamics: DVD recordables, IP, wireless LAN, etc. They show that change is usually driven by technical arguments, but that at the same time economic considerations lead to standards and standards constellations that are less than ideal. This is illustrated by the classic example of the Telefax standard. By 1989, the Comité Consultatif International Télégraphique et Téléphonique (CCITT, currently ITU-T) had developed the Group 3 for analogue networks and the Group 4 for digital networks. Problems started when a proposal was made for a Group 3 digital telefax standard. The main opposition to the new proposal came from the Group 4 supporters. To prevent acceptance of the Group 3 digital telefax standard, they came up with a compromise. In the resulting stalemate, the CCITT decided to accept the compromise as well as the proposal for a Group 3 digital telefax, creating rival technologies that could fragment the market (Schmidt and Werle 1998).

Although not all changes to standards are as politically motivated as the solution to the Telefax standard dilemma, the case illustrates that 'improvements' may well create difficulties. Those who are primarily affected by the changes are standards users (implementors) and IT consumers (end-users). What makes standards dynamics cumbersome is the fact that changes:

1. reduce transparency with regard to the functionality of a standard (e.g. lack of insight in the differences between versions or in the consequences for product interoperability complying with different versions), and thereby increase transaction costs;
2. increase costs (e.g. costs of updating the standard and devaluation of earlier investments, i.e. sunk costs);
3. diminish self-evident interoperability; in other words, there may be uncertainty concerning the interoperability of new standard-compliant IT with one's own installed base and with the installed base of others.

The referential property of standards and the difficulties that accompany change are strong arguments in favour of the value of stable standards as such. To gain greater insight into the current state of standards stability, this chapter asks which types of change are at stake, and how often change occurs. Because to date no systematic research has been conducted into the scale of standards dynamics – with the exception of Blind (see Chapter 10) – we use an explorative, quantitative research approach. The focus is on formal international IT standards, that is to say, on standards developed in JTC 1, the Joint Technical Committee 1 of ISO and IEC.

The structure of the chapter is as follows. Firstly, the terminology and procedures developed by JTC 1 regarding standards maintenance are introduced, since standard maintenance defines JTC 1's perspective on standards dynamics. Next, the characteristics of the dataset and the research methodology are described. Analysis has been carried out at two levels, the first of which provides an overall impression of the changes that have occurred, while the second level of analysis addresses specific themes of change. Finally, we present our conclusions and recommendations for follow-up research.

STANDARD MAINTENANCE IN JTC 1

JTC 1 was installed in 1987 to address the surge of work items in the field of information technology. It has a collaborative agreement with ITU-T, the part of the formal International Telecommunication Union that develops formal standards (i.e. recommendations) for telecommunications. Although JTC 1 is officially one of ISO and IEC's technical committees (e.g. the ISO central secretariat administers JTC 1 data), it operates as an autonomous body in certain respects. For example, it has its own website, its own directives, and, at the time of writing, 16 subcommittees. These produce international standards (ISs) and standard-type documents, namely technical reports (TRs) and international standardized profiles (ISPs).[3] In addition to developing and ratifying standards, they carry out maintenance work on standards. This maintenance starts with a periodical review. No more than five years after publication of the most recent edition of a standard a review is carried out to decide whether it should be confirmed, revised, declared as stabilized, or withdrawn (JTC 1 2004, Chapter 15.3.1). To start with the first option, a standard is confirmed if it has been implemented at the national level and is applied in practice.[4] A revision may involve supplementing a standard with a separate document called:

1. a 'technical corrigendum' (Cor), designed to correct a technical defect (i.e. a technical error or ambiguity in a standard that could lead to its incorrect or unsafe application);[5]
2. a 'technical amendment' (Amd), which is a technical addition or change;[6] or it may consist of:
3. a next 'edition' (Ed) (e.g. to correct editorial defects[7] or integrate supplements into the main body);
4. a 'replacement' (e.g., standards A, B, and C may merge into standard D, or D may be split into A, B, and C), and acquire a new project number; or
5. a 'change of document type', e.g. from an IS into a TR.

For example, the set of standards and standard-type documents on local and metropolitan area networks ISO/IEC 8802 consists of different parts (1–12 parts, parts 8 and 10 missing). All of them are ISs except for the first part, which is a TR. For most parts, new editions have replaced old ones (e.g. part 3 four times). Some parts also have corrigenda and/or amendments, which are sometimes replaced by a new corrigendum and/or amendment (e.g. part 2), or integrated into a new edition.

A standard may be withdrawn because it is replaced by a new edition, because it is given a new project number (the old standard project is then 'administratively' withdrawn), or because it has become obsolete (no replacement).

Finally, a standard may be declared as stabilized. Stabilized standards are not subject to periodic review. 'A stabilized standard […] will be retained to provide for the continued viability of existing products or servicing of equipment that is expected to have a long working life' (JTC 1 2004, Chapter 15.3.1).[8] That is to say, other standards and/or in-use implementations depend on them. An ISO document gives us two examples (ISO 2004):

1. The rationale to reinstate and stabilize the programming language Algol 60 (ISO 1538:1984), after withdrawal in 1990, was that the standard and algorithms in it are still referenced in textbooks and national standards.

2. The rationale to reinstate and stabilize a standard for Basic mode control procedures (ISO 2628:1973, ISO 2629:1973), after withdrawal in 1997, was that 'there are many terminals in existence operating TPAD and other similar protocols [...] that are based on ISO 2628 and ISO 2629', and that are character-oriented.

Since their market is no longer expected to evolve, no standards maintenance is needed (e.g. it is not necessary to keep a committee secretariat in place). In all, JTC 1 has 193 such stabilized standard documents (i.e. ISs, TRs, amendments and technical corrigenda, 27 April 2004).

The notion of a 'stabilized standard' already suggests that other standards may not be stable. It shows that JTC 1 also grapples with problems of legacy and standards dynamics. A second sign of this is the notion of a 'provisionally retained edition' (ISO 2004), which is an edition that has been updated but is still valid – instead of being withdrawn, as is common procedure.[9] For example, one of the standards for quality management and quality assurance, ISO 9000-1 (1994), was revised in 2003. However, because the certification market still works with it, the 1994 edition has been retained. The 'provisionally retained edition' procedure is a double-edged sword. It allows parties who value compliance to international standards but cannot or do not wish to update their implementations, to preserve their investment. However, the validity of successive editions may cause confusion and reduce the transparency of the standards market for newcomers.

A closer look at the use of procedures for stabilized standards and provisionally retained editions reveals that they are largely used to reconfirm the current relevance of earlier open systems interconnection (OSI) standards. All 27 provisionally retained editions (ISO, 15 August 2004), and a majority of the stabilized standards (i.e. 101 out of 193), are OSI-related. This does not fit well with the widely shared feeling that OSI, because of a lack of market, is out of date.

METHODOLOGY

The empirical results presented in the next section are based on quantitative analyses of the JTC 1 database. The database was accessed in the period 12–15 July 2004, at the ISO secretariat in Geneva, Switzerland and included two types of queries. Firstly, because not all JTC 1 data is publicly available, the central secretariat carried out a number of straightforward queries (lists and frequencies) for us (i.e. not hands-on). For example, they provided a list of revised standards. In most cases such data is not suitable for statistical analysis.

Secondly, permission was granted for a direct query of data that is also publicly available via ISO's website (http://www.iso.ch). This subset of the database contains all JTC 1 standards and standard-type documents (i.e. the whole population), but not all the variables (data fields). It includes basic document features, such as standard reference, date of publication, document number, document type, committee number, and technical area addressed. It also includes the most relevant fields for standards dynamics, such as the document review stage; the date, type and number of editions, as well as the number of amendments and corrigenda. According to the international classification for standards (ICS) level 1, the documents address the technical areas of 'telecommunications, audio and video engineering' (category 33) and in particular 'information technology / office machines' (category 35).

The JTC 1 database covers data from 1969 onwards, which means that it includes data from ISO TC97, JTC 1's predecessor. Data has been gathered systematically and rigorously since 1998. Earlier data can be conflicting or missing.[10] For example, in the course of our research we discovered that the edition numbers of some standards were incorrect, not included, or included twice because the same standard document was assigned to different ICS areas. However, this is the exception rather than the rule. Moreover, due to the large number of documents, the statistical significance of the results was not affected.

SPSS 11.5 software was used to carry out the descriptive statistics (e.g. frequencies and cross tabulations), variance analysis (e.g. ANOVA and Kruskal-Wallis test) and post-hoc tests (e.g. Tamhane test). For the sake of readability, the arguments behind the choice of statistics are not discussed at length in this chapter. For a detailed account, we refer to Egyedi and Heijnen (2005).

Finally, we made a number of choices. As the reader will see, all graphs exclude the year 2004, because the data was gathered halfway through that year. Furthermore, sometimes the area which is covered by a standard is addressed by a set of document parts. In the following section, they are treated as separate standards because, for the purpose of examining standards dynamics, it is irrelevant whether an area is addressed by different standards or by different standards parts.

RESULTS

The JTC 1 database contains 2752 documents: 2318 of them are international standards (ISs), 264 are ISPs, and 170 are technical reports (TRs). In the following sections these are referred to as standards unless explicitly stated otherwise. The 2752 documents include active and withdrawn documents, different types of revisions and replacements, original documents and supplements, and old and new editions.

Below, we begin by examining these features of standards dynamics in a straightforward manner; i.e. by treating all documents equally (level 1 analysis), with the particular aim of gaining insight into developments over time. At a later point we study some of the level 1 findings in greater detail by aggregating the data with regard to main documents (level 2 analysis).

Dynamics Overall

As Figure 9.1 shows, the total number of documents published per year increases considerably from 1990 onwards, with a slight peak in 1992 and a more pronounced one in 1995, after which it decreases. The slight peak in 1992 corresponds to a deadline by the European Common Market. To remove technical barriers to trade, the European Commission put pressure on the European standards bodies to produce the required standards within the given timeframe. To increase their relevance for Europe, international standardization passed through a phase of Eurocentrism (1985–92) in formal international standards bodies (Egyedi 1996, see also Box 9.1). Both European and international standards activity increased as the deadline approached.

Taking a closer look at the peak in 1995 (N=286), 60 per cent (N=172) of the documents published in that year are related to OSI, the open system interconnection family of standards for data communication (ICS 35.100). Many of them are ISPs, i.e. OSI profiles (N=104).[11] This flurry of OSI activity is presumably caused by the rising popularity of a competing network solution: the Internet (e.g. Abbate 1994). From 1993 onwards, the implementation of Internet protocols (TCP/IP, SMTP, etc.) is gaining ground quickly.

Finally, we hypothesize that the decline in number of JTC 1 standards published after 1995 relates to the exponential growth of the number of standards consortia in the second half of the 1990s (Hawkins 1999). Where many newly founded forums and consortia previously adapted to or were assimilated in the overall formal structure (Genschel 1993), they play a more competitive role towards JTC 1 from the mid-1990s onward. They seem to represent timely and effective standardization. Although it is perhaps too early to say, it appears as if the decline in the number of JTC 1 standards published each year seems to have come to a halt. This suggests that an equilibrium has been reached between JTC 1 and the IT consortia with respect to standards work. Note: The argument may extend beyond the number of consortium standards, relative to formal standards, to the number of consortia, relative to formal bodies. Blind and Gauch (2008 forthcoming) provide indirect support by noting that the number of consortia most relevant for European IT standardization has declined since 2000.

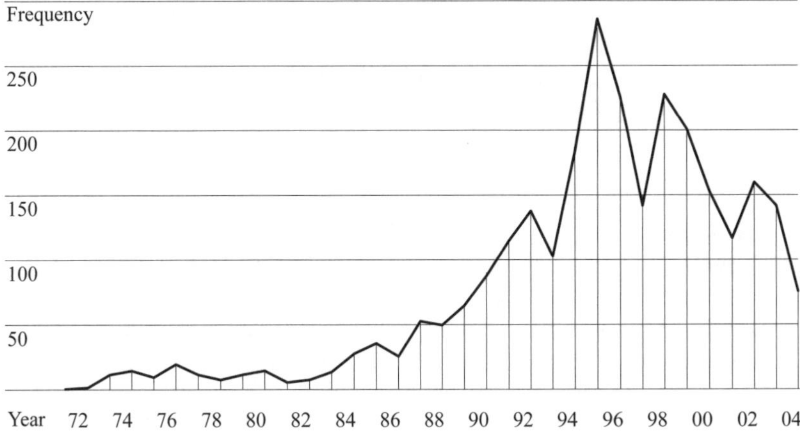

Figure 9.1 Number of standards documents published per year

Table 9.1 Overview of the changes at stake

Features of standards dynamics	Sub-category	N	Percentage of all documents
Withdrawals		990	36
Revisions	is revised by	999	36
	revises	559	20
Supplements		708	26
Editions 2–6		460	17
Replacements		132	5

Table 9.1 summarizes the scale of each type of standards change in absolute numbers and as a percentage of the total number of standards (N=2752). Below, each type of change is briefly discussed.

Withdrawals

Of the 2752 published standards, 1762 are still active, while 990 have been withdrawn (see Table 9.1). This suggests that JTC 1 takes the process of periodically reviewing standards seriously. Over time the number of withdrawn documents increases roughly proportionately to the overall number of publications (see Figure 9.2). Figure 9.2 also suggests that in the period 2001–03 the work involved with reviewing standards has been postponed to 2003 (i.e. the sharp decline in 2001–02 and the sudden increase in 2003).

BOX 9.1 EUROCENTRISM AND THE CO-OPERATION AGREEMENTS BETWEEN FORMAL EUROPEAN AND INTERNATIONAL STANDARDS BODIES

In the period leading up to the 1992 European Common Market deadline three co-operation agreements between European and International standards bodies were developed: the 'IEC-CENELEC agreement on exchange of technical information between both organisations' (IEC/CENELEC 1989), the 'IEC-CENELEC agreement on common planning of new work and parallel voting' (Dresden Agreement, IEC/CENELEC 1991) and the 'agreement on technical cooperation between ISO and CEN (Vienna Agreement, ISO/CEN 1991). Two features in these agreements are of interest. Firstly, if a European body considers new standards work, it first ascertains that the work cannot be accomplished within an international standards body. Secondly, draft international standards (DIS) automatically become European drafts (prEN). The drafts are voted upon in parallel internationally and at a European level. Likewise, a European prEN is put to a parallel vote at the international level.

The agreements offer the European partners the possibility to intervene in international standardization where work items of European origin show slow progress. In the IEC-CENELEC agreement (IEC/CENELEC 1991, p. 6), a failure of planning is grounds for withdrawing an item and continuing its standardization at a European level. Between ISO and CEN, apart from timing, reasons of technical and procedural nature are also grounds for intervention: 'CEN reaffirms the primacy of international standardization work, [...] and use of international results wherever possible [...]. However, it is to be acknowledged that CEN [...] chooses, according to the advice of its interested parties, amongst [...] possibilities.'[12] At stake is a conditional commitment of the European partners, a conditionality based on reference to European mandates and standards for European regulatory purposes.

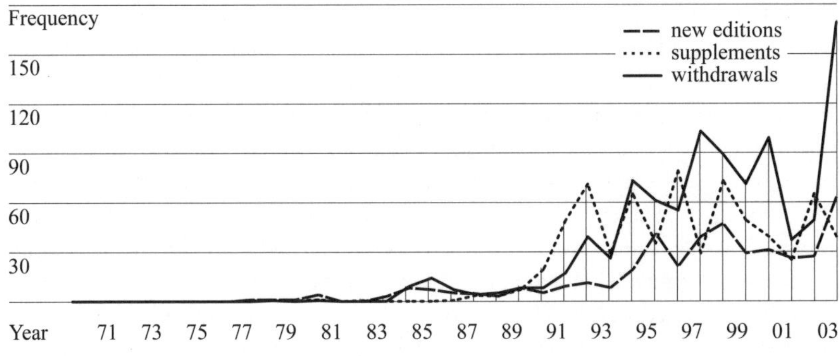

Figure 9.2 Number of changes over time: withdrawals, supplements and editions

Table 9.2 Example of a forward document revision ('revised by')

Reference	Stage started	Revised by
ISO/IEC 7816-4:1995 JTC 1/SC 17/WG 4	2001-02-23	ISO/IEC 7816-5 ISO/IEC 7816-4 ISO/IEC 7816-8:2004 ISO/IEC 7816-9:2004

Source: ISO Secretariat.

Table 9.3 Example of a backward document revision ('revises')

Reference	Stage Started	Revises
ISO/IEC 7816-9:2004 JTC 1/SC 17/WG 4	2004-06-11	ISO/IEC 7816-9:2000 ISO/IEC 7816-4:1995 ISO/IEC 7816-5:1994 ISO/IEC 7816-6:1996 ISO/IEC 7816-8:1999 ISO/IEC 7816-4:1995/Amd 1:1997 ISO/IEC 7816-5:1994/Amd 1:1996 ISO/IEC 7816-6:1996/Cor 1:1998 ISO/IEC 7816-6:1996/Amd 1:2000

Source: ISO Secretariat.

Revisions

The changes that are categorized as revisions include changes of document type, integration of or a split into several documents, etc. Some documents revise previous documents and are themselves revised by new documents later on. The result can be quite complex. For example, in 2004, part 4 of a standard for smart cards (IS 7816-4), active since 1995, is revised by a new part 4, a part 5, a part 8, and a part 9 (Table 9.2), while the new part 9 of IS 7816, active since 2004, revises and integrates several other parts as well as part 4, including the amendments and corrigenda belonging to these parts (Table 9.3). In all, 999 documents have been revised, while 559 documents have been revised into one or more other documents. The difference between the two numbers indicates that it is more common for documents to be integrated and merged than to be split up.

Replacements

In all, there are very few replacements (N=132). From the administrative angle, there are two types of replacement.[13] Firstly, there are standards that receive a new document number but that are still of the same document type. There are 109 such cases, all published between 1980 and 2004. It is striking that 70 of them have the same year of publication (i.e. 1994), which is something that neither we nor the people we talked to could explain. Secondly, 23 replacements retain their number but change document type, all published between 1988 and 2004.

Supplements

One in four (25.7 per cent, N=708) of all documents are supplementary documents: i.e. corrigendum (N=413), amendment (N=278) or addendum (N=17, addenda were only published between 1977 and 1991). The use of supplementary documents really takes off in 1990 (see Figure 9.2). From then on, the average number of supplements roughly remains stable over the years – although there are considerable variations between the years in question. Supplements also undergo changes. Half of the time they are withdrawn (53.2 per cent), which means they are less stable than main documents (30 per cent withdrawal rate).

New editions

Most documents are first editions (N=2292, i.e. 83.3 per cent). Only 16.7 per cent are higher editions (i.e. editions 2–6). The number of new editions has remained stable over the years.

Comparison and overall assessment

When we compare the various types, we see that all types of changes occur to a significant degree, with the exception of replacements and addenda. Furthermore, supplements and new editions to high degree address similar needs. Figure 9.2 shows, however, that JTC 1 prefers the use of supplements. Possibly, the work of drawing up a supplement is less demanding, given its narrower scope in comparison to a new edition.

Between 1989 and 1992, ISO/IEC procedures were adapted to shorten the standard process from seven to three years for a draft international standard (see Table 9.4). It is possible that the use of supplements has become a systematic way to deal more efficiently with complex standardization (i.e. by dividing the work and addressing difficult issues in supplementary documents).

One could also expect that, due to a) the extra time pressure and workload in 1992 and 1995, and b) a shortening of standards development time, JTC 1 may have developed less robust standards that would require a new edition

Table 9.4 Designated time for standards development

From date of inclusion project in programme of work to:	1989	1992
Working draft stage	2 years	1.5 years
Committee draft stage	5 years	2 years
Draft international standard stage	7 years	3 years

Source: ISO/IEC 1989 and 1992.

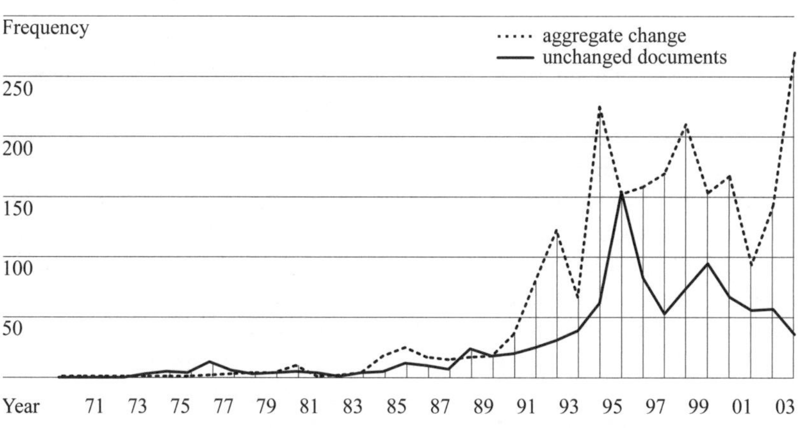

Notes:
Aggregate change: i.e. withdrawals, new editions, supplements and replacements.
Unchanged documents: no supplements, still active, first editions.

Figure 9.3 Aggregate number of changes per year and the number of unchanged main documents

more quickly, leading to an increase in the withdrawal rate. Figure 9.2 gives no indication that this is the case.

The dotted line in Figure 9.3 shows the total number of changes made to standards over the years, including replacements but excluding revisions (see earlier explanation). If we contrast this to the number of documents that have remained stable, we can conclude that the number of maintenance projects is higher than the number of pure standards development projects in JTC 1.

Dynamics of Main Documents

In the previous section the aim was to acquire a first overview of the number and type of changes at stake, treating a main document as equal to its supplements and new editions. Below, we turn to the core question as to how much change the main 'parent' documents undergo. To answer this question we need to aggregate the data on main documents, a process by which some information is lost. For example, with respect to document type, the aggregated database only contains the document type mentioned first (i.e. also information about change in document type, of which there are N=16 in all, is lost. However, because of the small number of cases to which this applies, the results will hardly be influenced.). We identify main documents by document number and part number combined, as argued in the methodology section.

There are 1527 such documents, 917 of which undergo no change (no new edition, supplement or withdrawal) – i.e. a small majority of 60.1 per cent. Throughout the period under investigation they have remained stable. The other documents, i.e. 39.9 per cent, together underwent 2158 changes in all, in some cases up to 49 changes per document (see Table 9.5).

Of the main documents, 33.9 per cent of the 'parents' have 'children' (i.e. supplements and/or new editions). Some have up to 24 children.

With regard to the distribution of changes across parents, 410 parents (26.8 per cent) are responsible for 90.7 per cent of the changes, representing an overwhelming majority of all dynamics involved. Furthermore, the changes occur primarily within ISs. That is to say, the percentage of parents with changes is significantly higher for ISs (45.9 per cent) than for ISPs (14 per cent) and TRs (28.1 per cent), as the parametric Tamhane test shows (see Table 9.6). More specifically, the difference in means between ISs and the other two types of documents is both fairly large and significant for supplements and withdrawals (see Table 9.7).

The difference in recognized status between ISs and TRs, and the level of maintenance review which ISs more likely elicit, provides one possible explanation; where ISs and ISPs are concerned, the former have a more generic focus and are therefore more open to criticism than ISPs, which have been developed for more specific purposes.

Table 9.5 Main documents

	Main documents without in %	Main documents with in %	Maximum number	Sum	Mean
Withdrawals	68.4	31.6	25	990	0.65
New editions	78.1	21.9	5	460	0.30
Corrigenda	87.4	12.6	12	413	0.27
Amendments	89.8	10.2	21	278	0.18
Addenda	99.3	0.7	3	17	0.01
Changes	60.1	39.9	49	2158	1.41
Children docs	66.1	33.9	24	1225	0.80

Table 9.6 Comparisons between types of standards and number of changes

(I) Type of standard document	(J) Type of standard document	Mean difference (I–J)	Sig.
International standard	International standard profile	1.18*	0.000
	Technical report	1.03*	0.000
International standard profile	International standard	–1.18*	0.000
	Technical report	–0.15	0.738
Technical report	International standard	–1.03*	0.000
	International standard profile	0.15	0.738

Note: * The mean difference is significant at the .05 level.

Table 9.7 Mean number of supplements, withdrawals and new editions

Type of standard document	Supplements Mean	Withdrawals Mean	New editions Mean	N
International standard	0.57	0.75	0.34	1184
International standard profile	0.12	0.22	0.14	215
Technical report	0.02	0.38	0.23	128
Total	0.46	0.65	0.30	1527

Age of Standards

How old do standards become? We restrict ourselves to the final age of parent and supplementary documents that have been withdrawn (i.e. year of

Table 9.8 Mean age of withdrawn standards

Standards	Mean	N
Main documents	*6.58*	*613*
Supplements		
Corrigendum	3.32	211
Amendment	3.11	149
Addendum	4.59	17
Total	5.33	990

withdrawal – year of publication). The average age of standards is five years (M=5.33 years; maximum age 27 years). The 5-year review procedure seems a compelling way to explain the 5-year mean. However, 'mean age' hides large differences. Most standard documents have already been withdrawn after three years (mode=3 years, N=155). This short life-span is largely attributable to the lower mean age of supplements which, as is to be expected, differs significantly from the age of main documents (since main documents precede possible supplements, and possibly outlive them – never the other way around,[14] see Table 9.8).

Over the years, the mean age of (withdrawn) standards remains relatively stable – that is to say, if one ignores the more erratic pattern in the early years caused by the low number of standards (see Figure 9.4). If we compare the average age of withdrawn standards to the average age of standards that are 'still active', the latter is much higher (M=7.35). Indeed, Figure 9.5 shows that the largest group of standard documents still active is already nine years of age (i.e. mode = nine years). The average age of the withdrawn documents is therefore not a good indicator for the expected age of still active standards.

Changes per Technology Area

Is the number of changes that a main standard document undergoes related to the technology area it addresses? We adopt the ICS categories used by JTC 1 to distinguish areas of technology. Because some areas are not sufficiently represented in the database (N<80), we have merged smaller ICS categories into new ones, and deleted others, wherever it made sense.[15] The recoded ICS categories are listed in Table 9.9.

There are significant differences between technology areas[16] (see Table 9.10). The differences show a pattern between two clusters of technology areas. One cluster consists of 35 080 (software development and system documentation), 35 220 (data storage) and 35 999 (recoded: hardware/

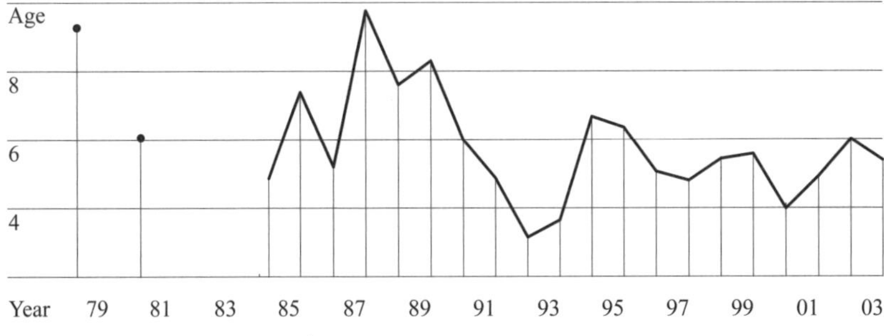

Figure 9.4 Mean age of withdrawn documents

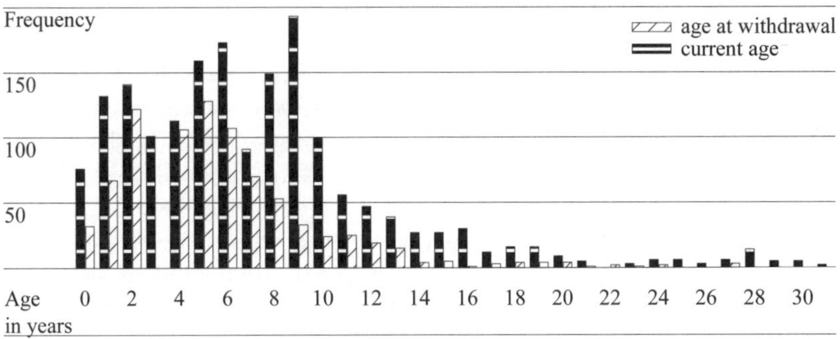

Figure 9.5 Comparison of computed age based on withdrawn standards and standards that are 'still active'

Table 9.9 Recoded ICS levels: number of changes

Recoded ICS Levels		Mean	N	Sum	Max.
33 040	Telecom systems; including network (system) aspects	1.31	114	149	10
35 020	IT in general; incl. general aspects of IT equipment	1.32	28	37	4
35 040	Character sets and Information coding	1.29	224	288	49
35 060	Languages used in IT	1.73	113	196	11
35 080	Software development and system documentation	0.21	84	18	2
35 100	Open systems interconnection (OSI)	1.82	496	904	27
35 220	Data storage	0.50	155	77	6
35 240	Applications of IT	2.33	181	422	34
35 999	Combined new category: hardware/equipment	0.52	113	59	13
Total		1.43	1508	2150	49

Table 9.10 Significant differences between means in technical areas

ICS recodes	33 040	35 040	35 060	35 080	35 100	35 220	35 240	35 999
33 040	–			x		x		x
35 040		–		x				
35 060			–	x		x		x
35 080	x	x	x	–	x		x	
35 100				x	–	x		x
35 220	x		x		x	–	x	
35 240				x		x	–	x
35 999	x		x		x		x	–

Note: x = The mean difference is significant at the 0.005 level.

equipment). In this cluster the average number of changes is low. The second cluster consists of 33 040 (recoded: networks), 35 060 (languages used in IT), 35 100 (OSI) and 35 240 (recoded: applications of IT). The hardware–software dichotomy only partly explains the difference between the clusters (the low mean of ICS category 'Software development and system documentation' and the high mean of 'networks' then remain to be explained). A better, but related, explanation is that the material feature of hardware leaves much less room for 'on the fly' improvements than software does.[17] Therefore, where hardware is concerned, standardization is more likely to occur ex-post, in other words, after the technology has been developed and tested. For software standardization, ex-ante standardization and parallel standards and technology development are more likely to occur, OSI (35 100) being a case in point. Since experience with the standard comes after the fact, more revisions can then be expected. That is to say, ex-ante (and parallel) standardization versus ex-post standardization next to the hardware–software dichotomy may in part explain cluster-specific standards dynamics. For a further analysis and discussion of technology allied standard dynamics, we recommend the next chapter by Blind.

CONCLUSION

Stability is an inherent value of standards. If we assume that stability should be the norm, we find that 40 per cent of the standards do not meet this norm. There is a clear tension between the need for stability and the need for change. Changes may be needed to support technical progress and develop new markets. However, change also creates complexity, as the revisions to the smart card standard illustrate. Complexity is more likely to create difficulties for standard implementers and possibly IT end-users. It typically decreases the transparency of a standard, makes implementation more difficult, and raises questions about the interoperability between versions.

The tension between stability and change is symbolized by the term 'stabilized standard' introduced by JTC 1. The term contains a contradiction in terms, and gives an inkling of the difficulty of addressing this tension. It also demonstrates that maintenance policy and procedures may not be workable if they are defined within the framework of standards development policy. The statistical analyses support the argument in favour of a distinct policy approach. The findings show that the number of standards maintenance projects (i.e. withdrawal, revision, supplement, etc.) outruns the number of standards development projects. Whether this also means that JTC 1 standardizers spend more time on standards maintenance than on development work requires different data.

Additional research is needed to determine whether the degree of standards change in JTC 1 is emblematic for ICT standardization in general, or even for all standards bodies. However, based on this study we can already recommend that JTC 1 draw up a policy that specifically focuses on standards maintenance. Such a policy should include addressing principled questions about the scale of standards dynamics (e.g. is a reduction in the number of changes feasible?) and about maintenance tools (e.g. is the impact of developing supplements less problematic for standardizers and end-users than developing a new edition?).

ACKNOWLEDGEMENTS

We are very grateful to Sun Microsystems who funded our research, to John Hill (Sun Microsystems), who came up with the research idea and helped us in many ways, to ISO for allowing us the use of certain JTC 1 data, for their hospitality and for helping us understand what the data signifies, and to the NO-REST colleagues Raluca Bunduchi and Knut Blind for their useful comments and suggestions.

NOTES

1. This chapter is a revised and abbreviated version of Egyedi and Heijnen (2005).
2. Transaction costs are costs that are not directly related to an economic exchange (e.g. the time and resources required to establish a common understanding). Standards reduce transaction costs of negotiation because 'both parties to a deal mutually recognize what is being dealt with' (Kindleberger 1983, p. 395).

3. An IS is a normative document, developed according to consensus procedure, which has been submitted for vote by all national bodies and approved by two-thirds of the P-members of the responsible technical committee with not more than one-fourth of all votes cast being negative. A TR is an informative document containing information of a different kind from that normally published in a normative document (e.g. collection of data), approved by a simple majority of the P-members of a technical committee or subcommittee. An ISP is an internationally agreed, harmonized document which identifies a standard or a group of standards together with options and parameters, necessary to perform a function or a set of functions (ISO 2004).
4. See the letter by Keith Brannon, ISO/IEC Information Technology Task Force, 12 February 2004, on systematic review of international standards.
5. Technical corrigenda are normally published as separate documents, the edition of the IS affected remaining in print. However, the ITTF shall decide whether to publish a technical corrigendum or a corrected reprint of the existing edition of the IS (JTC 1 2004).
6. A technical addition or change is an alteration or addition to previously agreed technical provisions in an existing IS (JTC 1 2004, Chapter 15.4.1).
7. An editorial defect is 'An error which can be assumed to have no consequences in the application of the IS, for example a minor printing error' (JTC 1 2004, Chapter 15.4.1).
8. '[H]owever, each Sub Committee shall periodically review a current list of its own stabilized standards to ensure that they still belong in stabilized status' (JTC 1 2004, Chapter 15.3.1).
9. 'Previous editions of standards (including their amendments and technical corrigenda) may be included in the ISO and IEC Catalogues on an exception basis as determined by the SC, noting that these documents should be used for reference purposes only' (JTC 1 2004, Chapter 15.1.5).
10. Private communication ISO Secretariat.
11. E.g. the ISP 10609 on 'connection-mode transport service over connection-mode network service' (N=27).
12. Revised 'Guidelines for TC/SC Chairmen and Secretariats for implementation of the Agreement on Technical Cooperation between ISO and CEN', 1992, p. 2.
13. Source: Printout provided by the ISO Secretariat (26 November 2004).
14. This is statistically confirmed (i.e. non-parametric Kruskal-Wallis test and the Tamhane post-hoc test; the category 'addendum' was excluded in the tests for its low frequency).
15. That is to say, the N for 33 050 is statistically negligible (N=1) [de-select]; there is no other category closely related to 35 260 (N=18) [de-select]; there is no obvious category closely related to 35 020 (N=28) [de-select if necessary]; both 33 040 and 35 110 (N=27) address networks [merge]; 35 140 (N=36) can be seen as an IT application area 35 240 [merge]; 35 160 (N=26), 35 180 (N=24) and 35 200 (N=63) can be captured in a new category 'hardware/equipment' [merge, recode 35 999]. A homogeneity of variances test shows that all categories are large enough to assume a normal distribution of the average number of changes – except for ICS 35 020, which is why we also leave this category out of the comparison.
16. Tamhane post-hoc test as a follow up of the non-parametric Kruskal-Wallis test.
17. The same reasoning would seem to apply to artifacts where network externalities play an important role. This needs to be examined further.

10. Factors Influencing the Lifetime of Telecommunication and Information Technology Standards

Knut Blind

INTRODUCTION

The dynamic technological changes in ICT influence the lifetime of standards, an important dimension of the dynamics of standards. The need to change or adjust standards according to new trends in ICT has definitely increased in the last decade. Furthermore, some standards became obsolete, because new technologies led to completely new generations of standards. Consequently, standards have a life cycle defined by their publication and withdrawal dates, which represents a core element of the dynamics of standards.

Despite the high level of dynamics in ICT and the importance of standards in the development of ICT and related sectors (Blind and Jungmittag 2008), there is no systematic quantitative attempt to investigate the lifetime of standards as an important dimension or indicator of the dynamics of ICT standards and their driving factors. An exception is the contribution by Egyedi and Heijnen (2005), who focus on the internal revision processes of ISO. In this chapter we compare different subcategories of ICT, looking at the situation in specific countries, based on the data of the PERINORM database published by the national SDOs British Standards Institute (BSI), Deutsches Institut für Normung (DIN) and Association Française de Normalisation (AFNOR).

In contrast to relative lack of quantitative studies, we can rely on a long tradition of conceptual analyses conducted by economists starting in the 1980s by the work of Arthur (1989), applied in David's (1985) study of the typewriter keyboard standard QWERTY and Farrell and Saloner's (1985, 1986) game theory approach. Based on network externalities, increasing returns and information asymmetries, these authors mainly explain the lock-in effects of standardization and the missing or insufficient dynamics of standards. Another kind of evolution of standards is discussed and illustrated by Swann (2000), who analyses the interplay between innovation and standardization. Starting with a basic standard, which defines the specifications of some platform technology, the field for further innovation is set in using this basic technology for various applications.

In addition to these very conceptual or theoretical approaches to standards dynamics, there are several case study analyses that focus on standard maintenance and succession in an attempt to answer the question how to deal with heritage relationships between standards (Egyedi and Loeffen 2002) and with standard integrity (Egyedi and Hudson 2005), and to discuss control mechanisms that safeguard the integrity of (*de facto*) standards. This chapter adds a methodological dimension to the analysis of the dynamics of standards by focusing on the lifetime of standards. The contribution of this chapter to the emerging research on the dynamics of standards is twofold. First, the descriptive presentation of lifetimes of standards focusing both on average publication years and survival times reflects, on the one hand, the historical development of ICT over time and, on the other hand, its dynamics in the various subfields. So far other indicators like scientific publications or patent applications have been used to describe the development especially of new technologies, e.g. biotechnology or nanotechnology. The analysis of publications of standard documents extends the former exercises by a new, more market- and diffusion-related dimension. Second, the characteristics of standard documents are used to explain their lifetimes. Here we borrow for the first time general approaches from bibliometrics and patent analysis in order to explain lifetimes of standards as an indicator of their value by document characteristics.

The remainder of the chapter is structured as follows. First, we analyse the average lifetimes of standards in a quantitative manner, taking into account differences between countries. Since the simple approach of calculating the average lifetimes of historical standards does not allow us to include standards which are still alive, we have to apply a more sophisticated methodology, the so-called survival analysis, which was initially applied mainly in medical science. The application of this statistical approach produces average lifetimes of standards, taking into account the expected lifetime of standards that are still being used. This approach is crucial, especially for the analysis of ICT standards, because the number of actively used standards is relatively high compared to historical standards. Because of the very high relevance of international standards in the ICT sector and the high quality of this subsample, we concentrate the survival analysis especially on international standards, including the standards released by the European standardization bodies. The results of this analysis provide us with new insights into the expected lifetimes of standards differentiated by technology in the ICT area. As a final step in our analysis, we try to answer the question which causal factors influence the lifetime of standards in the ICT sector. We present our initial insights by applying the so-called Cox regression, which allows us to determine whether some selected characteristics of a standard, like cross-references or references to international standards, have a significant impact on its actual or expected lifetime. The approach to assessing the importance of a technical document by analysing its references to or in other documents is part of a long tradition in evaluating the value of patents by counting and analysing their citations.[1] On the basis of the new insights, we conclude with a brief summary of the main results, and provide a number of general recommendations regarding standardization processes and the maintenance of standards.

METHODOLOGICAL ISSUES

To tackle the two major dimensions of our contribution, we apply different methodological approaches. Firstly, we perform simple descriptive statistics of average publication and withdrawal years, then continue with survival time analyses, which allow us to take into account the numerous still valid documents, and finally conduct Cox regression analyses to identify significant factors influencing the lifetimes of standards, at least in areas where sufficient statistical information is available.

For our analysis we use the PERINORM database edited by the three major national standardization bodies in Europe: BSI in the United Kingdom, DIN in Germany and AFNOR in France. The main characteristics of PERINORM edition 2004 relevant to our analysis are the following. Due to our focus on the ICT sector, we select only the documents in the field of telecommunication and information technology, including office machines, by relying on the ICS. Telecommunication is identified by ICS code 33, information technology by ICS code 35. The next level of subdivision of the two ICT-related fields is illustrated in the tables presented in this chapter. In total, we rely on more than 78 000 documents in the field of telecommunication and more than 31 000 documents in the field of information technology and office machines. The majority of the documents have been published since the beginning of the 1990s.

In our analysis, we cover the following European countries: Austria (AT), Belgium (BE), Czech Republic (CZ), Switzerland (CH), Germany (DE), Denmark (DK), Spain (ES), France (FR), Great Britain (GB), Italy (IT), Netherlands (NL), Norway (NO), Poland (PL), Russia (RU), Sweden (SE), Slovakia (SK) and Turkey (TR). In addition, international and European standards are included (IX).

The quality of the data is fairly heterogeneous, since the databases of the founding countries France, Germany and Great Britain are of higher quality than those of most other countries. The information regarding the standards that has been released by the international bodies is also of good quality.

It has to be noted that the European and international standards have to be included in the set of national standards, because of the requirement to CEN and ISO members to integrate and implement the European and international standards respectively.

Although each document is described by almost 50 characteristics, we rely mainly on the following search areas: classification, cross references, expiry date, international relationship, issuing body, origin code, publication date, replaced by, replaces, status, withdrawal date.

In the more sophisticated analyses, we have to restrict ourselves to countries that provide high quality data for most of the relevant classification fields. Because of the differences between telecommunication and information technology and due to the large number of documents and descriptors, we have set up two separate databases.

DESCRIPTIVE RESULTS

We began by analysing the average publication and withdrawal dates, differentiated both by technological area and by country. We concentrate on all standards documents, i.e. including drafts and pre-standards, by calculating the average of their publication date. In calculating withdrawal dates, we are able to consider only those documents that have already been withdrawn. The difference between the average publication and withdrawal dates provides an initial indication of the dynamics of standards in the different subfields.

In Table 10.1, we present the average publication and withdrawal dates for the various technological areas in telecommunication technology. The average publication dates vary between 1993 and 1998. The oldest documents can be found in the area of measuring equipment to be used in telecommunication, with an average publication date as far back as 1993. On average, standards regarding components and accessories for telecommunication equipment were published in 1994, those on telecommunication terminal equipment in 1995. By contrast, if we look at the standardization fields with more recent average publication dates, we find standards for fibre optic communications, with an average year of publication of 1999. On average, standards for telecommunication services and mobile services are published in 1998. This initial picture is in line with the technological and market-related development in telecommunication. First, standards are needed to solve the general measurement and testing problems, then to secure the compatibility between components of the equipment and the terminal equipment itself. As the technology and the market itself mature, we observe a shift in the focus from fixed to mobile telephony. This is also reflected by the delayed publication of standards for mobile services. Furthermore, the telecommunication

Table 10.1 Average publication and withdrawal dates in telecommunications differentiated by area of standardization

Categories	Publication date	Withdrawal date
Telecommunications in general including infrastructure	1996.59	1998.13
Telecommunication services	1998.34	2000.56
Telecommunication systems including network (system) aspects	1996.25	1998.14
Telecommunication terminal equipment	1995.25	1999.18
Radio communications	1996.61	1998.06
Mobile services	1998.08	1998.11
Integrated services digital network (ISDN)	1997.27	1998.27
Electromagnetic compatibility (EMC) including radio interference	1998.19	1999.63
Components and accessories for telecommunications equipment	1994.59	1998.73
Special measuring equipment for use in telecommunications	1993.28	1997.88
Audio, video and audiovisual engineering	1995.57	1997.66
Television and radio broadcasting	1996.76	1998.32
Fibre optic communications	1999.03	1999.43
Telecontrol telemetering including supervising, control and data acquisition	1997.11	1997.94

industry experiences a further shift toward service-related applications, i.e. at a later stage we observe the publications of standards structuring telecommunication services. In summary, the ranking of the average publication dates reflects the historical development of the telecommunication technology, which means that in telecommunication the development of standards follows the technology life cycle.

Although Egyedi and Heijnen (2005) indicate that the average withdrawal dates are not good indicators for the expected lifetime of standards, in this section we report also the average withdrawal dates. However, we perform a more sophisticated analysis which allows us to calculate the expected lifetimes of standards in the next section. In general, we observe a rough correlation between average publication and withdrawal dates. However, the fields of standardization which started relatively early are characterized by larger differences between withdrawal and publication dates. In the emerging fields of telecommunication standardization, the differences between average withdrawal and publication date are smaller, which is caused by the fact that the

Table 10.2 Average publication and withdrawal dates in telecommunications for various countries

Country	Number of standards	Publication date	Withdrawal date
International standards	18154	1995.26	1997.46
Austria	8377	1998.31	1999.27
Belgium	4679	1999.76	2001.64
Switzerland	1663	1995.18	1998.23
Czech Republic	3374	1998.25	2002.48
Germany	6983	1994.64	1997.30
Denmark	5355	1999.02	2000.21
Spain	1792	1996.13	1999.69
France	2927	1996.90	1999.17
United Kingdom	2029	1997.26	1999.77
Italy	19	1994.89	2002.33
Netherlands	5785	1997.44	1999.53
Norway	2467	1998.00	1998.44
Poland	1122	2000.02	2003.00
Russia	446	1988.95	1999.70
Sweden	4405	1997.46	1998.33
Slovakia	4654	1999.71	2000.69
Turkey	1422	1998.16	2002.00

majority of the standards in these areas are still operational. An exception is the area of telecommunication services, where a significant share of standards has obviously already been withdrawn.

In Table 10.2 we present the average publication and withdrawal dates differentiated by country. The overview confirms that the country-specific databases vary significantly. On the one hand, there are only small differences between the averages of the large central European countries. On the other hand, the data of the eastern European countries indicate that Russia has relatively old standards documents based on an average publication date prior to 1990, whereas the Czech Republic, Slovakia, Poland and Turkey have a rather young set of standards, with an average publication year close to 2000. Whereas the Russian case is certainly influenced by a rather old and small national stock of standards, which has only recently been linked to the international standardization activities, the other four countries have by now been linked to CEN or in case of telecommunication to ETSI, which means that they implement the stock of European standards in their national standardiz-

Table 10.3 Average publication and withdrawal dates in information technology differentiated by area of standardization

Categories	Publication date	Withdrawal date
IT in general	1995.33	1995.16
Character sets and information coding	1996.19	1997.69
Languages used in information technology	1996.01	1998.22
Software including software development, documentation, internet applications and use	1995.12	1996.08
OSI	1995.75	1998.11
Networking including LAN, MAN, WAN	1995.80	1998.11
Computer graphics	1994.53	1998.20
Microprocessor systems including PCs, calculators, etc.	1992.44	1997.19
IT terminal and other peripheral equipment including modems	1994.75	1996.77
Interface and interconnection equipment	1993.98	1995.26
Data storage devices	1990.49	1994.70
Applications of information technology	1996.88	1998.39
Office machines	1986.26	1993.52

ation system. Since they possessed only a small stock of domestic standards, the implementation of the European stock of telecommunication standards rejuvenated the national stock of standards drastically. The European effect can also be observed in Belgium, which has no significant standardization activities of its own.

In the next step, we look at the dynamics of standards in the field of information technology. In Table 10.3 we are again able to detect the life cycle of information technology in the averages of the publication dates. Standardization obviously began in the field of office machines in general, with an average publication date in 1986. Standards in the area of data storage devices have an average publication date of just after 1990. Microprocessor systems underwent a standardization phase with an average publication date of 1992. There are no significant differences in the remaining average publication dates, which are all in the interval between 1994 and 1996, with the exception of information technology, where standards on average were published in the year 1997.

The average withdrawal dates correlate fairly closely with the average publication dates. Obviously, the historical standards for office machines are characterized by the largest difference between average publication and

Table 10.4 Average publication and withdrawal dates in information technology differentiated by country

Country	Number of standards	Publication date	Withdrawal date
International standards	9429	1995.44	1997.14
Austria	1552	1995.97	1997.65
Belgium	740	1996.07	2002.11
Switzerland	860	1993.14	1996.54
Czech Republic	1412	1998.22	2002.64
Germany	3396	1992.88	1995.41
Denmark	2384	1997.81	2000.10
Spain	642	1997.32	2001.72
France	1508	1993.57	1998.95
United Kingdom	2510	1996.67	1999.48
Italy	721	1995.02	2002.27
Netherlands	2086	1997.55	1993.58
Norway	484	1993.97	2000.45
Poland	493	1998.24	2003.00
Russia	519	1992.25	1999.76
Sweden	1561	1992.55	1997.04
Slovakia	814	1996.96	1999.39
Turkey	663	1996.93	n.a.

withdrawal date. Historically, software standards have much shorter lifetimes. The differentiation of information technology standards by country (Table 10.4) reveals a much more heterogeneous picture than in the field of telecommunication. The average publication year varies from 1992 to later than 1998.

For the eastern European countries, we find a pattern similar to that found in telecommunications of relatively late publication and withdrawal dates. Again, Russia is characterized by a relatively early average standard publication year. In the case of the Netherlands, we even find that the average publication year is later than the average withdrawal year, which is caused by the fact that only a few documents were withdrawn during the 1990s, while a majority of the documents was published since the end of the 1990s.[2] However, the homogeneous picture among the central European countries observed in the telecommunication sector cannot be detected in the information technology sector. Consequently, country-specific analyses are required in the following analytical steps.

RESULTS OF THE SURVIVAL ANALYSIS

As indicated in the previous section, comparing average withdrawal and publication dates is not a robust and reliable enough method to provide indications about the average lifetimes of standards. Furthermore, the survival times indicate the dynamics within a field of standardization, i.e. the higher the dynamics, the shorter the survival times. Complementary, the average publication dates of standards may provide information about the development of a technology, e.g. which starts out with standards for hardware components and moves later to applications and services. In order to determine the survival times, we apply the so-called Kaplan-Meier survival analysis (for technical details, see Norusis 1996). Survival analyses have their origin in the testing of the effectiveness of medical treatments, especially on the survival times of patients. However, by now the methodology is also used to analyse the duration of unemployment and other economic phenomena, e.g. the expected lifespan of companies (Cantner et al. 2004).

In the following section, we present the results of survival analyses as applied only to the final standard documents differentiated by country and technological area. In an explorative analytical step we compared the expected survival times of draft or pre-standards with those of standards themselves. We found very short survival times for all the draft and preliminary documents, irrespective of the country and area of technology to which they applied. Because of this artificial phenomenon, we restrict our analysis to the sub-sample of final standard documents in contrast to the approach presented in the previous section. Because in this analysis we differentiate on the basis of countries and areas of technology, the number of observations is sometimes reduced to a level that does not allow us to apply the survival analysis. As we observed earlier, significant differences between the countries in the average publication and withdrawal dates, exist with regard to the expected survival times.

In Figure 10.1, we present the expected survival times of telecommunications and information technology standards differentiated by country. On average, international standards survive for 22.5 years in telecommunications and 16.5 years in the field of information technology.[3] Poland, Russia and Slovakia are characterized by expected survival times of over 30 years; the same is true for Belgium, with an expected survival time of over 40 years. In the database of these countries, there is a dominance of relatively old standards, which are still being used. However, these results can also be generated by a very few standards published early, which are still alive, and a majority of rather new and probably international and European standards, which are also not yet withdrawn. Whereas the results of these countries are rather biased by some special effects, the calculations for the other European

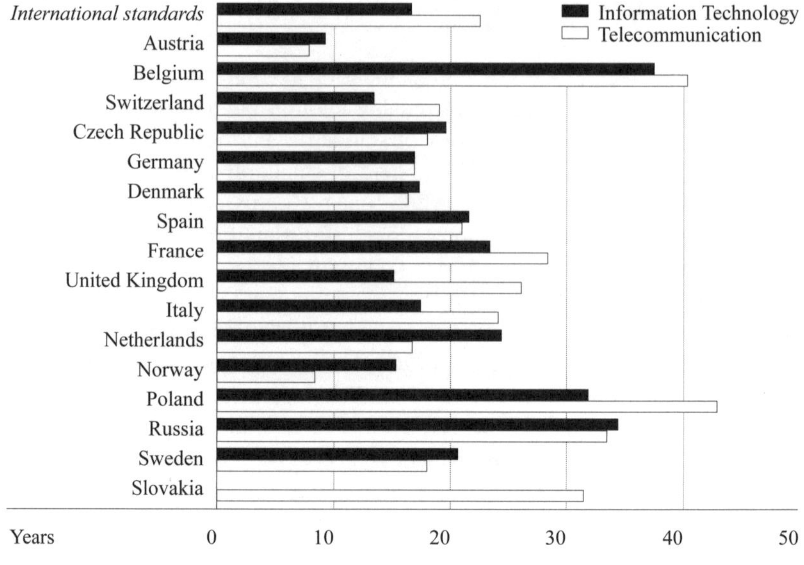

Figure 10.1 Survival times of telecommunication and information technology standards in years by country

countries are more reliable. We observe three clusters of countries. The survival times of standards in France and Great Britain are longer than the European standards. The Nordic and central European countries, including the Czech Republic, have lower survival times. Whereas France and Great Britain still have a significant and slightly older stock of national standards, the other countries are obviously more heavily influenced by the standardization activities at European and international levels, which require the withdrawal of existing national standards. Here, we also observe a difference between Germany , on the one hand, and France and Great Britain on the other; Germany is obviously under a stronger international and European influence when it comes to telecommunication standards. In general, the survival analysis confirms the country-specific heterogeneity of the standards life cycle data already observed by analysing the average publication and withdrawal dates.

The variation of the survival times between countries can also be observed among the information technology standards. For most of the countries, we observe partly similar patterns as in the telecommunication area. On the one hand, Belgium, Poland and Russia are again characterized by very high expected survival times. On the other hand, in most central European countries, for instance Germany, the survival times of information technology standards are not very different from those of international and European standards.

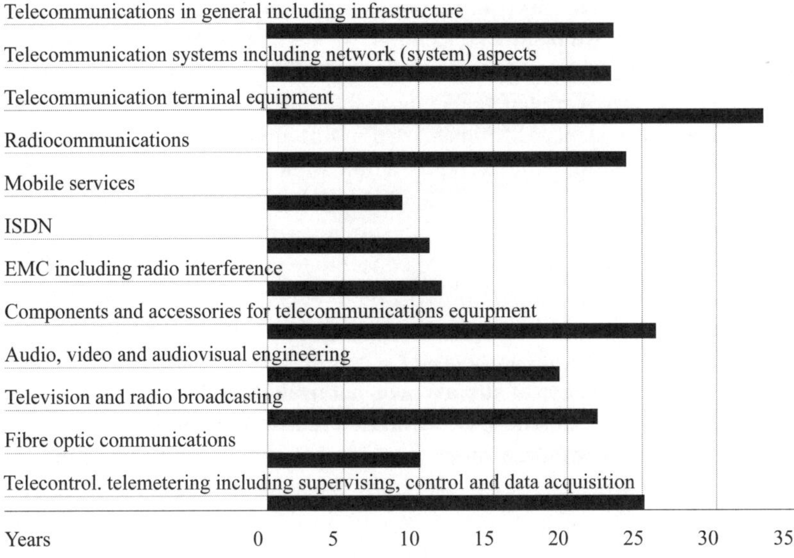

Figure 10.2 *Survival times of international telecommunication standards by area of standardization*

Again, with survival times of less than ten years, Austria represents an exception. In contrast to the general pattern of shorter survival times among information technology standards compared to the telecommunication standards, the Dutch information technology standards on average last more than seven years longer than the Dutch telecommunication standards. The same is true for Norwegian and, to a limited extent, Swedish standards.

Comparing the survival times of telecommunication and information technology standards reveals the country-specific influence by the high correlation of the survival times in both areas of technology. The major conclusion here is that we should calculate the data in a country-specific way. In the next step, we check whether – as expected and already indicated by the average publication and withdrawal dates – we find also technology-specific differences in the survival times.

In our presentation of the survival times differentiated by area of standardization (Figure 10.2), we concentrate on the European and international standards, because for telecommunication and information technology European and international standards are much more relevant than national standardization activities. Furthermore, the database of the European and international standards is much larger and more complete than the databases of the national standards, which allows for much more differentiated analyses. Keeping in mind that the average survival time of telecommunication standards in general is 22.5 years, we mainly concentrate on the largest deviations from this mean value. The expected survival times for telecommunication terminal equipment standards are ten years longer than the average. On the one hand, this indicates that standardization started in this area earlier than in the other sub-areas. Furthermore, the average lifetime of historical documents that are already withdrawn has to be sufficiently long. Both explanations are consistent with reality. Since there is no other sub-area with significantly longer survival times than the average, we now concentrate on the sub-areas with rather short survival times. First, we observe the relatively short survival times of standards for mobile services, which are even lower when we take the very recent ETSI standards into account. This conforms to the explanation already provided in the context of the average publication and withdrawal dates. The development of mobile services started relatively late in comparison to telecommunication standardization in general, and as a consequence the expected survival times are relatively short. Whereas the development of services always occurs at a rather late stage of the development of a technology and industry, in telecommunications we observe the emergence of fibre optic communication since the late 1990s. Consequently, standardization activities started later than in telecommunications in general. The standardization activities to ensure 'electromagnetic compatibility (EMC)' also started rather late, as we can see from the average publication dates presented earlier. Therefore, the expected survival times of these standards are around ten years, which is much shorter than those of telecommunication standards in general. Finally, the relatively short survival times of standards related to 'integrated services digital network (ISDN)' must be discussed. Although standardization started quite early in this field, the expected lifetimes are shorter than they are in comparative sub-areas (see Table 10.1 with the publication dates). Obviously, there have been more revisions of standards, leading to withdrawals of existing standards and to a shortening of lifetimes.

If we now summarize the results of the survival analysis of international telecommunication standards, three main results have to be noted. Firstly, the average survival times depend to a large extent on when the respective standardization activities were started, i.e. since standardization for telecommunication hardware took place before the 1990s, the expected survival times of these standards is much higher than those of mobile services standards, which were mostly released after the mid-1990s. This also confirms that telecommunication standards were published relatively early and turned out to be fairly stable. Secondly, the survival times of standards in telecommunications reflect – in the same way as the average publication years – the life cycle of telecommunication technology areas, which started out with traditional hardware and equipment, followed by application and services. Since fibre optic

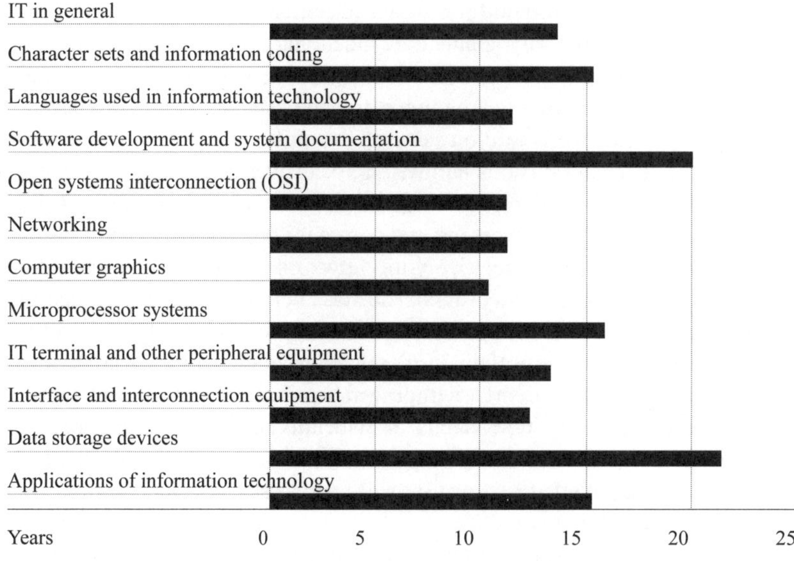

Figure 10.3 Survival times of international information technology standards by area of standardization

communication technology emerged only recently, the respective standards appeared in recent years, causing relatively short survival times. Thirdly, we find some technology-specific dynamics in the survival times, i.e. there are sub-areas in which standards are more frequently revised and withdrawn than in other areas. One example of such a sub-area is the international ISDN standards, which have much shorter survival times than standards in other fields, which were published on average at the same time.

After presenting and analysing the survival times of the international telecommunication standards, we now have a look at the survival times of the international information technology standards (Figure 10.3). On average, the survival time of an international information technology standard is 16.5 years, which is five years less than the average telecommunication standard. This underlines the fact that the level of dynamics is higher in the information technology standardization compared to the telecommunication technology standardization.

In contrast to the average survival times, we find an expected survival time of more than 20 years for standards for data storage devices. This is caused by the fact that standardization in this area started relatively early, as early as the 1980s. Standards for software development and system documentation also have a survival time of 20 years, but the standardization activities in this area on average were initiated five years later than they were for data storage devices. From this, we are able conclude that in the latter field standards are revised, adjusted to new generations of storage devices or even storage technologies more frequently than the more basic standards for software development, which focus more on general principles and terminologies, and obviously need fewer revisions and withdrawals over time.

If we focus on standardization sub-areas with relatively short survival times, we identify OSI, networking and computer graphics. The latter field is obviously characterized by relatively high dynamics, especially triggered by a rapid technical change, since standardization activities had already started relatively early. The OSI-related standards have also a relatively limited lifetime. In addition, if we use the additional information on the average withdrawal dates, we find an early withdrawal year relative to the publication year. If we compare the OSI standards with the networking standards, we see a similar survival time, but a much later average withdrawal date, which allows us to conclude that in the latter sub-area a larger number of standards has already been withdrawn.

A summary of the survival analysis of international telecommunication and information standards yields the following main new insights. The survival times of telecommunication standards are much longer than those of information technology standards, although the average publication dates do not differ significantly. Consequently, the dynamics within standards of information technology are much higher than those in telecommunication technology. In the latter field, survival times are much more heterogeneous, with relatively low survival times in the case of standards for mobile services, and high survival times in the case of telecommunication terminal equipment. In information technology, we merely observe that standards for data storage devices, software development and system documentation have a much higher survival time than the average for information technology standards. In the next section, we try to identify factors influencing the lifetimes of standards.

FACTORS INFLUENCING THE SURVIVAL TIMES OF STANDARDS: RESULTS OF THE COX REGRESSION ANALYSIS

In the previous section, we calculated and interpreted the survival times of telecommunication and information technology standards. Despite the fact that there are differences between the various countries, in some cases caused by country-specific data quality, the analysis of the European and international standards indicates that technology-specific reasons influence the survival times. In this final section, by applying the Cox regression methodology for a small selection of countries, we analyse which influences standard-specific characteristics have on the survival times of standards.

Based on the data which is available for each standard document, we developed the following hypotheses:

1. If a standard amends another standard, then the expected lifetime is increased, because it has the character of a more basic and therefore longer lasting standard.
2. If a standard is amended by another standard, then the expected lifetime of the latter is decreased, because the likelihood of a full substitution by another standard is higher.
3. If a standard replaces another standard, its expected lifetime is higher, because the weaknesses of the predecessor standards have been solved.
4. If a standard is replaced by another standard, its expected lifetime is lower, because of the replacement.
5. If a standard has a cross reference to another standard, its expected lifetime is higher, because it is embedded in a whole network of standards, which is more stable than single and isolated standards.
6. If a standard has a cross reference to another standard, its expected lifetime is lower, because it is embedded in a whole network of standards, which is more likely to be affected by external influences.
7. If a standard has a reference to an international standard, its expected lifetime is lower, because the international standard is likely to change faster.
8. If a standard has a reference to an international standard, its expected lifetime is higher, because changing an international standard is likely to take more time.
9. If a standard has a reference to regulation, its expected lifetime is higher, because changes in legislation take longer and its relevance is higher.
10. If a standard contains more pages, its expected lifetime is higher, because the volume of codified knowledge is higher, which may cause further inertia (it may even represent the merger of various standards).

Since some data fields are not filled out for the countries we selected, we had to restrict ourselves to testing some hypotheses only for a few countries or even a single country. Furthermore, in general, we do not differentiate on the basis of the sub-areas, because the number of observations is then too low to generate significant results.

In order to test the above hypotheses, we apply the so-called Cox regression model. This approach allows us to investigate whether and in what direction exogenous variables influence the survival probability of the standards documents. The methodology is a multiple regression or logistic regression analysis, which allows the inclusion of documents that are still being used, like the Kaplan-Meier survival analysis.

The cumulative survival function $S(t)$, i.e. the proportion of the surviving cases at a particular point of time t, is the dependent variable. In a further step, the cumulative survival function at point t is calculated under the influence of the exogenous variables x_1 to x_n, which relate to the hypotheses above, as:

$$S(t) = [S_0(t)]^p \tag{10.1}$$

with $S_0 = S_0(t)$ as baseline survival function at time t, the exponent p is determined by:

$$p = e^{(Bixi)} \tag{10.2}$$

with $i = 1$ to n explaining variables.

The estimation of the coefficients B_1 to B_n will be solved by the Cox regression analysis. If all coefficients B_1 to B_n were equal to zero, then p would have the value of one and the baseline survival function would not be influenced by the exogenous variables (covariates). Positive coefficients B_i reduce the survival probability, negative ones increase the survival probability.

In Table 10.5, the exogenous variables for explaining the survival times of standards documents are summarized.

First, we calculate separate regression models for each variable. In Tables 10.6 and 10.7 the results for the telecommunication and information technology standards are summarized. We concentrate our analysis on the data of international, Austrian, Swiss, German, French, British and Dutch standards, but have to restrict ourselves to a sub-set of these countries for the variables ‘amended’, ‘amended by’ and ‘legislation’.

The results for the variables ‘amended’ and ‘amended by’ confirm for the selected countries that both documents which amended and were amended by another document have a significantly higher survival time than documents that do not have this kind of cross references. Therefore, the first hypothesis, that if one standard amends another standard, the expected lifetime is increased, is confirmed. Obviously amended standards have the character of a more basic and therefore longer lasting standard. However, if a standard is amended by another standard, its expected lifetime is increased and not decreased. The explanation for this phenomenon, which we observed in some countries, may be that amendments obviously stabilize a standard in general and reduce the likelihood of a general withdrawal.

Table 10.5 Meanings and names of exogenous variables

Meaning	Name of variable
Standard amends another standard	B_1 amends
Standard is amended by another standard	B_2 amended by
Standard replaces another standard	B_3 replaces B_{3a} number of replacements
Standard is replaced by another standard	B_4 replaced by
Standard has a cross reference to another standard	B_5 cross reference B_{5a} number of cross references
Standard has a cross reference to an international standard	B_6 international reference B_{6a} number of international references
Standard has a reference to legislation	B_7 legislation
Number of pages	B_8 pages

With regard to the second pair of hypotheses, focusing on replacements, we find a consistent picture for the evident hypothesis that if a standard is replaced by another standard, its expected lifetime is lower. However, the hypothesis that if a standard replaces another standard, its expected lifetime should be higher, because the weaknesses of the predecessor standards have been solved, can only be confirmed for half of the countries considered. In the Netherlands, we even find a confirmation for information technology and a rejection for telecommunication standards. In telecommunication technology the hypothesis is rejected only in Great Britain, in information technology also in France and Switzerland.

Testing the hypotheses focusing on cross and international references reveals rather ambivalent results. For the standards in telecommunication technology, the hypothesis that if a standard has a cross reference to another standard, its expected lifetime is lower, because it is embedded in a whole network of standards, which is more likely to be affected by external influences, is confirmed by international, German and British standards. The analysis including instead the continuous variable of number of cross references confirms this result. However, the data from Austria, Switzerland, France and the Netherlands confirm the opposite hypothesis. For the standards in information technology, the latter hypothesis is confirmed for all countries except Germany and France. If we use the number of cross references, the data for Great Britain also confirm the hypothesis that the expected survival time of a standard will decrease with an increasing number of cross references.

The reference to an international standard reduces the expected lifetime of a telecommunication standard for the international, the Austrian and the

Table 10.6 Results of Cox regression analysis for telecommunication standards

Variable	International standards		Austria		Switzerland		Germany		France		UK		Netherlands
	B	Sig	B	Sig	B	Sig	B	Sig	B	Sig	B	Sig	B
B_1 amends	−0.136	0.006	n.a	n.a.	n.a	n.a.	n.a	n.a.	n.a	n.a.	n.a.	n.a.	−3.622
B_2 amended by	−0.558	0.000	n.a	n.a.	n.a	n.a.	n.a	n.a.	n.a	n.a.	0.238	0.124	−3.612
B_3 replaces	−0.432	0.000	−0.671	0.000	0.358	0.324	−0.473	0.000	0.379	0.250	0.375	0.009	0.547
B_{3a} number of replacments	−2.341	0.000	−0.403	0.000	0.146	0.529	−0.253	0.000	0.171	0.088	0.158	0.108	0.290
B_4 replaced by	3.600	0.000	5.139	0.000	3.075	0.000	2.538	0.000	4.402	0.000	2.829	0.000	6.143
B_5 cross reference	0.142	0.000	−1.053	0.000	−0.350	0.014	0.183	0.000	−0.458	0.001	0.467	0.025	−4.682
B_{5a} number of cross references	0.003	0.000	−0.025	0.000	−0.026	0.002	0.005	0.000	−0.002	0.685	0.020	0.000	−1.334
B_6 international reference	0.047	0.039	0.600	0.000	1.064	0.142	0.779	0.000	0.241	0.160	−0.356	0.027	−0.214
B_{6a} number of international references	−0.096	0.000	0.303	0.000	0.084	0.219	0.102	0.000	0.067	0.295	−0.130	0.145	−0.604
B_7 legislation	n.a	n.a.	n.a	n.a.	n.a	n.a.	0.338	0.000	n.a	n.a.	n.a	n.a.	n.a
B_8 pages	0.001	0.000	−0.002	0.000	0.002	0.170	0.003	0.000	0.002	0.264	0.005	0.001	0.000

Table 10.7 Results of Cox regression analysis for information technology standards

Variable	International standards		Austria		Switzerland		Germany		France		UK		Netherlands	
	B	Sig	B	Sig	B	Sig	B	Sig	B	Sig	B	Sig	B	Sig
B_1 amends	−0.267	0.000	n.a.	n.a.	n.a.	n.a.	n.a.	n.a.	0.276	0.181	n.a.	n.a.	−3.085	0.002
B_2 amended by	−0.615	0.000	n.a.	n.a.	n.a.	n.a.	n.a.	n.a.	−0.167	0.512	−0.291	0.004	−3.065	0.002
B_3 replaces	−0.710	0.000	−0.630	0.000	0.382	0.027	−0.498	0.000	0.586	0.000	0.266	0.005	−0.449	0.000
B_{3a} number of replacments	−0.372	0.000	−0.427	0.000	0.075	0.561	−0.248	0.000	0.294	0.000	0.143	0.001	−0.257	0.010
B_4 replaced by	2.862	0.000	2.421	0.000	1.741	0.000	2.103	0.000	2.393	0.000	2.142	0.000	7.508	0.000
B_5 cross reference	−0.086	0.008	−1.091	0.000	−0.372	0.004	0.234	0.001	0.538	0.000	−0.354	0.001	−4.709	0.000
B_{5a} number of cross references	−0.008	0.000	−0.053	0.000	0.001	0.949	0.006	0.001	0.015	0.000	0.010	0.000	−1.095	0.000
B_6 international reference	−0.218	0.000	0.400	0.030	1.072	0.011	0.215	0.000	0.449	0.001	0.131	0.265	−0.813	0.008
B_{6a} number of international references	−0.046	0.000	0.013	0.733	−0.064	0.048	0.043	0.004	0.137	0.000	−0.018	0.764	0.067	0.433
B_7 legislation	n.a.	n.a.	n.a.	n.a.	n.a.	n.a.	−0.238	0.175	n.a.	n.a.	n.a.	n.a.	n.a.	n.a.
B_8 pages	0.001	0.000	−0.001	0.041	0.002	0.001	0.000	0.275	0.001	0.059	0.001	0.062	0.001	0.043

German sample, whereas the longevity of standards increases in the British database. In information technology, international references lead to a reduction of the lifetime, with the exception of the international[4] and the Dutch databases. If we use the counts of international references, only the expected lifetime of standards of the Swiss and international databases increases with the number of international references.

Due to data restriction, we are only able to test the hypotheses that if a standard has a reference to regulation its expected lifetime is higher, because changes in legislation take longer and their relevance is higher, for Germany. We find this hypothesis is rejected in the telecommunication area and that there is no significant relationship for information technology. One explanation for this rejection may be that the liberalization and deregulation of the telecommunication sector has caused a relatively frequent change of regulations, which also causes the pressure to adapt the referred standards more often.

Finally, we wanted to test whether the quantity of content in standards, measured by the number of pages, has an impact on their survival times. In contrast to our hypothesis, that the more pages a standard contains, the higher its expected lifetime is, the opposite hypothesis is confirmed for most of the regressions. Only in Austria did larger standard documents correspond to a longer expected life. The reason for this counterintuitive result is the recent trend to produce larger standards documents.

Because of the fairly heterogeneous results between the few countries we have considered, we had a more in-depth look at the sub-areas of the international standards.[5] We then find relatively strong empirical evidence for some of the previous hypotheses. Whereas there is no empirical support for the hypothesis that standards that amend other documents have a longer expected survival time, standards that are amended by other documents have a longer life expectancy in a majority of the subclasses. This contrasts with our hypothesis that a standard amended by another standard has a reduced expected lifetime, because the likelihood of a general substitution might be higher. In line with our hypothesis, there is strong empirical support to suggest that standard documents that replace existing documents have a longer life expectancy. Consequently, the number of documents being replaced increases the survival time of the respective standards. In addition, the ambivalent role of the existence of cross references or international cross references supports the two contradicting aspects of cross references. On the one hand, a standard with cross references to other standards is embedded in a whole network of standards, which should be more stable than single and isolated standards. On the other hand, a standard with cross references to other standards may be also influenced by changes in the area of the referenced standards. The link to a regulation is negative as far as German telecommunication standards are concerned, but it is slightly positive for German information technology standards. This means that our hypothesis, that the expected lifetime is higher with a link to regulation, because changes in legislation take longer and its relevance is higher, is not confirmed only for the latter area. Finally, in most countries the survival time in the two areas decreases with an increasing number of pages representing a larger volume of codified knowledge even the merger of various standards.

A summary of the results of the Cox regression yields the following general new insights. Firstly, the document-specific information on predecessor and successor documents confirm, on the one hand, for the majority of countries and technological sub-areas that standards which replace a preceding document have a longer survival time compared to documents without a predecessor. Secondly, as was expected, standards with a successor document have a shorter expected lifetime. Thirdly, the existence and number of cross references have a heterogeneous influence on the lifetimes of standards, depending on the country and technological area involved. References to international information technology standards reduce the lifetime of standards at least for the majority of country-specific documents. Finally, the length of standard documents measured in number of pages correlates negatively with their survival time, which at face value is counter-intuitive. However, this result can be explained by the fact that standard documents published earlier are much shorter than documents that have been published recently.

CONCLUSION

We performed an analysis of the telecommunication and information technology standards published by formal international, European and national standardization bodies in an attempt to identify patterns within the dynamics of standards and factors influencing those dynamics. We were able to detect the patterns of dynamics based on quantitative statistics regarding average publication and withdrawal years, and expected survival times, which are consistent with well-known technological and market-related characteristics. However, we have also found country-specific patterns that are caused either by institutional reasons, like the participation in the European standardization activities, or by the quality of the database.

The analysis of factors influencing the dynamics of standards is restricted by two dimensions. Firstly, we have to rely in general on the additional information provided by the database. Consequently, only a limited number of hypotheses could be tested. Secondly, the quality of document-specific information tends to be quite heterogeneous. This means we have had to restrict our analysis to a few selected countries and to international and European standards. Nevertheless, the results of the analysis confirmed some of our hypotheses, as well as providing new insights. Generally speaking, the dynamics of standards depend both on the country under investigation and on the characteristics of the technology involved.

Since both the institutional framework, i.e. the processes in the national standardization bodies, and the characteristics of technology, e.g. platform technology or application, affect the lifetime of standards, these two dimensions have to be further taken into account when analysing information in this area of research. Furthermore, approaches have to be developed that will allow us to match additional information to each standard document systematically, because this facilitates the testing of further more sophisticated hypotheses about the causes influencing the dynamics of standards.

In addition, it has to be pointed out that the new insights can be used to improve standardization processes. The observations that the lifetimes of standards are influenced both by related technology and the institutional framework should be considered by the standardization bodies. Firstly, different technologies obviously require specific adjustment or withdrawal strategies in standardization. Consequently, standardization bodies should be more aware of the heterogeneity involved and adapt their processes accordingly, always taking into account the continuous changes that take place in science, technologies and markets. The differences between countries call for two strategies. Firstly, benchmarking exercises may help identify best practices in the adaptation of processes to adjust, modify or even withdraw existing standards. Secondly, and even more importantly, is the necessity to homogenize the maintenance processes among countries, to avoid inconsistencies that may jeopardize the development of technologies, but also common markets. This also includes a more homogeneous implementation or transfer of international and European standards into the body of national standards.

ACKNOWLEDGEMENTS

The author wants to express his gratitude for the financial contribution to the NO-REST project (507626) by the European Commission within the 6th Framework Programme. The chapter was developed within the workpackage on the dynamics of standards of the NO-REST project. A previous version of this chapter was published in the proceedings of the IEEE SIIT 2005 conference in Geneva and in a special issue of the *International Journal of IT Standards and Standardization Research*. Valuable comments from the co-editor of this special issue, Mostafa Hashem Sherif, and from the co-editor of this book, Tineke Egyedi, significantly increased the quality of this chapter. Remaining shortcomings are the sole responsibility of the author.

NOTES

1. See, for example, the recent publication by Hall et al. (2001).
2. The standard data of Turkey do not provide even one document with a withdrawal date, which questions the quality of the Turkish data.
3. The higher values in telecommunication technology are caused by the fact that the ETSI standards issued since 1998 are not included in the category of international standards.
4. For the subset of international standards, an international reference is equal to a simple cross reference.
5. The tables with the results are available from the author.

PART FIVE

Conclusion

11. Conclusion

Tineke M. Egyedi

Clearly, the value of standards depends on their functionality and quality. However, this volume demonstrates that stability is equally important. Because standards are points of reference for producers and consumers, change is inherently problematic. Indeed, in most cases stability is a prerequisite to adopt, invest in and implement standards.

Standards' change is a very common occurrence in the field of ICT (Chapter 9). If change can create serious problems, as the chapters illustrate, why do standards change? And is change always necessary? In the previous chapters we have addressed these questions from different angles covering all phases in the standard's life cycle: from its development to its implementation in products and services, and to the adoption of such products and services by organizations. Here, the different causes of change (maintenance, succession and implementation) investigated in these studies are categorized and presented together with a few final reflections and recommendations for future research. With this book we hope to have awakened the reader's interest in this relatively uncharted, new area of standardization research.

STANDARDS DYNAMICS AND CHANGE

Recapitulating, the concept 'standards dynamics' refers to what happens to standards once they have been set, that is, to changes to and interaction between standards (Chapter 1). Apart from the changes which standards undergo, standards' dynamics includes competition between standards and the friction between complementary standards. The overall focus in this book has been on standards' change, although standards competition plays an equally important role in Chapters 4 and 5.

Four types of change are distinguished:

1. Maintenance change or 'horizontal dynamics' (Chapter 4): standards' change that results from maintenance activities of standards bodies (e.g. new editions, revisions, withdrawals, etc.).

2. Formalization or 'vertical dynamics' (Chapter 4): when a formal standards body ratifies a *de facto* standard or a consortium standard; vertical dynamics also includes ratification of a *de facto* standard by a consortium. In both cases, increased recognition and endorsement of the *de facto* or consortium standard is at stake.
3. Succession: the replacement of one standard by another one in an area of standardization. It includes what retrospectively may be seen to be a next generation standard.
4. Implementation change: a change introduced to the standard specification during its implementation in, for example, a product. This includes extensions and omissions to the standard.

Table 11.1 provides an overview of the type of dynamics which the case studies, quantitative studies, and the feature study in the previous chapters foremost address.

CAUSES OF MAINTENANCE CHANGE AND SUCCESSION

In order to know how to prevent, reduce and/or cope with the negative impact of standards' change, better insight is required into their causes. The sources of change mentioned in the previous chapters roughly fall into three complementary explanations, each with its own flow of reasoning:

1. standards change as part of innovation;
2. standards change as a market strategy; and
3. standards change as a natural phase in the standard's life cycle.

Innovation

Standards change is an intrinsic part of technological innovation and as such an unavoidable derivative thereof. The cases illustrate that the pressure for technological change and standards' change in its wake may stem from:

1. 'Evolving user requirements', that is, changes in the needs of consumers and organizations. Examples are the requirement for higher speed and more bandwidth in the case of wireless LAN (IEEE 802.11, Chapter 7); for more internet addresses in the case of IPv4 (Chapter 5); or for extended facilities (ODA, Chapter 2). In addition, the use of standards leads to new problems that also need to be solved (e.g. routing and multi-homing in IP, Chapter 5).

Table 11.1 Areas of dynamics which the chapters primarily address

Types of Dynamics	Study of	Chapter	Authors
Maintenance change	ODA/ODIF	2	Van der Meer
	Dublin Core to Qualified DC	2	Van der Meer
	Updates to DVD recordables + and −	4	Gauch
	IPv4 to IPv4 + NAT	5	Vrancken et al.
	IEEE 802.11b to IEEE 802.11g	7	Jakobs
	ISO/IEC JTC 1 standards: Quant. study	9	Egyedi and Heijnen
	IT and Telecom standards PERINORM: Quantitative study	10	Blind
Formalization	DVD recordables + and −: *de facto* to consortium and formal standards	4	Gauch
Succession	IPv4 to IPv6	5	Vrancken et al.
	SGML succeeded by XML	6	Egyedi and Loeffen
	IT and Telecom standards PERINORM: Quantitative study	10	Blind
Implementation change	Z39.50	2	Van der Meer
	OSI > partial implementation	3	Egyedi
	UML	3	Egyedi
	802.11b > 802.11b+	7	Jakobs
	STEP	8	Thomas et al.
	Implementation change: feature study	3	Egyedi
Competition	DVD recordables + vs. −	4	Gauch
	IPv6 vs. IPv4 + NAT	5	Vrancken et al.

2. The 'expected' importance of a new functionality is enough reason to instigate standards change – although in practice the functionality may never be used (e.g. added proprietary standard features such as encryption in the WLAN case, Chapter 7).
3. The emergence of 'a new technical context': A new context-of-use sets different requirements, such as the new possibilities that the web-based environment offered for using standardized markup languages (Chapter 6).
4. The identification of 'new application domains': A new application domain sets different requirements, such as the use of a markup language for company-external document exchange (business-to-business, Chapter 6); the expected use of IEEE 802.11 for imaging and voice transmission (IEEE 802.11a, Chapter 7); and expansion of the Dublin Core to make it

better suited for more types of digital objects, including software components and cultural heritage materials (Chapter 2).

These developments have led to intensified standards maintenance as well as to more radical types of standards succession.

Market Strategy

ICT companies that compete typically use standardization as instruments of their market strategy. A company policy on standards' change is part of such a strategy. However, standards' change can also be an outcome of market competition. Thus, in the case of wireless LAN, competing technologies have led to different standard specifications (IEEE 802.11, 802.11a and 802.11b, Chapter 7). Gauch's study of changes in the area of DVD recordables illustrates how competition can even spur a standard's race, and the high extent of change which may be involved. He describes two largely stable, competing groups of companies tied together by patents and shared market interests. The two groups engage in R&D for increased speed and disc capacity to prolong revenue streams from their respective patents. This, in turn, leads to a string of competing standard versions and initiatives to formalize them ('horizontal' and 'vertical dynamics', Chapter 4). Standards change is here an outcome of market competition as well as part of a market strategy.

Standardization Factors

The relevance of standards' maintenance in the life cycle of standardization is often ignored in standardization studies. In addition to innovation- and market-related factors that give rise to standard updates and revisions, factors intrinsic to the activity of standardization occasion maintenance change. Difficulties may occur during standardization that later give rise to changes. For example, sometimes revisions are desired because experience with implementing the standard has uncovered ambiguities and omissions. Such flaws can emerge in any phase of standardization. There may be a flaw in the way the standard's scope has been defined, in aspects of the standards development process, in how the specification was written, and/or in the implementation process (Chapter 3). For example, a standard which is perceived as too complex for implementers may signal not only that the standard's scope was too wide (Chapter 8) but also that too many compromises clouded the standards process.

A number of factors influence the level of maintenance change. Most salient is, the timing of standardization with respect to the technology life cycle. The maturity of the technology to be standardized is important. Standards for immature technologies sooner need revisions (Chapter 9).

Technical immaturity not only increases the likelihood of change, it also leads to more radical changes. The same applies to standards that switch development environment and are elaborated in a different standards setting – that is, a different committee or standard body. Such a switch also facilitates the adoption of more radical – and incompatible – changes to the original standard (e.g. XML, Chapter 6).

Finally, although one might assume a direct relation between a low quality standards process, a dire need for maintenance and a high level of maintenance activity, this line of reasoning needs to be put into perspective. For, some standards bodies adopt a more elaborate and intensive maintenance policy, and therefore are likely to show a higher number of revisions.

Timing of Change and Standard's Lifetime

Innovation, market strategy and standardization factors highlight different causes of standards' change and clarify, in part, the radical quality of changes. However, these factors tell us little about when standards' change is likely to take place. Gauch notes that in the case of the DVD recordables, in periods of low competition standards' change serves the purpose of resolving standards implementation issues. However, when competition is intense, new updates (horizontal dynamics) and increased international recognition of the technical specifications (vertical dynamics) occur in parallel with the market entry of new products. Vertical and horizontal standards' dynamics are then used to distinguish one's products from competitors and increase one's market share (Chapter 4).

Blind's quantitative study shows that the lifetime of standards is technology-specific. For example, the level of technology dynamics – and therefore of the dynamics of standards – is much higher for IT standards than for telecommunication standards. Telecommunication standards have a longer life (Chapter 10).

Context of Implementing and Adopting Standards

Implementation change refers to a situation in which standards are not implemented as expected or intended, and therefore leads to incompatible implementations. As Egyedi's study shows, there are various causes for this process. Implementation change can be a conscious company strategy (e.g. in the case of an embrace-and-extend strategy), but the standard itself may also give rise to incompatible implementations (see also the discussion of standardization factors as cause of maintenance change above).

Complex standards may only be partially implemented (as in the case of OSI standards, Chapter 3); they may be implemented in different ways, for example, due to ambiguities (as in the case of Z39.50, Chapter 2); they may be implemented with proprietary extensions or be otherwise 'improved' (as in the case of IEEE 802.11b+ implementations and 'access point' that supports 128 bit link layer encryption, Chapter 7); or, organizations may implement a standard prematurely and comply to a draft standard which is subsequently changed (Chapter 7).

Past experiences with incompatible implementations adversely affect standard adoption decisions. They shape the attitudes of implementers and end-users of standards, both individuals and organizations, and sometimes lead to counter-intuitive dealings (Chapters 7 and 8). Rather than risk incompatibility between the standard implementations of different vendors, an organization may voluntarily and knowingly risk being locked-in by one vendor (Chapter 7).

Thomas et al. (Chapter 8) distinguish between primary adoption (i.e. the decision to adopt) and secondary adoption (i.e. implementation of standard-compliant products in an organization). Primary adoption is more likely to occur if, for example:

1. The standard solves a real problem and has local, short-term benefits, independent of whether or not the standard is adopted by others (Chapter 5).
2. The standard has an official status and is being defined and supported by an official or well-known standards body (ISO, W3C, IETF, etc., Chapter 5).
3. The standard is already widely used and is likely to become dominant in the market (Chapter 5).
4. Implementation and maintenance is not too costly or difficult (Chapters 2, 7 and 8), and the standard's scope and specification is not too complex (Chapter 8).
5. Implementation support is available (Chapter 8).
6. The standard is compatible with its predecessor (Chapter 7).
7. The (*de facto*) standard product is compatible with existing solutions (Chapter 5).
8. Little extra education is required for the end-user and continuity in daily operations (Chapters 6 and 8).
9. Standard-compliant products are available (Chapter 7).

Vendor lock-in based on proprietary standards is a common phenomenon. Once having successfully created a lock-in situation, it becomes difficult for the organization to change to an open standard – even when the same vendor is invited to implement the open standard (STEP, Chapter 8). Vendors argue strongly against such a decision for explicit fear of future vendor-independence. In the case study of Thomas et al. the vendor negotiated a gain-share contractual arrangement with the government in return for evolving the government's system towards the open STEP standard.

However, vendor lock-in can also occur with open standards. The findings show that vendor lock-in can take place in three ways: by monopolising tacit knowledge about the standard gained during the standards process (e.g. router protocols, Chapter 3); by unintentionally – but prematurely – implementing draft standards (WLAN project, Chapter 7); and by introducing change to the standard once it has been set (extension in the WLAN project, Chapter 7).

Addressing the Impact of Change

Sometimes standards' change has little negative impact. For example, the users of the Aachen Wireless LAN had few problems with the transition from IEEE 802.11b to IEEE 802.11g (Chapter 7). However, in most of the cases studied, revision of and extensions to standards have created difficulties. For example, different standards versions become competitors, as in the case of the compatible short-term solution to IPv4 addressing problems (i.e. NAT) and the incompatible long-term solution (i.e. IPv6). Or, to mention another difficulty, different standard implementations may, for example, lead to different query results. If a query result is later needed to account for an important decision, and cannot be reproduced, this may have legal repercussions (e.g. Z39.50, Chapter 2).

What means are there to avoid or reduce the adverse impact of standards' dynamics? Roughly, the suggestions made in the previous chapters can be divided into those that try to prevent problems from occurring and those that address them ex-post. Most chapters view downward compatibility as the key means to mitigate the negative impact of revisions (e.g. Dublin Core, Chapter 2) and standards' succession (XML, Chapter 6). In particular where the longevity of digital archival data is concerned, grafting would seem the most viable ex-ante strategy (Chapter 2).

However, backward compatibility is easier said than done (Chapter 8), and not always the most optimal solution (Chapter 6). Moreover, the backward compatibility effort itself can become a source of problems. For example, in the STEP case, end-users doubted the usefulness of the efforts made because they saw too few differences between the implemented versions and, because compatibility was not fully successful, extra work was required and project delays occurred (i.e. editions of AP224; 1999, 2001, 2006, Chapter 8).

Furthermore, the term 'bugward compatibility' is widely used to denote the problem of seeking backward compatibility with legacy systems that contain bugs – as in the case of AP224 with UNIX (Chapter 8) and CSS1 in Internet Explorer (Chapter 3). It puts a burden on present and future interoperability with other systems.

If standards' change cannot be prevented, the main problem implementers and end-users must face is market fragmentation and lack of compatibility between different standards versions, generations or implementations. Solutions exist depending on the type of incompatibility concerned. In data communication, for example, bridges, multiprotocol stacks and routers are used to re-create interoperability between competing standard (Chapter 6). In the field of consumer electronics, devices are made which contain competing standards (i.e. multiprotocol implementations, Chapter 4). In all of these solutions, producers and users of one standard maintain access to the market segment of the competing standard and its externalities. They reduce the consumers' fear that the market will tip towards the competing standard leaving them with an obsolete technology. However, apart from the extra costs involved, Gauch argues that these solutions sustain market competition and fragmentation. Because they allow consumers to benefit from the externalities of both markets, there is no urgent need to integrate standards or markets (e.g. DVD recordables, Chapter 4). A similar phenomenon is at stake with the dual stack implementation of IPv4 and IPv6 (Chapter 5). Although aimed to ease migration from IPv4 to IPv6, the dual stack lessens the need to migrate because it allows co-existence.

Where the sustainability of digital data is concerned, there are a number of partial and temporary solutions (Chapter 2): data refreshment, migration and conversion, and the emulation of earlier data handling devices. The emulation option is required if there is no strategy to archive and update the data handling devices, as was the case with tools that could handle ODA/ODIF (Chapter 2).

Although the development of crosswalks between a standard and its successor sometimes seem possible (e.g. from DC to DCQ, Chapter 2), such compatibility efforts are likely to be ambiguous – as were the results of multiple efforts to re-establish compatibility between SGML and its successor XML (Chapter 6).

In principle these ex-post measures temporarily solve the adverse effects of standards dynamics. Moreover, in rapidly evolving fields of technology, temporariness need not always pose a problem. However, ex-post measures are usually costly and laborious, and often unsatisfactory because they only solve part of the problem and do so in an inadequate way.

Research Recommendations

To conclude, the conceptual contribution of the chapters to the new field of standards' dynamics, and in particular to standards' change and competition dynamics is of a fundamental nature. It includes theory about types and causes of change, explanations regarding the timing of change, discussions about the impact which standards' change can have, and ways to address the adverse impact of change. A fundament has been laid, but it needs to be strengthened. Certain findings, in particular, require further investigation. For example:

1. In the introductory chapter, the contention is that 'the impact of incompatibility between different implementations of the same standard' is comparable to that between different standard versions and between incompatible standards. Additional research is needed to corroborate this claim.
2. The relation between innovation and standards dynamics differ among technologies. Further examination in this area is needed to understand, for example, which technology and market characteristics define these differences.[1]
3. Although the issue of how to cope with change has incidentally been addressed in different chapters, systematic research on how users and end-users of standards handle change is lacking.
4. In the introductory chapter we argued our choice of focus in this book. However, standards dynamics is a ubiquitous phenomenon. To know the degree to which the finding are generalizable, the research should be extended to other areas of standardization than ICT, to case studies of *de facto* standards, and to additional areas of standards' dynamics, such as the interaction between standards.

In this volume, we have focused foremost on the problematic side of standards' dynamics because it has been neglected in standards research. However, immutable static standards also represent a risk. The relative stability required from standards shows a tense relationship with the necessity of standards to keep up with technology, market and regulatory developments. The tension between these two pressures is well-captured by Cargill's (1989) IT architecture example: 'By definition, a standard is reasonably unchanging; therefore, the only time that an architecture should be standardized is when it is no longer subject to change – and when an architecture is no longer subject to change, it is dead' (Cargill 1989, p. 70).

NOTE

1. Since this chapter was written, Egyedi and Sherif (2008) have published a study that relates standards' dynamics to different categories of innovation, i.e. incremental, architectural, platform and radical innovation.

Bibliography

Abbate, J. (1994), *From ARPANET to INTERNET: A History of ARPA-sponsored Computer Networks, 1966–88*, dissertation, Pennsylvania: University of Pennsylvania.

Allen, P. and S. Frost (1998), *Component-based Development for Enterprise Systems: Applying the Select Perspective*, Cambridge University Press.

Anderson, P. and M. Tushman (1990), 'Technological discontinuities and dominant designs: a cyclical model of technology change', *Administrative Science Quarterly*, **35** (1), 604–33.

Aoun C. and E. Davies (2007), *RFC4966*, http://rfc.net/rfc4966.html.

Appelt, W. (1993),'The ODA standard 1993 and future extensions', *Computer Standards and Interfaces*, **15** (4), 343–51.

Arthur, W.B. (1989), 'Competing technologies, increasing returns, and lock-in by historical events', *The Economic Journal*, **99**, 116–31.

Atkinson, C., J. Bayer, O. Laitenberger and J. Zettel (2000), *Component-based Software Engineering: The KobrA Approach*, 3rd international workshop on component-based software engineering, Limerick, IE.

Attewell, P. (1992), 'Technology diffusion and organizational learning: the case of business computing', *Organization Science*, **3** (1), 1–19.

Bagozzi, R.P., F.D. Davis and P.R. Warshaw (1992), 'Development and test of a theory of technological learning and usage', *Human Relations*, **45** (7), 659–86.

Beall, J. (2004), 'Dublin Core: an obituary', *Library Hi Tech News*, **8**, 40–41.

Beijnum, van I. (2002), *BGP*, Cambridge, MA: O'Reilly.

Beijnum, van I. (2005), *Running IPv6*, Berkeley, CA: APRESS.

Beijnum van I. (2007), *IPv6 Firewalling Knows No Middle Ground*, Ars Technica, 7 May 2007, http://arstechnica.com/articles/paedia/ipv6-firewall-mixed-blessing.ars.

Belleflamme, P. (1999), 'Assessing the diffusion of EDI standards across business communities', in M.J. Holler and E. Niskanen (eds), *EURAS Yearbook of Standardization*, Munich: Accedo, pp. 301–24.

Berners-Lee, T. and D. Connolly (1995), *Hypertext Markup Language – 2.0*, Network Working Group, Request for Comments 1866, Freemont, CA: IETF.

Besen, S.M. and J. Farrell (1991), 'The role of the ITU in standardisation', *Telecommunications Policy*, **15**, 311–21.

Blind, K. (2004), *The Economics of Standards: Theory, Evidence, Policy*, Cheltenham, UK and Northhampton, MA, USA: Edward Elgar.

Blind, K. and S. Gauch (2008, forthcoming), *Trends in ICT Standards in European Standardization Bodies and Standards Consortia Telecommunication Policy*.

Blind, K. and A. Jungmittag (2008), 'The impact of patents and standards on macroeconomic growth: a panel approach covering four countries and 12 sectors – the empirical economics of standards', *Journal of Productivity Analysis*, forthcoming.

Bonino, M.J. and M.R. Spring (1991), 'Standards as change agents in the information technology market', *Computer Standards & Interfaces*, **12**, 97–107.

Booch, G. (1991), *Object Oriented Analysis and Design with Applications*, 1st edition, Redwood City, CA: Benjamin/Cummings.

Bosak, J. (1996a), *Re: Welcome to w3c-sgml-wg@w3.org!*, one of the first submissions to the discussion list of the W3C SGML working group, contribution to w3c-sgml-wg@w3.org discussion list, 28 August 1996.

Bosak, J. (1996b), *W3C SGML WG: The Work Begins*, contribution to w3c-sgml-wg@w3.org discussion list, 5 September 1996.

Bowker, G.C. and S.L. Star (1999), *Sorting Things Out: Classification and Its Consequences*, Cambridge, MA: MIT Press.

Bray, T. (1996), *XML, HTML, SGML, Life, the Universe, and Everything*, contribution to w3c-sgml-wg@w3.org discussion list, 8 November 1996.

Bray, T. (1997), 'Recent ERB votes', in C. M. Sperberg-McQueen (ed.), *Reports from the W3C SGML ERB to the SGML WG and from the W3C XML ERB to the XML SIG*, compiled for the use of the WG and SIG, 4 December 1997.

Bray, T., J. Paoli and M. Sperberg-McQueen (1998), *Extensible Markup Language (XML) 1.0*, W3C recommendation, 10 February 1998.

Brunnermeier, S.B. and S.A. Martin (1999), *Interoperability Cost Analysis of the U.S. Automotive Supply Chain*, project number 7007-03, Research Triangle Park, NC: Research Triangle Institute.

Byrne, B.M. and P.A. Golder (2002), 'The diffusion of anticipatory standards with particular reference to the ISO/IEC information resource dictionary system framework standard', *Computer Standards and Interfaces*, **24** (5), 369–79.

Cantner, U., K. Dressler and J. Krüger (2004), 'Verweildaueranalysen in der empirischen Wirtschaftsforschung', *Das Wirtschaftsstudium*, **10**, 1287–93.

Cargill, C.F. (1989), *Information Technology Standardization, Theory, Process and Organizations*, Newton, MA: Digital Press, Digital Equipment Corporation.

Carr, R. (1988), 'ODA – the electronic standard for document interchange', *Computer Standards and Interfaces*, **7** (3), 297–301.

Castek (2000), *Component-based Development: the Concepts, Technology and Methodology*, Castek company's white paper, http://www.castek.com.

Chen, M. (2003), 'Factors affecting the adoption and diffusion of XML and Web services standards for e-business systems', *International Journal of Human-Computer Studies*, **58** (3), 259–79.

Christensen, C.M. (1997), *The Innovator's Dilemma: When New Technologies Cause Great Firms to Fail*, Boston, MA: Harvard Business School Press.

Clark J. (1997), *Comparison of SGML and XML*, W3C Note, 15 December 1997, http://www.w3.org/TR/NOTE-sgml-xml.html (accessed 16 May 2007).

Coad, P. and E. Yourdon (1991), *Object Oriented Analysis*, 2nd edition, Englewood Cliffs, NJ: Yourdon Press.

Connolly, D. (ed.) (1997) 'XML. Principles, tools and techniques', *WWW Journal*, **2** (4).

Dankbaar, B. and R. van Tulder (1992), 'The influence of users in standardization: the case of MAP', in M. Dierkes and U. Hoffmann (eds), *New Technologies at the Outset – Social Forces in the Shaping of Technological Innovations*, Frankfurt/M. and Boulder, CO: Campus and Westview, pp. 327–50.

David, P.A. (1985), 'Clio and the economics of QWERTY', *American Economic Review*, **75**, 332–36.

Davis, F.D., R.P. Bagozzi and P.R. Warshaw (1989), 'User acceptance of computer technology: a comparison of two theoretical models', *Management Science*, **35** (8), 982–1003.

DCMI (2007), *Dublin Core Metadata Initiative*, http://dublincore.org/documents/dces/ (accessed 16 May 2007).

DCQ (2007), *Using Dublin Core – Dublin Core Qualifiers*, http://dublincore.org/documents/usageguide/qualifiers.shtml (accessed 16 May 2007).

Dedrick, J. and J. West (2003), 'Why firms adopt open source platforms: a grounded theory of innovation and standards adoption', in J.L. King and K. Lyytinen (eds), *Proceedings of the Workshop on Standard Making: a Critical Research Frontier for Information Systems*, 12–14 December 2003, Seattle, WA, pp. 236–57.

Deering, S. and R. Hinden (1995), *Internet Protocol, Version 6 (IPv6) Specification*, RFC1883, superseded by RFC2460, Fremont, CA: IETF.

Deering S. and R. Hinden (1998), *Internet Protocol, Version 6 (IPv6) Specification*, RFC2460, Fremont, CA: IETF.

Dobson, B. (2005), 'Greater efficiency, reduced cost', *Defence Management Journal*, **28**, 25–26.

Dosi, G. (1982), 'Technological paradigms and technological trajectories. A suggested integration of the determinants and directions of technical change', *Research Policy*, **11** (3), 147–62.

Dranove, D. and N. Gandal (2000), *The DVD vs. DIVX Standard War: Empirical Evidence of Vaporware*, Competition Policy Center, paper CPC01-016.

Dranove, D. and N. Gandal (2003), 'Surviving a standards war: lessons learned from the life and death of DIVX', *CEPR Discussion Paper*, **3935**.

Dranove, D. and N. Gandal (2005), *The DVD vs. DIVX Standard War: Empirical Evidence of Network Effects and Preannouncement Effects*, Evanston/Chicago, IL: Northwestern University.

Dreverman, M. (2005), *Adoption of Product Model Data Standards in the Process Industry*, Eindhoven, NL: Eindhoven University of Technology.

DTI (2005), *The Empirical Economics of Standards*, No. 12, UK: Department of Trade and Industry.

Durand A. (2001), 'Deploying IPv6', *IEEE Internet Computing*, January–February, 79–81.

Durand A. (2006), *IPv6 @ Comcast, Managing 100+ Million IP Addresses*, www.apricot.net/apricot2006/slides/conf/wednesday/Alain_Durand-Architecture-external.ppt.

Durand, D.G. (1996), *Last Unstructured Discussion: SGML Compatibility*, contribution to w3c-sgml-wg@w3.org discussion list , 9 October 1996.

DVD6C (1999), 'DVD6C Starts to License Recordable DVD License', in DVD6C (ed.), *DVD6C Patent Licensing*, Redwood Shores, CA: DVD6C.

ECITC (1993), *ECITC Guide to IT&T Testing and Certification*, Brussels: ECITC.

Egevang K. and P. Francis (1994), *The IP Network Address Translator (NAT)*, RFC1631, May 1994, obsoleted by RFC3022, Fremont, CA: IETF.

Egyedi, T.M. (1996), *Shaping Standardisation: A Study of Standards Processes and Standards Policies in the Field of Telematic Services*, Delft: Delft University Press.

Egyedi, T.M. (1997), 'Examining the relevance of paradigms to base OSI standardisation', *Computer Standards and Interfaces*, **18**, 431–50.

Egyedi, T.M. (1999), *Examining the Relevance of Paradigms to Base OSI Standardisation*, reprinted in J.L. Berg and H. Schumny (eds), *Best Papers of Computer Standards & Interfaces, 1986–1998*, **20** (4/5), 355–74.

Egyedi, T.M. (2002), *Trendrapport Standaardisatie. Oplossingsrichtingen voor problemen van IT-interoperabiliteit*, Delft: Ministerie van Verkeer en Waterstaat, Rijkswaterstaat/Meetkundige Dienst.

Egyedi, T.M. (2006), 'Beyond consortia, beyond standardization? Redefining the consortium problem', in K. Jakobs (ed.), *Advanced Topics in Information Technology Standards and Standardization Research*, 1, pp. 86–104.

Egyedi, T.M. and A. Dahanayake (2003), 'Difficulties implementing standards', in T.M. Egyedi, K. Krechmer and K. Jakobs (eds), *Proceedings of the 3rd IEEE Conference on Standardization and Innovation in Information Technology*, SIIT 2003, 22–24 October 2003, Delft, pp. 75–84.

Egyedi, T.M. and P. Heijnen (2005), 'Scale of standards dynamics: change in formal, international IT standards', in S. Bolin (ed.), *The Standards Edge: Future Generation*, Felton, CA: Bolin Communications, pp. 289–308.

Egyedi, T.M. and J. Hudson (2005), 'A standard's integrity: can it be safeguarded?', *IEEE Communications Magazine*, **43** (2), 151–5.

Egyedi, T.M. and A.G.A.J Loeffen (2002), 'Succession in standardization: grafting XML onto SGML', *Computer Standards & Interfaces*, **24** (4), 279–90, copyright Elsevier.

Egyedi, T.M. and M.H. Sherif (2008), *Standards' Dynamics Through an Innovation Lens: Next Generation Ethernet Networks*, paper presented at the proceedings of the first ITU-T Kaleidoscope Academic Conference 'Innovations in NGN', 12–13 May 2008, pp. 127–134.

Eijk, I. van (2007), *Practical Implementations of Internet Protocol Version 6* (in Dutch), report ordered by the Dutch Ministery of Economic Affairs, Maart.

ESPRIT (1990–93), *ESPRIT: the European Strategic Programme for Research and Development in Information Technology. First programme: 1990–93.*

ETSI (2005a), *Making Better Standards*, http://portal.etsi.org/mbs/.

ETSI (2005b), *Impact of Standards?! – New Insights*, lectures by J. Friis (ETSI) and Z.A. Lozinski (Parlay), NO-REST conference, 27 May 2005, Sophia Antipolis, France.

European Union (1985), 'Council Resolution of 7 May 1985 on a new approach to technical harmonization and standards', *Official Journal C 136*, 4 June 1985, 1–9.

Farrell, J. (1990), 'The economics of standardization: a guide for non-economists', in J.L. Berg and H. Schumny (eds), *An Analysis of the Information Technology Standardization Process*, New York, NY: Elsevier, pp. 189–98.

Farrell, J. and G. Saloner (1985), 'Standardisation, compatibility, and innovation', *The RAND Journal of Economics*, **16** (1), 70–83.

Farrell, J. and G. Saloner (1986), 'Installed base and compatibility: innovation, product preannouncements, and predation', *American Economic Review*, **76**, 943–54.

Farrell, J. and G. Saloner (1988), 'Coordination through committees and markets', *Rand Journal of Economics*, **29** (2), 235–52.

Ferné, G. (1995), 'Information technology standardization and users: international challenges move the process forward', in B. Kahin and J. Abbate (eds), *Standards Policy for Information Infrastructure*, Cambridge, MA: MIT Press.

Fichman, R.G. (1999), 'Information technology diffusion: a review of empirical research', in J.I. Degross, J.D. Becker and J.J. Elam (eds), *Proceed-*

ings of the Thirteenth International Conference on Information Systems, December 1992, pp. 195–206.

Fichman, R.G. and C.F. Kemerer (1993), 'Adoption of software engineering process innovations: the case of object orientation', *Sloan Management Review*, **34** (2), 7–22.

Fleck, J. (1994), 'Learning by trying: the implementation of configurational technology', *Research Policy*, **23**, 637–52.

Ford B. and P. Srisuresh (2005), *Peer-to-peer Communication Across Network Address Translators*, proceedings, USENIX Annual Technical Conference, pp. 179–92, http://www.usenix.org/events/usenix05/tech/general/full_papers/ford/ford.pdf.

Fuller V. and T. Li (2006), *Classless Inter-domain Routing (CIDR): The Internet Address Assignment and Aggregation Plan*, RFC4632.

Gallaher, M.P., A.C. O'Connor and T. Phelps (2002), *Economic Impact Assessment of the International Standard for the Exchange of Product Model Data (STEP) in Transportation Equipment Industries*, project number 07007.016., Research Triangle Park, NC: RTI International.

Gallivan, M.J. (2001), 'Organizational adoption and assimilation of complex technological innovations: development and application of a new framework', *SIGMIS Database*, **32** (3), 51–85.

Genschel, P. (1993), *Institutioneller Wandel in der Standardisierung von Informationstechnik*, PhD dissertation, Köln: University of Köln.

Goldfarb, Ch.F. (1990), *The SGML Handbook*, Oxford University Press.

Goldfarb, Ch.F. (1996a), *Re: XML, HTML, SGML, Life, the Universe, and Everything*, contribution to w3c-sgml-wg@w3.org discussion list, 10 November 1996.

Goldfarb, Ch.F. (1996b), *Re: Capitalizing on HTML (Was 'Re: Equivalent Power in SGML and XML')*, contribution to w3c-sgml-wg@w3.org discussion list, 19 September 1996.

Goldfarb, Ch.F. (1996c), *Re: Make DTDs optional?*, contribution to w3c-sgml-wg@w3.org discussion list, 30 September 1996.

Goldfarb, Ch.F. (1996d), *Re: Compliance with 8879, a moving target*, contribution to w3c-sgml-wg@w3.org discussion list, 12 September 1996.

Goldfarb, Ch.F. (1997), *Final Text of SGML TC, JTC 1/WG 4*, ISO 8879 TC 2, 4 December 1997.

Grindley, P., D.J. Salant and L. Waverman (1999), 'Standards wars: the use of standard setting as a means of facilitating cartels – third generation wireless telecommunications standards setting', *International Journal of Communications Law and Policy*, **3**, Summer 1999.

Hall, B., A. Jaffe and M. Traijtenberg (2001), *Market Value and Patent Citations: A First Look*, University of California, Berkeley: Institute of Business and Economic Research.

Hania S. (2006), *IPv6 en de business realiteit, XS4ALL en IPv6*, presentation at the IPv6 Summit, The Hague, 15 November 2006.

Hanseth, O., E. Monteiro and M. Hatling (1996), 'Developing information infrastructure: the tension between standardisation and flexibility', *Science, Technologies and Human Values*, **21** (4), 407–26.

Hawkins, R. (1999), 'The rise of consortia in the information and communication technology industries: Emerging implications for policy', *Telecommunications Policy*, **23**, 159–73.

Hoeven, J.R. van der, R.J. van Diessen and K. van der Meer (2005), 'Development of a universal virtual computer (UVC) for long-term preservation of digital objects', *Journal of Information Science*, **31** (3), 196–208.

Horik, R. van (2005), *Permanent Pixels, Building Blocks for the Longevity of Digital Surrogates of Historical Photographs*, DANS studies in digital archiving, The Hague: DANS.

Hovav, A., R. Patnayakuni and D. Schuff (2004), 'A model of Internet standards adoption: the case of IPv6', *Information Systems Journal*, **14** (3), 265–94.

Hunter, R., P. Kayser and F. Nielsen (1989), 'ODA: a document architecture for open systems', *Computer Communications*, **12** (2), 69–78.

Hurd, J. and J. Isaak (2005), 'IT standardization: the billion dollar strategy', *JITSR*, **3** (1), 68–74.

Huston G. (2004), 'Anatomy: a look inside network address translators', *The Internet Protocol Journal, Cisco Systems*, **7** (3), 2–32.

Huston, G. (2007), *The IPv4 Report*, http://ipv4.potaroo.net.

Huston, G. (permanently auto-generated), *IPv4 Address Report*, http://www.potaroo.net/tools/ipv4/index.html.

IANA (permanently updated), *Port Numbers*, http://www.iana.org/assignments/port-numbers, Internet Assigned Numbers Authority (IANA).

IEC/CENELEC (1989), *IEC-CENELEC Agreement Exchange of Technical Information Between Both Organisations*, Geneva: IEC.

IEC/CENELEC (1991), *Agreement on Common Planning of New Work and Parallel Voting, 'The Dresden Agreement'*, Geneva: IEC.

IEEE (1991), *802.11 Project Authorization Request*, http://grouper.ieee.org/groups/802/11/Documents/DocumentArchives/1991_docs/1191058.DOC.

Imperial College London, Distributed Software Engineering Section, *List of references in Pervasive Computing*, http://www.doc.ic.ac.uk/~mss/pervasive.html.

INSPEC (2007), *INSPEC® Bibliographic Information Service for Physics, Electronics and Computing*, http://www.iee.org/publish/inspec/ (accessed 16 May 2007).

ISO (2001), *ISO Strategies 2002–2004: Raising Standards for the World*, ISO/Gen 15:2001, http://www.iso.org/iso/en/aboutiso/strategies/isostrategies2002-E.pdf.

ISO (2004), *ISO Catalogue 2004*, Geneva: ISO.

ISO (2006), *ISO Website*, http://www.iso.org/iso/en/ISOOnline.frontpage (accessed February 2006).

ISO (2007), *Vote Closes on Draft ISO/IEC DIS 29500 Standard*, ref. 1070, 4 September 2007, http://www.iso.org/iso/pressrelease.htm, Geneva: ISO.

ISO/CEN (1991), *Agreement on Technical Cooperation Between ISO and CEN, 'The Vienna Agreement'*, Geneva: ISO.

ISO/IEC (1991), *ISO/IEC Guide 2*, Geneva: ISO/IEC.

ISO/IEC (1993), *ISO/IEC 10646-1993 (E), Information Technology – Universal Multiple-octet Coded Character Set (UCS), Part 1: Architecture and Basic Multilingual Plane (plus amendments AM 1 through AM 7)*, Geneva: ISO.

ISO/IEC (1996), *ISO/IEC 10179.2:1996, Document Style Semantics and Specification Language (DSSSL), International Standard*, Geneva: ISO.

ISO/IEC (1997), *ISO/IEC 10744:1992. Hypermedia/Time-based Structuring Language (HyTime)*, Geneva: ISO, revised edition (ed. 2).

ISO/IEC (2004), *ISO/IEC Directives, Part 2: Rules for the Structure and Drafting of International Standards*, Geneva: ISO/IEC.

ISO/IEC (2007), *ISO/IEC JTC 1/WG4: Recent changes to ISO 8879*, http://xml.coverpages.org/wg4-n1960.html#annex-k (accessed 16 May 2007).

ISO/IEC JTC 1/SC 18 (1996), *Document Processing and Related Communication – Document Description and Processing Languages, N1855, Third Interim Report on the Project Editor's Review of ISO 8879*, SGML Review Group, WG 8, 24 May 1996.

ISO/IEC JTC 1/SC 18 (1996), *Fourth Interim Report on the Project Editor's Review of ISO 8879, N1893*, SGML Review Group, 23 December 1996.

ISO/IEC JTC 1/SC 18 (1997), *Draft SGML TC 2, N1929*, WG 8, Proposed TC for WebSGML Adaptations for SGML, Annex K (normative), WebSGML Adaptations, 1 June 1997.

ISO/IEC JTC 1/SC 18 (1997), *Final Text of SGML Technical Corrigendum, N1955*, WG 4, ISO 8879 TC 2, 4 December 1997.

ISO/IEC JTC 1/SC 18 (1997), *Report of the SGML Rapporteur Group (Barcelona Meeting), N1925*, WG 8, 9 May 1997.

Jacobson I., G. Booch and J. Rumbaugh (1999), *The Unified Software Development Process*, Reading, MA: Addison-Wesley-Longman.

Jakobs, K. (1989), 'ISO's directory proposal – evolution, current status and future problems', *Canadian Journal of Information Sciences*, **14** (1).

Jakobs, K. (2002a), *Even Desperately Needed Standards May Fail – the Case of E-mail*, proceedings of International Conference on the History of Computing and Networks, Grenoble.

Jakobs, K. (2002b), 'A proposal for an alternative standards setting process', *IEEE Communications Magazine*, **40** (7).

Jakobs, K. (2005a), *Installation of an IEEE 802.11 WLAN in a Large University Setting*, proceedings of the 4th International Conference on Standardization and Innovation in Information Technology, ITU, 21–23 September 2005, in Geneva, Switzerland, Aachen: Wissenschaftsverlag Mainz, pp. 171–84.

Jakobs, K. (2005b), 'The role of the "third estate" in ICT standardisation', in S. Bolin (ed.), *The Standards Edge: Future Generation*, Menlo Park, CA: The Bolin Group.

Jakobs, K. (2006), 'Shaping user-side innovation through standardisation – the example of ICT', *Technological Forecasting and Social Change*, **73** (1).

Jakobs, K., R. Procter, R. Williams and M. Fichtner (1996), 'Non-technical issues in the implementation of corporate e-mail: lessons from case studies', in M. Igbaria (ed.), *The Virtual Workplace: The Impact on Individuals, Organizations, and Societies*, ACM Conference of the SIG in Computer Personnel Research and MIS, Denver, Colorado, USA, 11–13 April 1996, New York, NY: ACM Press.

Jones, P. and J. Hudson (1996), 'Standardization and the cost of assessing quality', *European Journal of Political Economy*, **12**, 355–61.

Johnson, H.T. (1992), *Relevance Regained from Top-down Control to Bottom-up Empowerment*, New York, NY: The Free Press/Maxwell Macmillan International.

Johnson, S. (2001), *Emergence: The Connected Lives of Ants, Brains, Cities, and Software*, New York, NY: Scribner.

JTC 1 (2004), *ISO/IEC Directives*, 5th edition, Geneva: ISO/IEC.

Kahn, H., N. Filer, A. Williams and N. Whitaker (2001), 'A generic framework for transforming EXPRESS information models', *CAD Computer Aided Design*, **33** (7), 501–10.

Karrenberg D. (2006), *RIPE*, presentation at the IPv6 Summit, The Hague, 15 November 2006.

Katz, M.L. and C. Shapiro (1986), 'Technology adoption in the presence of network externalities', *Journal of Political Economy*, **94** (4), 822–41.

Kindleberger, C.P. (1983), 'Standards as public, collective and private goods', *Kyklos*, **36**, 377–96.

Kohler E., M. Handley and S. Floyd (2006), *Datagram Congestion Control Protocol (DCCP)*, RFC4340, March.

Kol, N.J.C., R.J. van Diessen and K. van der Meer (2006), 'An improved universal virtual computer approach for long-term preservation of digital objects', *Information Services & Use*, **26** (4), 283–91.

Kortum, S. and J. Lerner (1997), *Stronger Protection or Technological Revolution: What is Behind the Recent Surge in Patenting*, working paper 6204, Cambridge, MA: National Bureau of Economic Research.

Kotter, J.P., J. Collins, R. Pascale, J.D. Duck, J. Porras and A. Athos (1998), *Harvard Business Review on Change*, 6th edition, Boston, MA: Harvard Business School Publishing.

Krechmer, K. (1998), 'The principles of open standards', *Standards Engineering*, **50** (6), 1–6.

Krechmer, K. (2006), 'Open standards requirements', in K. Jakobs (ed.), *Advanced Topics in Information Technology Standards and Standardization Research Vol. 1*, Hershey: Idea Group, pp. 27–48.

Kretschmer, T. and K. Muehlfeld (2004), *Co-opetition in standard-setting: the case of the Compact Disc*, working paper #04-14, London: LSE.

Kuhn, T.S. (1970), *The Structure of Scientific Revolutions III*, 2nd edition, Chicago: University of Chicago Press.

Lawrence, S. and C.L. Giles (1999), 'Accessibility of information on the web', *Nature 400*, 8 July 1999, 107–9.

Lea, G. and P. Hall (2004), 'Standards and intellectual property rights: an economic and legal perspective', *Information Economics and Policy*, **16** (67), 89.

Lear E. (2006), *Procedures for SCTP, TCP, and UDP Port Assignments by IANA*, http://www.ietf.org/internet-drafts/draft-lear-iana-no-more-well-known-ports-02.txt.

Linn, R.J. and M.U. Uyar (eds) (1994), *Conformance Testing Methodologies and Architectures for OSI Protocols*, IEEE Computer Society Press.

Lint, O. and E. Pennings (2000), *The Recently Chosen Digital Video Standard: Playing the Game Within the Game*, Eindhoven Centre for Innovation Studies, Rotterdam: Eindhoven University of Technology.

Lint, O. and E. Pennings (2002), *The Option Value of Developing Two Product Standards Simultaneously when the Final Standard is Uncertain*, Vlerick working papers 2002/10, Gent: Vlerick Leuven Gent Management School.

LSC Group (2002), *RAMP White Paper – The UK Navy Mechanical RAMP Project*, Issue 1, UK MoD Warships Support Agency, http://www.lsc.co.uk/downloads/documents/eit-wp-01%20RAMP%20White%20Paper.pdf (accessed November 2003).

Lu, Y., Y. Zhang, L.T. Yang and H. Ning (2008), *The Internet of Things: From RFID to the Next-Generation Pervasive Networked Systems (Wireless Networks and Mobile Communications)*, Boca Raton, FL: Auerbach Publications.

Maler, E.L. (1996), *Compatibility Issues and Principle #3*, contribution to w3c-sgml-wg@w3.org discussion list, 16 September 1996.

Männistö, T., H. Peltonen, A. Martio and R. Sulonen (1998), 'Modelling generic product structures in STEP', *Computer-Aided Design*, **30** (14), 1111–18.

Mansell, R. and R. Hawkins (1992), 'Old roads and new signposts: trade policy objectives in telecommunication standards', in F. Klaver and P. Slaa (eds), *Telecommunication: New Signposts to Old Roads*, Amsterdam: IOS Press, pp. 45–54.

Mapping (2007), *Dublin Core Metadata Element Set Mapping to MODS Version 3*. http://www.loc.gov/standards/mods/dcsimple-mods.html (accessed 16 May 2007).

Meeuws, R.J., B.R. Sodoyer and K. van der Meer (2003), *Digital Longevity*, Delft: Delft University of Technology.

Meister, D. (2004), *STEP through 20 Years: Lessons and Theoretical Implications*, working paper edition, Faculty of Information Systems, Richard Ivey School of Business, Ontario: University of Western Ontario.

Meloan, S. (2003), *Toward a Global 'Internet of Things'*, http://java.sun.com/developer/technicalArticles/Ecommerce/rfid/.

MoD (2002), *General MoD Article*, http://www.dstan.mod.uk/MOD%20stan%202002.pdf (accessed June 2005).

MoD (2005), *Recent Trends in Service and Civilian Personnel Numbers*, http://www.dasa.mod.uk/natstats/ukds/2005/c2/table21.html (accessed November 2005).

MoD AMS (2003), *AMS Additional Information – Addressing Standardization*, http://www.ams.mod.uk/ams/content/docs/addrstan.doc (accessed July 2005).

MoD CDMA (2004), Ministry of Defence Policy on the Use of XML, http://www.cdma.mod.uk/suppinfo/XMLpolicy-v1_0.doc (accessed June 2005).

MoD SSE (2005), *Support Solutions Envelope*, http://www.ams.mod.uk/ams/content/docs/sse/eam/gp_4_ed1.htm (accessed March 2005).

MODS (2007), *Metadata Object Description Schema*, US Library of Congress, Library of Congress' Network Development and MARC Standards Office.

Moseley, S., S. Randall and A. Wiles (2003), 'Experience within ETSI of the combined roles of conformance testing and interoperability testing', in T.M. Egyedi, K. Krechmer and K. Jakobs (eds), *Proceedings of the 3rd IEEE Conference on Standardization and Innovation in Information Technology*, SIIT 2003, 22–24 October 2003, Delft, pp.177–90.

Mustonen-Ollila, E. and K. Lyytinen (2003), 'Why organizations adopt IS process innovations: a longitudinal study using diffusion of innovation theory', *Information Systems Journal*, **13** (3), 275–97.

Needleman, M. (2000), 'Z39.50 – a review, analysis and some thoughts on the future', *Library Hi Tech*, **18** (2), 158–65.

Nelson, R.R. and S.G. Winter (1977), 'In search of useful theory of innovation', *Research Policy*, **6** (1), 36–76.

Nilakanta, S. and R.W. Scamell (1990), 'The effect of information sources and communication channels on the diffusion of innovation in a data base development environment', *Management Science*, **36** (1), 24–40.

Norusis, M. (1996), *SPSS Advanced Statistics 6.1*, Chicago, IL: SPSS Incorporated.

Oksala, S., A. Rutkowski, M. Spring and J. O'Donnell (1996), 'The structure of IT standardization', *StandardView*, **4** (1), 9'22.

OMG (1998), *Unified Modelling Language Specification*, Framingham, MA: Object Management Group, www.omg.org.

Optical Disc Systems (2004), *DVD+/−RW Market Survey of Recorders + Discs*, Mumbai: Optical Disc Systems.

Over, P., W.E. Moen and R. Denenberg (1995), *Z39.50 Implementation Experiences*, US National Institute of Standards and Technology, Computer Science Laboratory. Washington: US GPO.

Prescott M.B. and S. Conger (1995), 'Information technology innovations: a classification by IT locus of impact and research approach, *Special Issue of Technological Diffusion of Innovations*, **26** (2–3).

Raggett, D., A. Le Hors and I. Jacobs (1999), *HTML 4.01 Specification*, W3C Recommendation, 24 December 1999.

Raz D., J. Schoenwaelder and B. Sugla (2000), *An SNMP Application Level Gateway for Payload Address Translation*, DRFC2962, October.

Reddy, N.M. (1990), 'Product of self-regulation. A paradox of technology policy', *Technological Forecasting and Social Change*, **38**, 43–63.

Rogers, E.M. (1995), *Diffusion of Innovations*, 4th edition, New York: The Free Press.

Rogers, E.M. (2003), *Diffusion of Innovations*, 5th edition, New York: Simon & Schuster International.

Rosenberg J., H. Schulzrinne, G. Camarillo, A. Johnston, J. Peterson, R. Sparks, M. Handley and E. Schooler (2002), *SIP: Session Initiation Protocol*, http://www.ietf.org/rfc/rfc3261.txt.

Schmidt, S.K. (1998), 'International standardisation processes in telecommunications as example of closure', in J. Esser, G. Fleischmann and T. Heimer (eds), *Soziale Schließung im Prozess der Technologieentwicklung*, Frankfurt/Main: Campus, pp. 157–75.

Schmidt, S.K. and R. Werle (1998), *Co-ordinating Technology. Studies in the International Standardization of Telecommunications*, Cambridge, MA: MIT Press.

SGML (1999), *ISO 8879:1986/Cor 2:1999*, Geneva: ISO.

Shapiro, C. and H.R. Varian (1999a), 'The art of standards wars', *California Management Review*, **41** (2), 8–32.

Shapiro, C. and H.R. Varian (1999b), *Information Rules – A Strategic Guide to the Network Economy*, Boston: Harvard Business School Press.

Sherif, M.H, T.M. Egyedi and K. Jakobs (2005), 'Standards of quality and quality of standards for telecommunications and information technologies', in T.M. Egyedi and M.H. Sherif (eds), *Proceedings of the 4th International Conference on Standardization and Innovation in Information Technology*, ITU, 21–23 September 2005 in Geneva, Switzerland, Aachen: Wissenschaftsverlag Mainz, pp. 221–30.

Sherif, M.H., K. Jakobs and T.M. Egyedi (2007), 'Standards of quality and quality of standards for telecommunications and information technologies', in M. Hörlesberger, M. El Nawawi and T. Khalil (eds), *Challenges in the Management of New Technologies*, Singapore: World Scientific Publishing Company, pp. 427–47.

Shlaer, S. and S.J. Mellor (1988), *Object-Oriented Systems Analysis: Modelling the World in Data*, Englewood Cliffs, NJ: Yourdon Press.

Söderström, E. (2004), *B2B Standards Implementation: Issues and Solutions*, dissertation, Department of Computer and System Sciences, Stockholm University, Sweden, Edsbruk: Akademitryck AB.

Souza, D.F.D and A.C. Wills (1999), *Objects, Components and Frameworks with UML: The Catalysis Approach*, Reading, MA: Addison-Wesley.

Spath, M. (2003), *Why DVD+R(W) Is Superior to DVD−R(W)*, http://www.cdfreaks.com/reviews/Why-DVDRW-is-superior-to-DVD-RW.

Srisuresh P. and K. Egevang (2001), *Traditional IP Network Address Translator (Traditional NAT)*, RFC3022, January.

Stirling, A. (2001), 'Standardization systems and defence procurement', in European Commission (ed.), *Proceedings European Commission's Conference 'European Defence Procurement in the 21st Century'*, Brussels.

Stojanovic, Z., A. Dahanayake and H. Sol (2001), *A Methodology Framework for Component-based Systems Development Support*, proceedings of the 6th CAISE/IFIP8.1 International Workshop on Evaluation of Modelling Methods in Systems Analysis and Design.

Swann, G.M.P. (2000), *The Economics of Standardization*, final report for Standards and Technical Regulations, Directorate Department of Trade and Industry, Manchester: University of Manchester.

Tan, G. and J. Guttag (2004), *Time-based Fairness Improves Performance in Multi-rate Wireless LANs*, The USENIX Annual Technical Conference, Boston, MA.

Themistocleous, M. (2002), *Enterprise Application Integration*, Uxbridge, UK: Brunel University.

Thiard, A. and Pfau, W. (1991), *Forschung & Entwicklung und Normung*, Luxembourg: Office for Official Publications of the EC.

Timmermans, S. and M. Berg (1997), 'Standardization in action: achieving local universality through medical protocols', *Social Studies of Science*, **27** (2), 273–305.

Tsirtsis, G. and P. Srisuresh (2000), *Network Address Translation – Protocol Translation (NAT-PT)*, RFC2766, February.

Tsuchiya, P.F. and T. Eng (1993), 'Extending the IP internet through address reuse', *ACM SIGCOMM Computer Communication Review*, **23** (1), 16–33.

Unicode (2006), *The Unicode Standard, Version 5.0*, Addison-Wesley.

Uniface (2000), *Compuware Corporation Uniface Products*, http://www.compuware.com/products/uniface/.

United Nations (1949), *Protocol on Road Signs and Signals*, http://www.geocities.com/bkkriders/law/unc/sign1949.html.

Upward, F. (1996), 'Structuring the records continuum, part one: post-custodial principles and properties', *Archives and Manuscripts*, **24** (2), 268–85.

Upward, F. (1997), 'Structuring the records continuum, part two: structuration theory and recordkeeping', *Archives and Manuscripts*, **25** (1), 10–35.

US Department of Justice (2005), *Justice Department Approves Joint Licensing of Patents Essential for Making DVD-Video and DVD-Rom Discs Players*.

US Government (1990), *Taking a Byte Out of History: The Archival Presentation of Federal Computer Records*, report of the United States House of Representatives Committee on Government Operations 101–978, 6 November 1990, Washington: US Government Printing Office.

Vercoulen, F. and M. van Wegberg (1998), *Standard Selection Modes in Dynamic, Complex Industries: Creating Hybrids Between Market Selection and Negotiated Selection of Standards*, Maastricht: University of Maastricht, pp. 1–14.

Voip-info.org, *Domain Name Server (DNS) SRV*, http://www.voip-info.org/tiki-print.php?page=DNS+SRV.

Vrancken, J.L.M. (1994), 'Bottom-up processen in de automatisering', *Informatie*, December (Dutch).

Vries, H.J. de (1999), *Standardization: A Business Approach to the Role of National Standardization Organizations*, Dordrecht, The Netherlands: Kluwer Academic Publishers.

Vries, H.J. de (2006), 'IT standards typology', in K. Jakobs (ed.), *Advanced Topics in Information Technology Standards and Standardization Research*, vol. 1, Hershey: Idea Group, pp. 1–26.

W3C (1998), *Extensible Markup Language (XML) 1.0*, W3C recommendation, 10 February 1998, http://www.w3.org/TR/1998/REC-xml-19980210.

W3C (2000), *XHTML™ 1.0: The Extensible HyperText Markup Language: a Reformulation of HTML 4 in XML 1.0*, W3C recommendation, 26 January 2000.

Wapakabulo, J., R. Dawason, S. Probets and T. King (2005), 'A STEP towards the adoption of data-exchange standards: a UK defense community case', in T.M. Egyedi and M.H. Sherif (eds), *Proceedings of the 4th International Conference on Standardization and Innovation in Information Technology*, ITU, 21–23 September 2005 in Geneva, Switzerland, Aachen: Wissenschaftsverlag Mainz, pp. 255–66.

Warner, A.G. (2003), 'Block alliances in formal standard setting environments', *International Journal of IT Standards and Standardization Research*, **1** (1), 1–18.

Weiss, M.B.H. (1990), 'The standards development process: a view from political theory', *StandardView*, **1** (2), 35–41.

Weitzel, T. (2003) 'A network ROI', in J.L. King and K. Lyytinen (eds), *Proceedings of MISQ Special Issue Workshop on Standard Making: a Critical Frontier for Information Systems*, Seattle, 12–14 December 2003, pp. 62–79.

Weizsacker, C.C. von (1982), 'Staatliche Regulierung – positive und normative Theorie', *Schweizerische Zeitschrift für Volkswirtschaft und Statistik*, **2**, 325–43.

Weizsacker, C.C. von (1984), 'The costs of substitution', *Econometrica*, **52** (5), 1085–116.

West, J. (1999), 'Organizational decisions for I.T. standards adoption: antecedents and consequences', in IEEE (ed.), *Proceedings of the 1st IEEE Conference on Standardisation and Innovation in Information Technology*, Aachen, September 1999, pp. 13–18.

West, J. (2003), 'The role of standards in the creation and use of information systems', in J.L. King and K. Lyytinen (eds), *Proceedings of MISQ Special Issue Workshop on Standard Making: a Critical Frontier for Information Systems*, Seattle, 12–14 December 2003, pp. 314–25.

Xia, M., K. Zhao and M.J. Shaw (2003), 'Open e-Business standard development and adoption: an integrated perspective', in J.L. King and K. Lyytinen (eds), *Proceedings of MISQ Special Issue Workshop on Standard Making: a Critical Frontier for Information Systems*, Seattle, 12–14 December 2003, pp. 222–35.

Yin, R.K. (2002), *Case Study Research: Design and Methods*, Newbury Park: Sage Publications.

Zaltman, G., R. Duncan and J. Holbek (1973), *Innovations and Organizations*, New York: Wiley & Sons.

Zhang, J. and A. Dimitroff (2004), '"Internet search engines" response to metadata Dublin Core implementation', *Journal of Information Science*, **30** (4), 310–20.

Zhou, X., M. Jacobsson, H. Uijterwaal and P. van Mieghem (2007), 'IPv6 delay and loss performance evolution', *International Journal of Communication Systems*, accepted 30 October 2007.

Index

Aachen University, RWTH, *see* RWTH Aachen
addressing, Internet 68–81
adopter-centric research 120, 123
adoption of standards 186
  motivation 125
  size of organization, effect on 125
age
  JTC 1 standards 149–50
  see also lifetime of standards; longevity
amendments, effect on standard survival time 170
Anderson, P. 69
Arthur, W.B. 155

Bagozzi, R.P. 123
Beall, J. 22
Berners-Lee, T. 88
Besen, S.M. 48
Blind, K. 59, 138, 142, 152, 155, 185
bottom-up processes 76–7
  adoption of standards 77–8
Byrne, B.M. 118, 124

Carr, R. 18
change 4–8
  causes 182–5
  costs 7–8
  problems 6–8
  reducing impact of 187–8
  resistance to 126
  timing of 185
  types of 4–6, 181–2
Chen, M. 123, 125
committee standards 2–3
compatibility
  backward 26, 187
  bugward 37, 187–8
  downward 66
  effect on RAMP project implementation 130–31
  of successive standards 82–6
  SGML and XML 32–3, 89–96
competition 83
  DVD standards 47–8
  and dynamics of DVD standards 58–62
complexity
  and adoption of RAMP project 124, 128
  and implementation of RAMP project 130
Conger, S. 125–6
costs of standards change 7–8
Cox regression analysis 156–7, 168–70, 172–3, 175
cross referencing, effect on survival time 171, 174

David, P.A. 155
Davis, F.D. 123
de facto standards 2–3, 7–9, 57, 182–3
DECT (digital enhanced cordless telecommunications) standard 36
Dedrick, J. 121
DePietro, R. 120
diffused implementation strategy 63–4
diffusion of innovation (DOI) theory 119
digital archival objects 15–16
digital data sustainability 15–27
digital enhanced cordless telecommunications (DECT) standard 36
Dimitroff, A. 22
Dreverman, M. 118, 120
drivers (motivation) for adoption 125
DSSSL standards 87
Dublin Core metadata element set 21–3, 25
Durand, D.G. 94
DVD
  actors 47–8, 50–51, 53, 56–7, 64–5

competition 47–50, 58–9, 62, 64–6
development of 50–51
dynamics 56–8
Forum 52
history 50–51, 57, 60
standards 47–66
DVD+RW Alliance 52–4
DVD6C Patent Pool 54
dynamics of standards
dimensions of 109, 111–14
DVD standards 56–66
horizontal 58–9, 181
JTC 1 standards 142–8
vertical 59, 62, 182

ECMA Technical Committee 31 54–5
economic costs of standards change 7
economics of standards approach 119
Egyedi, T.M. 17, 155, 159
end-to-end principle 75
environmental-related factors
adoption of RAMP project 127–8
implementation of RAMP project 132
Esperanto 82
eurocentrism and co-operation agreements 144

Farrell, J. 48, 155
fees, effect on implementing standards 131
Fichman, R.G. 119–20, 126
firmware patching 66
flat name space addressing 69–70
formalization 182
functional equivalents 83

Gallivan, M.J. 123, 133
Giles, C.L. 22
Golder, P.A. 118, 124
Goldfarb, C. 91, 93
grafting 84–5
XML onto SGML 89–95

Heijnen, P. 155, 159
heritage relationships 84
hierarchical name space addressing 69–71
Hovav, A. 127
HTML 88, 94
HyTime standard 87

ICT standards 8–9, 99–101
factors affecting lifetime 155–76
and incompatibility 28–42
lifetime analysis 161–2, 163–6, 167–8
stability of 137–53
IEC-CENELEC co-operation agreements 144
IEEE 802.11 standard 102–4
WLAN project, RWTH Aachen 105–15
implementation
change 5, 182, 185–7
dynamics of 111, 112–13
independence 31–2
multiple 63–5
of RAMP project 129–33
stages 29–30
incompatibility 28–42, 82–96
causes of 29–39
consensus decision-making and standards 31
recommendations 39–41
SGML and XML 32–3, 89–96
tacit knowledge and standards 37–8
incremental innovation 84
information objects, longevity requirements 24–5
infrastructure and adoption of RAMP project 127
innovation as cause of change 182–4
innovation-centric research 120
installation, dynamics of 111, 113–14
institutions, *see* standards institutions
interface 3, 4, 9, 100, 161, 167
international standards bodies agreements 144
Internet
addressing standards 68–81
IPv4 68
IPv6 72–3, 78–81
ISO
ISO 10303-224 122
ISO-CEN co-operation agreements 144
IT standards, *see* information technology standards

Jakobs, K. 7–8, 128

Joint Technical Committee 1 (ISO/IEC)
  provisionally retained edition, JTC 1 140
  standard maintenance 138–40
  standard stability analysis 140–53

Kaplan-Meier survival analysis 163–8
Kemerer, C.F. 119–20
Kortum, S. 64
Kotter, J.P. 126
Kuhn, T.S. 6

language and standards incompatibility 36
Lawrence, S. 22
Lerner, J. 64
lifetime of standards 155–76
  and standard characteristics 168–75
  and timing of change 185
  see also longevity; survival of standards
Loeffen, A.G.A.J. 17
longevity 24–6
  digital data standards 24–6
  digital information objects 15–16
  see also lifetime of standards

maintenance change 181, 182–5; *see also* horizontal dynamics
maintenance of standards 5
  in JTC 1 138–40
Maler, E. 90
market effects of standards change 188
market strategy as cause of standards change 184
markup languages 86–9
Meister, D. 117–18, 120, 124, 125, 126
Metcalfe's law 68–9
MMCD (multimedia compact disc) 50–51
Mobile Professors and Students (MoPS) project, RWTH Aachen 102
MoD (Ministry of Defence) 121–2
MoPS project, *see* Mobile Professors and Students (MoPS) project
multimedia compact disc (MMCD) 50–51

NAT (Network Address Translation) 73–5, 78–81
  compared with IPv6 78–9
network effects 127–8

ODA/ODIF 17–19, 25
options and standards incompatibility 37
organization-related factors
  adoption of RAMP project 125–7, 128
  implementation of RAMP project 131–2
OSI model 33–4

Prescott, M.B. 125–6
primary adoption 186

RAMP project 122
  adoption process 123–9
  implementation 129–33
  resource availability 127
rapid acquisition of manufactured parts, *see* RAMP project
rational unified process (RUP) 35
read–write media 49
replacements
  effect on standard lifetime 171
  JTC 1 standards 146
revision of standards, JTC 1 139, 146
Rogers, E.M. 119, 123, 124
routing, Internet addressing 69–73
RUP (rational unified process) 35
RWTH Aachen 101
  MoPS project 102
  WLAN project 105–15

Saloner, G. 155
Schmidt, S.K. 31
SD (super density) digital video discs 50–51
secondary adoption 186; *see also* implementation
SGML 19–21, 86–8
  and XML 19–21, 25, 32–3, 89–95
Sherif, M.H. 28–9
stabilized standards, JTC 1 139–40
standard for the exchange of product model data (STEP) 117–33
standard generalized markup language, *see* SGML
standard (technology)-related factors
  adoption of RAMP project 123–4
  implementation of RAMP project 130–31

standardization
as cause of maintenance change 184–5
dynamics of 111–12
standards
change, *see* change
competition 4, 47–50, 58–9, 62, 64–6, 68–81, 83–4, 96, 100, 181, 183–5
definition 2–3
dynamics of, *see* dynamics
implementation, *see* implementation
lifetime, *see* lifetime of standards; longevity
maintenance, *see* maintenance of standards
succession, *see* succession
value of 3–4, 99–101
standards institutions
and compatibility 31–2
co-operation agreements 144
remoteness, effect on RAMP project implementation 132
STEP (standard for the exchange of product model data) 117–33
observability and adoption of STEP project 124
RAMP project 122–33
succession 5–6, 83, 182
and compatibility 82–6
XML and SGML 86–96
super density (SD) digital video discs 50–51
supplements, JTC 1 standards 146
survival analysis, ICT standards 163–8
survival of standards
analysis, ICT standards 163–8
legislation references, effect on survival time 174
length of standards, effect on survival time 174
time 174
see also lifetime of standards; longevity
Swann, G.M.P. 118, 155
switching costs 7
system installation, dynamics of 111, 113–14

technical maturity, effect on standards change 185
technology acceptance model 123
technology areas, and standards stability 150–52
telecommunications standards
lifetime analysis 158–61, 163–7
Themistocleous, M. 125
TOE framework 120
top-down processes 76–7
Tushman, M. 64

UK Ministry of Defence 121–2
unified modelling language (UML) 34–5
universality benefits of standards 100
users
attitudes towards standards 126
bearing costs of standards change 7–8

vendor lock-in 186–7
RWTH 113–14
vertical dynamics 182
DVD standards 59, 62

Weitzel, T. 131
Werle, R. 31
West, J. 120, 121
withdrawals, JCT standards 143
WLAN project, RWTH Aachen 105–15
write once read many times (WORM) media 49

XML 83, 88–9
and SGML 19–21, 32–3, 89–95

Z39.50 protocol 23–4, 25
Zaltman, G. 123
Zamenhof, L.L. 82
Zhang, J. 22